Econometric Models of the Euro-area Central Banks

Edited by

Gabriel Fagan

Head of Monetary Policy Research Division, Directorate General Research, European Central Bank, Germany

Julian Morgan

Deputy Head of Econometric Modelling Division, Directorate General Research, European Central Bank, Germany

Edward Elgar
Cheltenham, UK • Northampton, MA, USA

Published by
Edward Elgar Publishing Limited
Glensanda House
Montpellier Parade
Cheltenham
Glos GL50 1UA
UK

Edward Elgar Publishing, Inc.
136 West Street
Suite 202
Northampton
Massachusetts 01060
USA

A catalogue record for this book
is available from the British Library

ISBN 1 84542 486 7

Printed and bound in Great Britain by MPG Books Ltd, Bodmin, Cornwall

Contents

Foreword

This book presents the main macroeconomic models used in the central banks of the euro area. These include models of individual countries, multi-country models and aggregate euro-area models. In my view the important contribution of this volume is that it is the first attempt to provide a systematic comparison of these models in terms of their structures, main features and properties. In line with the Eurosystem policy of openness and transparency, we have decided to publish, in many cases for the first time, the details of these models. I believe that this information will be of interest to central bankers, academics, ECB watchers and the many others interested in learning more about the functioning of the euro-area economy.

The interest in this volume will stem from the fact that these tools provide an important input into policy formulation within the Eurosystem. Of course, as the overview chapter indicates, these models are not used in a mechanical fashion. The information they provide complements that from other sources, including smaller scale models, monetary and financial indicators, survey evidence and judgmental assessments. Nevertheless the models described in this volume are a crucial element in the preparation of economic projections, helping to ensure consistency within and across countries. They are also extensively used for scenario analysis aimed at assessing the impacts of shocks on the economy and for rapidly updating projections in the light of new information.

This volume has been prepared through the cooperation of experts in the Working Group on Econometric Modelling (WGEM). This working group provides a forum in which technical experts from around the Eurosystem can exchange ideas and experiences in relation to model development. Through such cooperation we have been able to exploit important synergies in model development. The result has been a considerable improvement in the quality of our modelling infrastructure and a greater degree of convergence in the underlying approaches to model building. Complete harmonization has not been achieved, but, so long as there are open issues in macroeconomics, this would be neither realistic nor desirable. Nevertheless cooperation has enabled us to learn much from one another, and this volume is one of the fruits of this endeavour.

Jean-Claude Trichet
President of the European Central Bank
Frankfurt am Main, April 2005

Contributors

Olivier de Bandt, Head of Division, Macroeconomic Analysis and Forecasting, DG Research and International Relations, Banque de France, Paris

Véronique Brunhes-Lesage, Research Analyst, Macro-economic Analysis and Forecasting Division, DG Research and International Relations, Banque de France, Paris

Pablo Burriel, Economist, Servicio de Estudios, Banco de España, Madrid

Fabio Busetti, Economist, Econometric Unit, Research Department, Banca d'Italia, Rome

Gabriela Lopes de Castro, Economist, Economic Research Department, Banco de Portugal, Lisbon

Alistair Dieppe, Senior Economist, Directorate General Research, European Central Bank, Frankfurt am Main

Peter van Els, Head of Department, Research Division, De Nederlandsche Bank, Amsterdam

Ángel Estrada, Head of Labour Market and Modelling Unit, Servicio de Estudios, Banco de España, Madrid

Gabriel Fagan, Head of Monetary Policy Research Division, Directorate General Research, European Central Bank, Frankfurt am Main

Gerhard Fenz, Economist, Economic Analysis Division, Oesterreichische Nationalbank, Vienna

Paolo Guarda, Economist, Monetary, Economics & Statistics Department, Banque Centrale du Luxembourg, Luxembourg

Britta Hamburg, Economist, Economic Research Centre, Deutsche Bundesbank, Frankfurt am Main

Philippe Jeanfils, Economist, Research Department, National Bank of Belgium, Brussels

Tohmas Karlsson, Principal Economist, Directorate General Research, European Central Bank, Frankfurt am Main

Mika Kortelainen, Economist, Monetary Policy and Research Department, Bank of Finland, Helsinki

Alberto Locarno, Head of the Econometric Unit, Research Department, Banca d'Italia, Rome

Hanna-Leena Männistö, Adviser, Economics Department, Bank of Finland, Helsinki

Peter McAdam, Principal Economist, Directorate General Research, European Central Bank, Frankfurt am Main

Kieran McQuinn, Economist, Economic Analysis, Research and Publications Department, Central Bank and Financial Services Authority of Ireland, Dublin

Libero Monteforte, Economist, Econometric Unit, Research Department, Banca d'Italia, Rome

Julian Morgan, Deputy Head of Econometric Modelling Division, Directorate General Research, European Central Bank, Frankfurt am Main

Nuala O'Donnell, Economist, Economic Analysis, Research and Publications Department, Central Bank and Financial Services Authority of Ireland, Dublin

Mary Ryan, Senior Economist, Economic Analysis, Research and Publications Department, Central Bank and Financial Services Authority of Ireland, Dublin

Martin Spitzer, Economist, Directorate General Economics, European Central Bank, Frankfurt am Main

Karl-Heinz Tödter, Senior Economist, Deputy Head of Economic Research Centre, Deutsche Bundesbank, Frankfurt am Main

Javier Vallés, Head of the Forecasting and Conjunctural Division, Servicio de Estudios, Banco de España, Madrid

Jean-Pierre Villetelle, Deputy Head of Division Macroeconomic Analysis and Forecasting, DG Research and International Relations, Banque de France, Paris

Nicholas Zonzilos, Head of the Domestic Economy Division, Economic Research Department, Bank of Greece, Athens

Abbreviations

AGG EUR-12	Aggregate of the 12 euro area countries
AT	Austria
BE	Belgium
BIS	Bank for International Settlements
BMPE	broad macroeconomic projection exercises
CBFSAI	Central Bank and Financial Services Authority of Ireland
CES	constant elasticity of substitution
CPI	consumer price index
DE	Germany
EARP	Economic Analysis, Research and Publications at the Central Bank and Financial Services Authority of Ireland
ECB	European Central Bank
ECM	error correction mechanism
EMU	economic and monetary union
ES	Spain
ESA	European System of Accounts
ESCB	European System of Central Banks
FI	Finland
FR	France
FRB/US	United States of America Federal Reserve Bank
GR	Greece
HICP	harmonized index of consumer prices
HWWA	Hamburgisches Welt-Wirtschafts-Archiv
IE	Ireland
IMF	International Monetary Fund
IT	Italy
LU	Luxembourg
MCM	multi-country model
MPC	Monetary Policy Committee
MPS	MIT, University of Pennsylvania, and Social Science Research Council
NAIRU	non-accelerating inflation rate of unemployment
NAWRU	non-accelerating wage rate of unemployment

NBB	National Bank of Belgium
NCB	national central bank
NFNE	Non-farm, non-energy
NL	Netherlands
NPISH	non-profit institutions serving households
OECD	Organization for Economic Cooperation and Development
OPEC	Organization of the Petroleum-Exporting Countries
PAC	polynomial adjustment costs
PPP	purchasing power parity
PT	Portugal
Q	Quarter
SUR	seemingly unrelated regression
Tbonds	Treasury bonds
TCE	trade consistency exercise
TFP	Total factor productivity
UIP	uncovered interest parity
ULC	unit labour costs
VAR	vector auto regression
VAT	value-added tax
WGEM	Working Group on Econometric Modelling
WS–PS	Wage-setting, price-setting model

Acknowledgments

We are grateful to members of the Working Group on Econometric Modelling (WGEM) and the Monetary Policy Committee (MPC) of the European Central Bank (ECB) for useful comments and suggestions on the material in this volume. In addition we would like to thank the following individuals who acted as referees for the chapters: Pedro Alvarez-Lois, Robert-Paul Berben, Pablo Burriel, Fabio Busetti, Heather Gibson, Heinz Glück, Paolo Guarda, Philippe Jeanfils, Juha Kilponen, Dan Knudsen, Malte Knüppel, Peter McAdam, Kieran McQuinn, Christian Nilsson, Alvaro Novo, Mary Ryan and Jean-Pierre Villetelle. Finally we are grateful for excellent administrative and editorial assistance from Christina Brandt, Kathrine McAleenan and Sabine Fuchs.

G.F.
J.M.

Acknowledgements

1. An overview of the structural econometric models of euro-area central banks

Gabriel Fagan and Julian Morgan[1]

This chapter provides a comprehensive overview of the main structural econometric models used by the European Central Bank (ECB) and the euro area national central banks (Eurosystem). It takes stock of the current macro-econometric modelling infrastructure available within the Eurosystem, high-lighting not only the structures and main features of the models used but also their purposes and underlying model-building philosophies. It also includes information on how the models respond to economic shocks, such as changes in monetary or fiscal policy.

The models described in this volume are used to assist in the preparation of economic projections and for scenario and policy analysis. They include national, multi-country and euro-area aggregate models. Chapters 2 and 3 describe two models which treat the euro-area as an aggregate single economy; Chapters 4 and 5 describe two linked multi-country models of euro-area economies, while Chapters 6–17 describe the national models of each of the individual euro-area economies. The above chapters provide a 'bird's eye view' of the key details of the design, structure and characteristics of each of the models.

Despite the number and variety of the models described in this volume, it is worth noting that these large-scale structural models form only a subset of the tools used in the Eurosystem. Many alternative approaches (such as time-series models, structural vector autoregressions and computable general equilibrium models) are available and are widely used. In addition, models are not used mechanically and expert judgment plays an important role in economic analysis and projections.[2]

This overview chapter takes a cross-model perspective, with a view to identifying important shared attributes as well as differences. To facilitate cross-model comparisons, a set of comparative tables is provided. The information in these tables ranges from basic details on the models, such as the number of equations, to the short and long-run determinants

of key behavioural equations. The next section contains a brief description of the underlying model philosophies before describing some of the
basic features of the models and the uses to which they are put in the
central banks. This is followed by a more detailed description of the
structures and main features of the models. In the third section there is
a discussion of the main determinants of the key behavioural relationships within the models. In the final section there is a discussion of
model properties. This compares the results from five standard simulation exercises, covering the estimated impacts of changes in interest
rates, government spending, foreign demand, the exchange rate and oil
prices.

Inevitably this chapter can only provide an overview of the 16 models
covered in this volume. More comprehensive information on each of the
models is provided in the individual model chapters.

1   THE MODELS AND THEIR USES

There is no single common modelling philosophy in the Eurosystem and a
range of theoretical and empirical approaches are employed. Nonetheless
some common features appear to characterize the models. Many have
evolved significantly in recent years, reflecting theoretical and empirical
advances. Most models now embody the 'neoclassical synthesis' featuring
a long-run vertical supply curve combined with an important role for
demand effects in the short run. While the models have this general design
feature, there can be important differences in the length of time it takes for
short-run demand effects to die out and for the long-run supply-side results
to dominate.

Intertemporal decision making and dynamic optimization play an
important role in the specification of some of the models considered in this
volume. The adoption of these techniques in the formulation of econometric models constitutes one of the major advances in economic modelling in the 1990s. As is discussed in the individual model chapters, some of
the models contain complex dynamic adjustment processes, including both
forward-looking and backward-looking elements. Another important issue
that has also been reflected in the development of macroeconomic models
is the use of monetary and fiscal policy rules. These features of the models
are considered in greater detail in the next section.

Tables 1.1a and 1.1b give some basic details relating to the models discussed in this volume. As can be seen in the first table, there are essentially
three types of model in terms of the geographical coverage. Most models
in this volume relate to a single country and seek to represent the national

Table 1.1a   Basic details of the models (1)

Central bank	Model name	Coverage	Number of equations	Number estimated
Belgium	NBB quarterly	Belgium	150	30
Germany	BbkM	Multi-country	691	292
Greece	Bank of Greece model	Greece	93	17
Spain	MTBE	Spain	150	23
France	MASCOTTE	France	280	60
Ireland	MCM block	Ireland	75	20
Italy	BIQM	Italy	886	96
Luxembourg	MCM block	Luxembourg	63	18
Netherlands	MORKMON	Netherlands	400	70
Netherlands	EUROMON[1]	Multi-country	1000	330
Austria	AQM	Austria	169	43
Portugal	AMM	Portugal	115	23
Finland	BOFMINI	Finland	240	40
Finland	EDGE	Euro area aggregate	40	11 (calibrated)
ECB	AWM	Euro area aggregate	84	15

economy for each of the euro area central banks. However some of the models are multi-country in the sense that they include a number of linked models for individual countries. The multi-country models reported in this volume are the Bundesbank's BbkM, De Nederlandsche Bank's EUROMON, and the Eurosystem's multi-country model (MCM). Finally, there are two models which treat the euro area as a single economy, namely the ECB's area-wide model (AWM) and the Bank of Finland's EDGE model.

The choice between modelling the euro area as an aggregate or modelling countries individually and then aggregating up raises a number of interesting issues (see, for instance, Fagan and Henry, 1998). Aggregate analysis has the benefit of simplicity and requires considerably fewer resources to use and maintain a model than is the case with a multi-country approach. In addition, modelling the euro area as a single economy has the advantage of linking in with the discussion of monetary policy, which is now conducted at the euro area level. Nevertheless there can be difficulties in obtaining timely data at the euro area level and using such data in estimating behavioural relationships may lead to aggregation biases. Moreover aggregate analysis can ignore important

Table 1.1b　Basic details of the models (2)

	Model name	Estimation period	Data	Periodicity	Simulation software
BE	NBB quarterly	1980q1–2000q4	ESA-95	Quarterly	TROLL
DE	BbkM	1970–2000	ESA-95 in the EU, Germany: ESA-79/ ESA-95	Quarterly	TROLL
GR	Bank of Greece model	1964–2000	ESA-95	Annual	TROLL
ES	MTBE	1980–1998	ESA-95	Quarterly	TROLL
FR	MASCOTTE	1975–2001	ESA-95	Quarterly	TROLL
IE	MCM block	1980–1995	ESA-79	Quarterly	TROLL
IT	BIQM	1970s– (late) 1990s	ESA-79/ ESA-95	Quarterly	Speakeasy/ Modeleasy+
LU	MCM block	1970–2000	ESA-79/ ESA-95	Annual	Eviews
NL	MORKMON	1970–1999	ESA-79/ Output ESA-95	Quarterly	TROLL
NL	EUROMON	1970–1999	ESA-79/ ESA-95	Quarterly	TROLL
AT	AQM	1980–2002	ESA79/ ESA-95	Quarterly	TROLL
PT	AMM	1977–2001	ESA-95/ ESA-79	Annual	Excel
FI	BOFMINI	1970–1994	SNA-68/93	Quarterly	CEF (LBS)
FI	EDGE	1997–1999	ESA-95	Quarterly	TROLL
ECB	AWM	1970–2003	Specially constructed	Quarterly	TROLL

differences between countries, for instance in the behaviour of their labour markets.

There is considerable variety in the size of the models. Not surprisingly, given their coverage, the multi-country models tend to be the largest, with 700–1000 equations. The Banca d'Italia's model (BIQM) is also relatively large, with 886 equations, of which 96 are estimated. However many of the remaining models are much smaller. The Greek, Luxembourg, Spanish, Irish and Portuguese models, the AWM and the various country blocks of the MCM have just 14–25 estimated behavioural equations. The Bank of Finland's EDGE model has no estimated equations as all relationships – including behavioural ones – are calibrated.[3]

As indicated by Table 1.1a, the models in this volume range from those which rely heavily on estimated behavioural equations to models which are completely calibrated. By calibrating models it is possible to ensure that they are consistent with economic theory and have model properties that are in accordance with some stylized facts about the way the economy in question works. On the other hand, by estimating models one can have greater confidence that they closely fit the data of the economy that they seek to represent. In most cases the modellers have chosen to estimate key behavioural relationships while keeping a close eye on the model properties required by theory (that is, constraining certain parameter values where necessary or imposing longer-term restrictions: in both cases such restrictions are normally tested).

The estimation periods for the behavioural relationships in each model can vary significantly in line with the availability of data across countries. The maximum estimation period generally runs from the mid-1960s or early 1970s to the present day. However some models, such as those from the central banks of Ireland, Belgium and Spain, have a shorter estimation period, starting in the 1980s. Where possible, the modellers have used European System of Accounts 1995 (ESA-95) data definitions, although comprehensive ESA-95 data sets are not always available and consequently some countries have had to rely wholly or partly on earlier ESA-79 data. The historical euro-area aggregate data for the AWM needed to be specially constructed by the ECB. The MCM database has been constructed by collecting data from the various national central banks (NCBs) who supplied information for their own countries. All the models under consideration are quarterly, with the exception of the models from the central banks of Greece, Luxembourg and Portugal, which are annual models.

Uses of the Models

In the central banks, the models are typically used for three basic purposes. The first is to aid the preparation of economic projections in the context of the Broad Macroeconomic Projection Exercise (BMPE) and other macroeconomic forecasting exercises (the procedures for the Eurosystem Staff Macroeconomic Projection Exercises are described by ECB, 2001). These are normally prepared in conjunction with expert judgment on the respective economies, but the models provide an important input. Not only do models combine economic theory and (usually) estimated relationships for each economy but they also provide consistency in a forecast by ensuring that projections for individual parts of the economy contribute to a consistent and coherent projection of the economy as a whole. In the specific context of euro-area projections, multi-country models also have a key role to play by checking consistency, in particular as regards intra-area trade flows. Finally models also allow for forecast updates in response to changes in exogenous variables or external assumptions.

The second key function of the models is to prepare various scenario analyses. Requests for simulations using the models typically come from the management of the respective central bank or from the working groups and committees of the Eurosystem and the European System of Central Banks (ESCB) (for example, the WGEM analysis of the Monetary Transmission Mechanism using macroeconomic models, see van Els *et al.*, 2003). However central banks are also sometimes requested to undertake simulation analyses for other national and international economic institutions (for example, in the context of IMF Article IV missions). Additional simulations may be undertaken to accompany economic projections by presenting variants which assess risks to a central projection. They can also be undertaken to analyse changes in policies, for example changes in monetary or fiscal policies, labour market policies or social security regulations, or changes in other economic variables, such as the exchange rate, foreign trade, oil and commodity prices or asset prices. The models are also sometimes used for tasks that are quite distinct from standard macroeconomic scenario analysis. For example, the models of the Central Bank and Financial Services Authority of Ireland, the Banco de Portugal, the Bundesbank and the Banco de España have been used to generate consistent scenarios as an input into stress test analysis of the stability of these countries' banking systems. As a further example, the model of the Bank of Greece has been used to evaluate the impact of structural funds on the Greek economy.

The third use of the models is for counterfactual analysis, where actual economic developments and government policies are compared with the outcome of alternative courses of action that could have been taken. This analysis helps to shed light on the costs and benefits of the policy actions taken.

Reflecting the different natures of the tasks to be undertaken, the models can be operated in different ways. Within the multi-country models, individual country blocks can be operated in an isolated mode, with the rest of the world exogenous. Where monetary or fiscal policy rules are available within the model, their use is usually optional, depending on the task at hand. Such rules are rarely used when preparing economic projections but may be used in scenario analyses and longer-term simulations.

2 THE STRUCTURES AND MAIN FEATURES OF THE MODELS

General Features

Tables 1.2 to 1.6 give key details relating to the supply side, use of forward-looking behaviour, policy rules and the government, along with information on monetary aggregates and interest rates.

Table 1.2   The supply side of the models

	Model name	Production function	Types of output	Types of factors	Long-run output determinants
BE	NBB quarterly	CES	Single	Capital, labour (hours)	Labour supply, labour augmenting technical progress, export markets growth
DE	BbkM	Cobb–Douglas	Single	Capital, labour (hours), imported inputs	TFP, labour force, capital stock
GR	Bank of Greece model	Cobb–Douglas	Single	Capital, labour	Labour force, technical progress and the NAWRU
ES	MTBE	Cobb–Douglas	Distinction value added market sector/ non-market sector	Capital, labour	Technical progress, population and NAIRU (real exchange rate and real interest rate are given with regard to the rest of the world)
FR	MASCOTTE	Cobb–Douglas	Single	Capital, labour	Exogenous labour productivity trend, labour force and equilibrium rate of unemployment
IE	MCM block	Cobb–Douglas	Single	Capital, labour	Labour force, technical progress, NAIRU, cost of capital
IT	BIQM	Cobb–Douglas	Multiple	Capital, labour	Technical progress, population growth (real exchange and interest rates fix the level with regard to the rest of the world)

Table 1.2   (continued)

	Model name	Production function	Types of output	Types of factors	Long-run output determinants
LU	MCM block	Cobb–Douglas	Single	Capital, labour	Technical progress, labour force and the capital stock
NL	MORKMON	CES	Distinction value added market sector/ semi-public sector	Capital, labour	Labour supply, capital stock, implicit equilibrium unemployment rate, technical progress
NL	EUROMON	CES	Single	Capital, labour (hours)	Labour force, capital stock, TFP, NAWRU
AT	AQM	Cobb–Douglas	Single	Capital, labour	Technical progress, labour force, NAWRU
PT	AMM	Cobb–Douglas	Public sector, farm and non-farm private sector	Capital, labour and oil as an intermediate input	Technical progress, labour force, NAIRU and real interest rate
FI	BOFMINI	CES	Single	Capital, labour (hours)	Technical progress, labour force and real interest rate
FI	EDGE	Cobb–Douglas	Single	Capital, labour	Technical progress, labour force, real interest rate and NAIRU
ECB	AWM	Cobb–Douglas	Single	Capital, labour	Technical progress, labour force, NAIRU and the steady-state real interest rate

The key building block of a macroeconomic model is an explicit *supply side*. As shown in Table 1.2, in nearly all cases the supply side of the model is based on a Cobb–Douglas production function. However, in the Belgian, Dutch and Finnish models, a constant elasticity of substitution (CES) production function is used. In most models there is just one type of output or sector of production. However, in the Belgian, Dutch, Spanish and Portuguese models, value added is disaggregated into the market sector and semi-public sector and in the Italian model there are multiple sectors. The factor inputs in the models typically consist of capital and labour.

Table 1.3   Forward-looking elements

	Model name	Forward-looking variables	Determination of forward-looking variables
BE	NBB Quarterly	(1) Labour demand, corporate investment, output price, (2) private consumption, residential investment, market value of housing, (3) human wealth, (4) market valuation of the capital stock, (5) long-term interest rate	(1)–(2) expected values of their respective long-run targets, (3) discounted sum of expected future labour incomes, (4) discounted sum of expected after-tax companies' incomes, (5) forward-looking term structure
DE	BbkM	(1) Short-term interest rate (2) Long-term interest rate (3) Exchange rate (4) Inflation	(1) EMU: deviation of money growth from its target; non-EMU countries: deviation of inflation from its target, (2) Term structure, forward-looking and backward-looking expectations (3) Short-term: UIP; long-term: PPP (4) As given in Table 11
GR	Bank of Greece model	None	
ES	MTBE	None	
FR	MASCOTTE	None	
IE	MCM block	None	
IT	BIQM	Exchange rate	Forward-looking UIP
LU	MCM block	None	
NL	MORKMON	None	
NL	EUROMON	None; yet to be developed	
AT	AQM	None	
PT	AMM	None	
FI	BOFMINI	(1) Private consumption, (2) fixed investment, (3) housing investment, (4) demand for labour, (5) price of housing, (6) producer prices, (7) price of exports of goods, (8) demand for money, (9) inventories, (10) negotiated wages, (11) long-run interest rates	(1), (8) utility-maximizing, household, (2) profit-maximizing firm, (3) profit-maximizing construction company, (4), (6)–(7) profit-maximizing firm, Rothembergian menu cost model, (5) demand and supply of housing, (9) cost-minimizing firm, (10) bargaining unions maximize expected real after-tax income, inflation expectations rational, (11) forward-looking term structure

Table 1.3   (continued)

	Model name	Forward-looking variables	Determination of forward-looking variables
FI	EDGE	(1) Private consumption, (2) fixed investment, (3) demand for labour, (4) inventories, (5) producer prices, (6) exchange rate, (7) long-run interest rates, (8) nominal wages, (9) market value of private wealth	(1) Utility maximizing household, (2) profit maximizing firm, (3), (5) profit-maximizing firm, Rotembergian menu cost model, (4) cost-minimizing firm, (6) forward-looking UIP, (7) forward-looking term structure, (8) Calvo contracts, (9) discounted present value of capital income
ECB	AWM	(1) Exchange rate (2) Long-term interest rate	(1) Forward-looking UIP (2) Forward-looking term structure

There is some heterogeneity in the long-run determinants of output. In all cases some measure of labour supply plays a role and the typical set-up is to include a measure of the labour force modified by some form of equilibrium unemployment rate, such as a non-accelerating inflation rate of unemployment (NAIRU) or non-accelerating wage rate of unemployment (NAWRU). In addition, a technical progress or total factor productivity term always plays a role. The role of capital is often included either directly via the capital stock (in the case of the MCM, AWM, EUROMON, German and Dutch models) or indirectly through the cost of capital or real interest rate. Finally, since the euro-area countries (individually) are generally considered small open economies, a number of foreign variables, such as the real exchange rate, can play a role (Italy and Spain). In the case of the Spanish model, the role of the real exchange rate is to affect price determination through its effect on firms' mark-ups over marginal costs.

An important feature of model design that has a major bearing on model properties is the treatment of *expectations* of variables such as long-term interest rates, the exchange rate and inflation. The traditional way of dealing with expectations in macro models was to assume that they are determined as a function of current and lagged values of some observed variables, often in the form of adaptive expectations. The theoretical development of the rational expectations hypothesis in recent decades has led many model builders to include expectations that are genuinely forward-looking in the sense that they are consistent with the future outcomes generated by the model. For this reason they are often called 'model-consistent' expectations. Around half of the models considered contain

Table 1.4   Determination of short-term interest rates

	Model name	Determination of short-term interest rates
BE	NBB quarterly	Exogenously determined (euro-area country model). When necessary a model for the eurozone is used: either NiGEM or a SDGEM built at the NBB
DE	BbkM	Monetary forecast targeting rule. For the euro-area countries a common targeting rule applies that is linked to euro-area aggregates
GR	Bank of Greece model	Exogenously determined (euro-area country model). However a Taylor rule can be used for the analysis of model properties
ES	MTBE	Exogenously determined (euro-area country model)
FR	MASCOTTE	Exogenously determined (euro-area country model). When necessary a model for the eurozone is used (NiGEM in most cases)
IE	MCM block	Exogenously determined (euro-area country model)
IT	BIQM	Exogenously determined (euro-area country model). However a Taylor rule can be used for the analysis of model properties
LU	MCM block	Exogenously determined (euro-area country model)
NL	MORKMON	Exogenously determined (euro-area country model). Model simulations can be made conditional on exogenously defined time path of policy controlled interest rates (for example, by using other models such as NiGEM and EUROMON that include Taylor rules)
NL	EUROMON	Taylor rule linked to euro-area aggregates
AT	AQM	Exogenously determined (euro-area country model)
PT	AMM	Exogenously determined (euro-area country model)
FI	BOFMINI	Exogenously determined (euro-area country model). However a real interest rate rule (unchanged compared to baseline) can be used to examine model properties
FI	EDGE	Taylor rule or Taylor rule conditional on central bank's model consistent forecast of euro-area aggregates
ECB	AWM	Taylor rule linked to euro-area aggregates

some *forward-looking elements*, as indicated in Table 1.3. The use of forward-looking behaviour is most common in the financial markets and particularly in the determination of long-term interest rates and the exchange rate. In some cases forward-looking behaviour characterizes the

Table 1.5   The monetary aggregates and interest rates in the model

	Model name	Monetary aggregates and their role	Interest rates present
BE	NBB Quarterly	None	3-month money market, over 6-year government bond, rates on credit to companies and to households
DE	BbkM	EMU: M3 (role: determination of long-run price level); Canada and US: M2; Japan: M3; UK: M4	3-month money market, 10-year government bond
GR	Bank of Greece model	None	3-month treasury bill rate, 3-year government bond, lending rates
ES	MTBE	None	3-months short-term (exogenous), long-term (10-year bonds) bank lending and mortgage rates
FR	MASCOTTE	None	Overnight money market rate, average long-term government bond rate
IE	MCM block	None	1-month inter-bank, 10-year government bond, credit interest rate to corporate sector
IT	BIQM	M1, M2, compulsory and free reserves, currency, bank and postal deposits	Overnight, inter-bank rate, T-bill rates, T-bond rates, loan and deposit rates
LU	MCM block	None	3-month money market and 10-year government bond
NL	MORKMON	Portfolio models for households, firms and pension funds (affect income channel of monetary transmission)	Market rates (3-month and 10-year) plus various deposit and loan rates
NL	EUROMON	M3 (demand-determined)	3-month money market, 10-year government bond

Table 1.5 (continued)

	Model name	Monetary aggregates and their role	Interest rates present
AT	AQM	None	3-month money market, 10-year government bond
PT	AMM	None	3-month money market rate plus various deposit and loan rates
FI	BOFMINI	M2 as part of private net wealth, M1 and M3 as post-recursive block	Market rates (3-month money market and 5-year government bond) plus various deposit and loan rates
FI	EDGE	None	3-month money market and 10-year government bond
ECB	AWM	M3 (recursive)	3-month money market, 10-year government bond

policy rules used for short-term interest rates. In the Belgian, Finnish and EDGE models there is a wide range of forward-looking elements in labour markets, output and price formation and in the determination of wealth.

Another practice that has become increasingly widespread in recent years has been the use of *monetary policy rules* in macroeconomic models. These can take a number of forms, including Taylor rules, inflation targets or money base targets. They are generally implemented as an 'optional' feature in that the model user can choose whether they are operational in simulation analyses. Policy rules are rarely used in preparing forecasts where it is more common to implement a predetermined exogenous path of interest rates. It is worth noting that, for the models describing individual countries of the euro area, a national monetary policy rule is clearly not consistent with the single euro-area monetary policy. This is not a problem for the euro area and multi-country models which include monetary policy rules that target euro area aggregates. As indicated in Table 1.4, in the single-country models, it is possible to use an exogenously defined path for policy interest rates taken from other models with policy rules that are linked to euro area aggregates. In addition, as shown in the table, a number of the models for euro-area countries include explicit monetary policy

Table 1.6   The government sector and fiscal policy rules

	Model name	Disaggregation of the government sector (categories)	Fiscal rule option	Target variable(s)	Instrument variable(s)
BE	NBB quarterly	6 expenditure (2 endogenous, 4 exogenous in real terms); 8 revenue (4 direct taxes, 1 indirect taxes, 3 social security contributions)	Yes	Deficit and debt to GDP ratios	Transfers to households
DE	BbkM	Germany: 7 revenue (6 endogenous) 6 expenditure (4 endogenous); other countries: 2 revenue, 2 expenditure	Yes	Deficit	Nominal government consumption
GR	Bank of Greece model	5 expenditure (4 exogenous) 3 revenue (1 exogenous)	Yes	Government debt to GDP ratio	Direct taxation
ES	MTBE	8 expenditure (2 exogenous) 19 revenue (4 exogenous)	Yes	Government debt to GDP ratio	Direct taxation on households
FR	MASCOTTE	13 expenditure (5 exogenous) 16 revenue	No		
IE	MCM block	6 expenditure (1 exogenous) 4 revenue (2 exogenous)	No		
IT	BIQM	13 expenditure (main items) 11 revenues (main items)	No		
LU	MCM block	4 expenditure (2 exogenous) 6 revenue (1 exogenous)	No		

Table 1.6 (continued)

	Model name	Disaggregation of the government sector (categories)	Fiscal rule option	Target variable(s)	Instrument variable(s)
NL	MORKMON	8 expenditure categories (3 exogenous) 5 main revenue categories: income taxes, corporate taxes, indirect taxes, employers' social security premiums, employees' social security premiums	Yes	Real expenditure target; deficit target	Tax rates as well as expenditure categories
NL	EUROMON	5 expenditure 4 revenues	Yes	Government deficit to GDP ratio	Personal income tax rates
AT	AQM	4 expenditure (1 exogenous) 5 revenue (1 exogenous)	Yes	Government debt to GDP ratio	Direct taxation on households
PT	AMM	22 expenditures 26 revenues	No		
FI	BOFMINI	Expenditures and revenues disaggregated (direct and indirect taxation, corporate taxation, social security contributions).	No		
FI	EDGE	3 expenditure 4 revenue	Yes	Government deficit and debt to GDP ratio	Direct taxation
ECB	AWM	6 expenditure (2 exogenous) 4 revenue (1 exogenous)	Yes	Government deficit to GDP ratio	Direct taxation

rules, usually in the form of a Taylor rule, which can be useful for analysing model properties or undertaking historical counterfactual analyses.

Treatment of Monetary and Fiscal Sectors

As regards the monetary aggregates and interest rates present in the models, Table 1.5 indicates that in many of the models there is no direct role for monetary aggregates in determining output and prices. Indeed where monetary aggregates are present they are usually treated as recursive; that is, they have no feedback on the rest of the model. The main exception is the German model, where M3 plays a role in the determination of the long-run price level. The models typically include both a short-term (three-month money market) and a long-term (ten-year bond) interest rate and many include other interest rates as well.

As shown in Table 1.6, most of the models disaggregate the government sector into a number of revenue and expenditure categories. Typically there are around four to six categories of expenditure in the models, with the French, Italian and Portuguese models being somewhat more disaggregated. As regards revenue categories, most models have between four and eight categories, with the French, Italian and the Portuguese models offering the most detailed disaggregation (16, 11 and 26 categories, respectively). Disaggregation may facilitate the use of the models for preparing more detailed projections for the public finances. It should be noted that, in most models, one or two of the expenditure and revenue categories are kept exogenous. Such exogenous categories nevertheless provide useful means by which fiscal policy shocks can be undertaken in the models.

It has long been recognized by macro-modellers that the intertemporal government budget constraint should be taken into account in simulations (especially those with a long horizon).[4] Therefore many models now incorporate explicit fiscal closure rules, which aim to maintain some level of fiscal solvency by adjusting fiscal variables to achieve a target specified in terms of either the deficit or the debt ratio. As with the monetary policy reaction function, activation of such rules is usually at the discretion of the model user.

As indicated in Table 1.6, in some cases the fiscal policy reaction function aims to achieve a target level specified in terms of the government deficit, whilst in other cases the government debt stock is the target (or, in the case of the Belgian and EDGE models, both aims are addressed simultaneously). The fiscal rule in the Dutch model also has a real expenditure target. The instrument variables used to achieve the target vary considerably across the models. In most cases some form of direct taxation is used, but in the Belgian and German models the adjustment takes place on the expenditure side. In the Belgian model transfers to households are adjusted to achieve the fiscal target, while in the German model the adjustment takes place via nominal government consumption. In the Dutch model both tax rates and expenditures are used as instrument variables.

3 A DESCRIPTION OF THE BEHAVIOURAL EQUATIONS

Aggregate Demand and Employment

The key behavioural equations in the models are reported in Tables 1.7 to 1.13. These tables give information on the long-run determinants in the behavioural equations and any additional variables that have an effect only in the short run. Table 1.7 gives some summary details of the determinants of *consumer spending*. Most models do not differentiate between different types of consumption. However, in the Portuguese and Italian models, a distinction is made between durables and non-durables and in the latter

Table 1.7   Treatment of consumption

	Model name	Disaggregation	Long-run determinants	Additional short-run determinants
BE	NBB quarterly	None	(1) Human and financial wealth (2) Unemployment rate as a proxy for countercyclical riskiness of income	Disposable labour income for liquidity-constrained consumers
DE	BbkM	None	Real disposable income; Germany (additionally): real net financial wealth	Real long-term interest rate
GR	Bank of Greece model	None	Real disposable income and real short-term interest rate	Inflation surprise
ES	MTBE	None	Real disposable income, real wealth of the private sector (financial and residential) and long-term real interest rates	

Table 1.7   (continued)

	Model name	Disaggregation	Long-run determinants	Additional short-run determinants
FR	MASCOTTE	None	The long run of the equation determines the saving ratio as a function of real disposable income growth, inflation and the ratio of the change in the outstanding level of cash loans to households over disposable income	
IE	MCM block	None	Wealth	Disposable income, short-term interest rates, credit
IT	BIQM	(1) Non-durables, (2) durables, (3) Tourism	(1) Disposable income, wealth and real interest rate, (2) non-durable consumption, relative price, real interest rate, female participation rate, (3) relative prices and relative incomes	
LU	MCM block	None	Real disposable income, real financial wealth, long-term real interest rates	
NL	MORKMON	None	Real disposable income, real financial and non-financial wealth, long-term interest rates	Change in the unemployment rate and the government budget balance
NL	EUROMON	None	Real disposable income, real financial and non-financial wealth, long-term interest rates	Change in the unemployment rate and the government budget balance; change in short- and long-term interest rates

Table 1.7 (continued)

	Model name	Disaggregation	Long-run determinants	Additional short-run determinants
AT	AQM	None	Real disposable income, real financial wealth, long-term interest rates	
PT	AMM	(1) Non-durables, (2) durables, (3) housing rents	(1) Real disposable income (adjusted by households' debt redemptions), potential output and interest rates, (2) real disposable income (adjusted by households' debt redemptions) and interest rates, (3) stock of housing	(2) Unemployment rate
FI	BOFMINI	None	Real disposable income, real net wealth (asset wealth plus discounted value of future income), real interest rate	Some consumers myopic or liquidity-constrained
FI	EDGE	None	Real disposable income, market value of assets, real interest rate	Expected future income
ECB	AWM	None	Real disposable income and wealth	Short-term interest rates and unemployment

model there are two additional equations for tourist expenditure. Most models find a role for both income and wealth as long-run determinants of consumption. However long-run wealth effects are not present in the Greek, French and Portuguese models, while long-run income effects are not present in the Belgian or Irish models. In the Belgian case a long-run income effect enters via the human wealth variable, which is the discounted value of current and future income. Around half of the models have direct interest rate effects in consumption in order to account for direct intertemporal substitution effects.

In terms of additional short-run determinants of consumption, some models include terms to capture cyclical factors which may affect consumer spending (for example, the change in the unemployment rate, employment and the deviation of inflation from trend).[5] The Belgian model allows disposable labour income to have a short-run impact for liquidity-constrained consumers and the Finnish model also assumes that some consumers are myopic or liquidity-constrained. Another specific feature worthy of mention is that consumers in the Dutch model increase expenditure when the government budget balance improves; a type of Ricardian effect.

Table 1.8 gives details of the treatment of *investment* in the models. As the table indicates, in nearly all of the models, there is some degree of disaggregation of investment. This varies across models, but the categories

Table 1.8   Treatment of investment

	Model name	Disaggregation	Long-run determinants	Additional short-run determinants
BE	NBB Quarterly	(1) Residential, (2) non-residential, (3) government	(1) Disposable income, excess mortgage rate, (2) output and relative factor prices and capacity utilization, (3) exogenous in real terms	(2) Accelerator and changes in Tobin's Q
DE	BbkM	Germany: (1) machinery and equipment investment (firms and government separately), (2) construction investment (firms and government separately), (3) residential construction investment; other countries: none	(1) Firms: final demand; government: exogenous in nominal terms; (2) Firms: firms' machinery and equipment investment; government: exogenous in nominal terms, (3) private consumption	(1) Firms: real long-term interest rate
GR	Bank of Greece model	Private, public	User cost of capital (marginal condition)	GDP, a measure of profitability
ES	MTBE	(1) Private productive, (2) residential, (3) public (exogenous)	(1) Output, relative factor prices (user cost of capital and wages), (2) private consumption and user cost of capital	(1) Cash-flow, (2) financial wealth and the unemployment rate

Table 1.8 (continued)

	Model name	Disaggregation	Long-run determinants	Additional short-run determinants
FR	MASCOTTE	(1) Equipment, (2) buildings, (3) housing, (4) public	(1) Value added and user cost, (2) equipment investment, (3) real disposable income, real LT interest rate and investment price relative to consumption price, (4) exogenous	Profits, capacity utilization rate, fiscal measures concerning housing investment
IE	MCM block	None	(Long-run equation refers to capital stock) Output, wages, technical progress, cost of capital	
IT	BIQM	(1) Equipment, (2) structures, (3) residential buildings, (4) public sector investment	(1) Optimal capital/output ratio, private-sector value added, (2) private- sector value added, real interest rate, (3) tax rate on houses, real interest rate, market price relative to replacement cost, stock of per capita houses, (4) level of economic activity and discretionary fiscal impulse	(1) Adjustment costs, delivery lags, business confidence and spread between lending rate and T-bond rate, (2) business confidence
LU	MCM block	None	Output, relative factor prices (user cost of capital and wages)	
NL	MORKMON	(1) Non-residential, (2) residential, (3) government	(1) User cost of capital, firms' profitability and output, (2) real disposable income, long-term interest rates, house prices, rents, (3) exogenous	(1) Total sales, capacity utilization

Table 1.8   (continued)

	Model name	Disaggregation	Long-run determinants	Additional short-run determinants
NL	EUROMON	(1) Non-residential, (2) residential, (3) government	(1) User cost of capital, capital–output ratio, (2) real disposable income, real long- and short-term interest rates, (3) exogenous	(1) Change in sales; change in interest rates; change in profitability
AT	AQM	Equipment, residential, other, government	Relative factor costs, capital–output ratio	Short-run accelerator mechanism
PT	AMM	(1) Non-residential, (2) residential, (3) public (exogenous)	(1) User cost of capital and real GDP, (2) real disposable income (adjusted by households' debt redemptions) and interest rate	
FI	BOFMINI	(1) Non-residential, (2) residential, (3) public (exogenous)	Marginal product of capital, user cost of capital, real price of investment	(2) Tobin's Q
FI	EDGE	Private, public	Marginal product of capital, user cost of capital, real price of investment	
ECB	AWM	Private, public	User cost of capital and marginal productivity of capital	GDP accelerator effects

include residential construction, business construction, machinery, inventories and government/public sector investment. Typically investment is determined by output and a user cost of capital variable. However, as shown in the table, there are differences in the long-run and short-run determinants of investment. These differences arise both across investment functions in different models and according to the treatment of different types of investment within individual models.

Turning now to the labour market, the determination of *employment* in the models is detailed in Table 1.9. In some cases there is no disaggregation of employment, while in others there is a split made between public and private sector employment. In a small number of cases there is a more detailed disaggregation into categories such as employees/self-employed

Table 1.9   Treatment of employment

	Model name	Disaggregation	Long-run determinants	Additional short-run determinants
BE	NBB Quarterly	(1) Private, (2) public	(1) Output and relative factor prices, (2) exogenous	Expected change in hours
DE	BbkM	Germany: residents in employment, commuters, self-employed; no sectoral disaggregation	Real final demand, real wage	
GR	Bank of Greece model	Total employment	Inverted production function	Real product wages and GDP
ES	MTBE	(1) Private, (2) public (exogenous)	(1) Output, capital, technological progress	Real wages
FR	MASCOTTE	(1) Business sector (financial, non-financial and unincorporated enterprises), (2) public sector, households, NPISH, self-employed	(1) Value-added in the private sector and real labour cost (in terms of the value added deflator), (2) all exogenous	Working time and capacity utilization rate
IE	MCM block	None	Output, capital/ labour ratio, technical progress	
IT	BIQM	(1) Non-farm non-energy sector, (2) farm, (3) Energy, (4) public sector (exogenous)	(1) Value added, technical progress, optimal labour/ output ratio, (2) total employment and trend decrease in farm employment share, (3) private sector value added, energy sector value added and total employment	(1) Adjustment costs and delivery lags for capital goods (3) Relative wage
LU	MCM block	None	Output, capital, technical progress (inverted production function)	Real wages

Table 1.9 (continued)

	Model name	Disaggregation	Long-run determinants	Additional short-run determinants
NL	MORKMON	Market-sector versus semi-public sector	Real product wages, output, technical progress, relative minimum wage	
NL	EUROMON	None	Real product wages, output, technical progress	
AT	AQM	Self-employed, employees, public	Capital labour ratio, output, technical progress (inversion of the production function)	Real wages, output
PT	AMM	Non-farm private sector, farm and public (exogenous)	Labour force and NAIRU	Real GDP, real wages and productivity
FI	BOFMINI	Hours disaggregated (private/government sector, employees/ self-employed)	Output, capital stock, technical progress	
FI	EDGE	None	NAIRU, labour force	Output, capital stock, technical progress
ECB	AWM	None	Output and the capital stock (inversion of the production function)	Real wage, productivity

and also in some cases a further disaggregation by sector, usually some measure of output adjusted for trend productivity and the price (or relative price) of labour function as the long-run determinants of employment. Models differ according to whether they have endogenous or exogenous long-run unemployment.

Costs and Prices

Table 1.10 provides details of the treatment of *wages*. The disaggregation of wages is typically along the same lines as the disaggregation in employment.

Table 1.10   Treatment of wages

	Model name	Disaggregation	Framework	Long-run determinants	Additional short-run determinants
BE	NBB quarterly	(1) Private, (2) public	(1a) Right to manage, (1b) legal wage norm, (2) demonstration effect from private wages	(1a) Unemployment rate, long-run, productivity tax wedge, price wedge, (1b) exogenous in real terms, (2) private gross wages	(1a)–(1b)–(2) Indexation mechanism
DE	BbkM	None	Phillips curve	Consumer price deflator	Deviation of unemployment from a smoothed unemployment rate
GR	Bank of Greece model	Whole economy average earnings	Wage bargaining	Real product wage equals average productivity	CPI inflation and deviation of unemployment from the NAWRU
ES	MTBE	(1) Private, (2) public (exogenous)	Wage-bargaining framework	GDP deflator, labour productivity, unemployment, tax wedge and replacement ratio	Private consumption deflator
FR	MASCOTTE	(1) Business, (2) public, households, NPISH, self-employed	(1) Wage-bargaining framework, (2) Functions of wages in the business sector	Consumption deflator, tax wedge, actual labour productivity, unemployment rate	Inflation (consumption and value added deflators), employers' social contribution rate
IE	MCM block	None	Long-run: mark-up; short-run: Phillips curve	GDP deflator and productivity (corrected for transfer pricing)	Deviation from NAIRU
IT	BIQM	Private-sector (3 equations) and public sector	Phillips curve for the private non-farm non-energy sector; identities for others	Inflation expectations, constant trend productivity growth	Unemployment and output gap, hours lost to strikes
LU	MCM block	None	Phillips curve	Marginal productivity condiion	Unemployment, direct tax rate

Table 1.10   (continued)

	Model name	Disaggregation	Framework	Long-run determinants	Additional short-run determinants
NL	MORKMON	(1) Firms, (2) Government	(1) Right to manage, (2) Government	(1) Producer and consumer prices, unemployment, productivity, replacement ratio, tax shifting employers and employees (2) firms' wages	
NL	EUROMON	(1) Firms, (2) Government	(1) Right to manage, (2) follows firms	(1) Producer prices, consumer prices, productivity, unemployment rate, tax shifting (2) firms' wages	
AT	AQM	None	Phillips curve	Consumer price deflator, marginal productivity condition	Inflation, productivity
PT	AMM	Public (exogenous), farm and non-farm private sector	Phillips curve	Inflation and productivity	Unemployment 'gap' (actual unemployment minus the NAIRU)
FI	BOFMINI	(1) Negotiated wages, (2) wage drift, private/ government sector	Right to manage, Phillips curve	(1) Inflation expectations, tax wedges, unemployment, (2) real wage gap, unemployment	(1) Unemployment (2) changes in MPL
FI	EDGE	None	Phillips curve (New Keynesian)	Marginal productivity condition	Unemployment, GDP deflator
ECB	AWM	None	Phillips curve	Marginal productivity condition	Unemployment, consumer price deflator

In most cases the underlying framework for the wage equation is provided by the (short-run) Phillips curve. The Belgian, Dutch, Finnish, Spanish and EUROMON models incorporate a 'right to manage' bargaining framework for the determination of private sector wages. The EDGE model incorporates the idea of 'overlapping contracts'. In most cases unemployment (or the deviation of actual unemployment from some measure of equilibrium) also has a role in the determination of wages although, since unemployment cannot permanently deviate from its equilibrium rate, such a role is only present in the short run. All models have a role for inflation or inflation expectations, usually in the short-run determination of wages. Structural factors, such as the tax wedge or the replacement ratio, are also found to affect wages in the short run in some models and can have long-run impacts on structural unemployment.

The treatment of *prices and deflators* is described in detail in Table 1.11. Most models assign a 'key' role to the GDP deflator measured either at market prices or at factor cost. Prices are generally set as a mark-up over

Table 1.11   Treatment of prices and deflators

	Model name	Key domestic Prices/deflators	Long-run determinants	Additional short-run determinants	HICP and breakdown
BE	NBB quarterly	(1) Output price, (2) consumption deflator, (3) import deflator, (4) export deflator	(1) Variable mark-up over marginal costs, a function of eurozone competitors' price and of capacity utilization, (2) output, import and energy prices augmented with indirect taxes, public consumption deflator, (3) competitors' price on the import side and domestic output price, (4) output price and competitors' price on the export side	(3) and (4) capacity utilization	Aggregate HICP and subcomponents for energy, unprocessed food
DE	BbkM	The central inflation equation determines the change in the deflator of domestic demand	Wage rate, import prices, inflationary expectations, additional in EMU: equilibrium price level P-Star	Output gap, additional in EMU: price gap	HICP not modelled

Table 1.11   (continued)

	Model name	Key domestic Prices/deflators	Long-run determinants	Additional short-run determinants	HICP and breakdown
GR	Bank of Greece model	GDP deflator at factor cost	Unit labour cost, import prices, ratio of tertiary sector value added to GDP		Satellite model for HICP and unprocessed food subcomponent
ES	MTBE	Private value-added deflator	Wages, external prices, output–capital ratio and technical progress	Import deflator	Energy and non-energy
FR	MASCOTTE	Value-added deflator (1), domestic demand deflators (excluding VAT) (2), export and import deflators (3)	(1) Unit labour cost and capacity utilization rate, (2) value-added deflator and import deflator, (3) production prices and competitors' prices		Non-energy component (bridge equation), energy (function of the oil price), aggregate HICP (definition)
IE	MCM block	(1) GDP deflator, (2) Consumption deflator	(1) Short-run marginal costs, degree of competition for output (mark-up over marginal costs), (2) GDP deflator and import deflator		HICP not modelled
IT	BIQM	(1) NFNE private sector value added deflator, (2) import deflator	(1) ULC, real exchange rate, (2) foreign prices and effective exchange rate	(1) Input prices, output gap, ratio of self-employed to dependent workers, (2) relative cycle	
LU	MCM block	GDP deflator at factor cost	Unit labour costs, output–capital ratio and technical progress	Import prices	
NL	MORKMON	Private consumption, non-residential and residential investment, goods and services exports;	Unit labour costs; capital costs; prices of imported commodities, services and energy all	Capacity utilization	Aggregate HICP

Table 1.11   (continued)

	Model name	Key domestic Prices/deflators	Long-run determinants	Additional short-run determinants	HICP and breakdown
		prices for all main expenditure categories treated similarly	weighted according to input–output structure; competitors' or import prices		
NL	EUROMON	Private consumption deflator	Unit labour costs; competitors' or import prices, oil price, indirect taxes	Output gap, and changes in wages, unemployment	Aggregate HICP
AT	AQM	GDP deflator at factor cost	Wages, technical progress, output–capital ratio	Import prices	Aggregate HICP, energy and non-energy component
PT	AMM	Consumption deflator	Wages, long-run productivity and import prices	Energy prices	HICP not modelled
FI	BOFMINI	(1) Producer price, (2) export prices	Marginal cost in private sector/ export production, (2) competitors' prices		Aggregate HICP
FI	EDGE	GDP deflator at factor cost	Marginal cost in production		
ECB	AWM	GDP deflator at factor cost	Trend unit labour costs	Import prices	Aggregate HICP

unit labour costs. In the German model the development of prices is influenced by the price gap, which comprises the output gap and the velocity gap. Also important are foreign prices captured through the import deflator or the effective exchange rate. In a number of cases there is a role for cyclical indicators, such as capacity utilization or the output gap, in explaining the short-run dynamics of prices.

Trade and Balance of Payments

As regards *trade*, Tables 1.12 and 1.13 describe the determination of export and import volumes. Around half the models analyse total trade in goods and services, while in the remainder there is some form of disaggregation.

Table 1.12   Treatment of export volumes

	Model name	Disaggregation	Long-run determinants	Additional short-run determinants
BE	NBB quarterly	None (at present)	Export markets and competitiveness	Degree of capacity utilization
DE	BbkM	None (includes intra-euro area trade)	World import demand, determined through the trading partners' import volumes expressed in the exporter's currency	
GR	Bank of Greece model	None	World demand and competitiveness	
ES	MTBE	(1) Euro-area goods, (2) rest of world goods, (3) services	World demand, competitiveness	
FR	MASCOTTE	Goods and services	World demand and competitiveness	
IE	MCM block	None	World trade, competitiveness	
IT	BIQM	(1) Goods (3 equations), (2) services	(1) World demand, competitiveness, (2) goods trade, competitiveness	Output gap
LU	MCM block	None	World demand and competitiveness	Exchange rate
NL	MORKMON	(1) Non-energy, (2) energy, (3) services	(1) World demand; relative export prices; rate of capacity utilization; labour income share; (2) world output; relative energy (oil) prices ; (3) competitiveness of services exports; exports of goods	
NL	EUROMON	None	World demand, relative export prices	
AT	AQM	None	Word demand, relative export prices	

Table 1.12   (continued)

	Model name	Disaggregation	Long-run determinants	Additional short-run determinants
PT	AMM	Goods, tourism and other services	World demand and competitiveness	Private consumption (to reflect the substitution between sales in domestic and external markets)
FI	BOFMINI	(1) Exports of goods, (2) exports of services	(1) World demand and competitiveness (default: finite price elasticity), (2) world demand and competitiveness	
FI	EDGE	None (includes intra-euro area trade)	World demand competitiveness	
ECB	AWM	None (includes intra-euro area trade)	World demand and competitiveness	

Usually this separates goods and services, but in the case of the Italian model there is a detailed sectoral breakdown. Some models isolate energy trade (or, more specifically, oil), particularly on the import side. The long-run determinants of exports typically include world demand and competitiveness, with a number of additional factors playing a role in the short run. Imports are usually linked to a measure of domestic demand and competitiveness, again with a number of specific short-term factors. In the trade blocs of the multi-country models a distinction is often made between intra- and extra euro-area long-run determinants, making it possible thereby to assess separately the role of extra-area as opposed to intra-area factors in determining the overall trade pattern for each country. For reasons of data availability, the euro-area aggregate models, AWM and EDGE, use gross trade (that is, including intra euro-area flows). In many models the long-run equilibrium exchange rate is determined from model conditions for stock-flow equilibrium in the domestic and external sectors.

Table 1.13   Treatment of import volumes

	Model name	Disaggregation	Long-run determinants	Additional short-run determinants
BE	NBB quarterly	None	Final demand weighted by import content and competitiveness	Degree of capacity utilization
DE	BbkM	None (includes intra-euro area trade)	Final demand, ratio of the final demand deflator (corrected for indirect taxation) and import prices	
GR	Bank of Greece model	None	Final demand weighted by import content, import deflator and GDP deflator	
ES	MTBE	(1) Euro-area goods, (2) Rest of world goods, (3) services	Final demand weighted by import content, competitiveness	
FR	MASCOTTE	Goods excluding energy, energy and services	Final demand weighted by the corresponding import contents, competitiveness and a time drift	Capacity utilization rate
IE	MCM block	None	Relative prices, import-weighted domestic demand	
IT	BIQM	(1) Goods (3 equations), (2) services	(1) Final demand weighted by import content and competitiveness, (2) goods trade, relative prices	Output gap
LU	MCM block	None	Final demand weighted by import content and competitiveness (import deflator and GDP deflator)	

Table 1.13 (continued)

	Model name	Disaggregation	Long-run determinants	Additional short-run determinants
NL	MORKMON	(1) Non-energy, (2) energy, (3) services	(1) Sales; relative import prices; rate of capacity utilization; openness indicator; inventories relative to sales, (2) sales; relative energy (oil) prices, (3) sales; relative price of services import	
NL	EUROMON	None	Sales and real import prices	Output gap and change in inventories-to-sales ratio
AT	AQM	None	Final demand weighted by import content, competitiveness	
PT	AMM	Goods excluding oil, oil and services	Final demand weighted by import content and relative prices	
FI	BOFMINI	(1) Imports of goods, (2) imports of services	(1) Exports of goods, at factor cost, producer prices and import prices, (2) exports of goods, production at factor cost, consumption, consumption deflator and import prices	Consumption, investment
FI	EDGE	None	Domestic demand, import deflator, GDP deflator	
ECB	AWM	None (includes intra-euro area trade)	Final demand weighted by import content, import deflator, GDP deflator	

4 SIMULATION PROPERTIES OF EUROSYSTEM MODELS

In this section some basic model properties are compared on the basis of the results from five simulations which have been conducted on a largely harmonized basis.[6] Some of the individual model chapters also report the elasticities from the key behavioural equations in the models. However, in order to better understand the properties of the models, it is most useful to compare whole model properties rather than single equation elasticities. The five simulations are as follows:

1. *A monetary policy shock* in which the short-term (typically three-month money market) interest rate is shifted upwards by 100 basis points for two years.[7]
2. *A fiscal policy shock* in which real government consumption (all elements) is increased by 1 per cent of initial real GDP for five years.
3. *A foreign demand shock* in which the level of real imports of each country's trading partners outside the euro area is increased by 1 per cent for five years.
4. *An exchange rate shock* in which the euro strengthens for five years by 1 per cent against all other currencies.
5. *An oil price shock* in which oil prices increase by 10 per cent in US dollar terms for five years.

A key element in this exercise was that the simulations were conducted on a largely harmonized basis. In particular, common practices were followed by modellers with respect to the treatment of monetary and fiscal policy and the exchange rate. These common practices entail monetary and fiscal policy rules being switched off. It should be kept in mind that this is likely to alter the stability properties of the models and hence will affect the persistence of the responses of prices and output. Full details of the agreed design of these harmonized simulations are provided in the Annex to this chapter.[8]

In relation to the transmission of monetary policy, van Els *et al.* (2003) identify five channels as being present in most of the participating models: the exchange rate channel, the substitution-effect-in-consumption channel, the cost-of-capital channel, the income/cash-flow channel and the wealth channel. Table 1.14 indicates which of these channels are present in each of the models. The exchange rate channel exists in all models. It feeds directly into the euro price of oil and other commodities (involving the euro–dollar exchange rate) and the foreign prices of other goods and services (involving the effective exchange rate). The change in

Table 1.14 *Conventional channels of monetary transmission in ESCB models*

	Model name	Exchange rate	Substitution	Cost of capital	Cash-flow/ income	Wealth
BE	NBB quarterly	P	S	P	S	P
DE	BbkM	P	P	P	P	N
GR	Bank of Greece model	P	P	P	N	N
ES	MTBE	P	P	P	P	P
FR	MASCOTTE	P	S	P	P	N
IE	MCM block	P	P	S	N	P
IT	BIQM	P	P	P	P	P
LU	MCM block	P	P	P	N	P
NL	MORKMON	P	P	P	S(1)	S(2)
NL	EUROMON	P	P	P	P	S(2)
AT	AQM	P	P	P	P	P
PT	AMM	P	P	P	P	N
FI	BOFMINI	P	P	P	P	S
FI	EDGE	P	P	P	S	P
ECB	AWM	P	P	P	P	P

Notes: P: channel present, S: channel present but has special feature, N: channel not present; (1) includes portfolio reallocation channel, (2) endogenous asset prices.

import prices and competitors' prices in euros initiates a change in domestic prices, which spreads through the price and wage system, thereby affecting competitiveness and real wages.

The substitution-effect-in-consumption channel also exists in all models and can affect both short-run and long-run consumption.[9] In some cases the driving variable is the short-term interest rate, while in others the effect comes via the long-term interest rate. In a small number of cases, a distinction is made between consumption expenditure on durables and nondurables. For example, in the Italian model, the former responds to the bank lending rate while the latter responds to real Treasury bond yields.

The cost-of-capital channel is also present in all models. However there are differences across the various models in the way this channel is incorporated. In many cases, the link between interest rates (generally long-term) and business investment is via the capital stock. A change in interest rates affects the user cost of capital, which affects the desired capital stock and thereby investment. Because of adjustment costs, investment can only gradually bring the actual capital stock to its desired level. The user cost of capital variable is designed to reflect long-term borrowing costs and its precise construction varies across models.

The combined cash flow/income channel exists in all models except those for Greece, Ireland and Luxembourg. The impact of this channel will depend on the financial position of households and firms at the time of the policy action. In the model for the Netherlands the income channel includes the effects of portfolio reallocation by households and firms.[10]

The wealth channel is not present in the models for Germany, Greece, Portugal and France. Changes in wealth are caused by (cumulated) changes in asset holdings (M3, bonds, shares and net foreign assets) as well as by valuation effects. Most countries have some form of endogenous bond price determination. In addition some other asset prices are endogenous in the models for Finland, Spain, EUROMON and the Netherlands (house and share prices). In the Portuguese case a particular feature of the model is the inclusion of a debt redemption correction for disposable income.

Finally there are a number of country-specific channels that are not shown in the table. In the German model there is a separate monetary channel which transmits interest rate impulses directly to inflation via the price gap, which is the deviation of the actual price level from the equilibrium price level P-Star. A rise in interest rates leads to a reduction in the monetary aggregate M3 and in P-Star, thereby leading to a fall in prices. In the Italian model two additional channels are operating: (a) the expectations channel capturing the direct impact of changes in policy-controlled interest rates on inflation expectations, and (b) the portfolio channel which includes the effects of portfolio reallocation by households. The latter channel is also present in the Dutch model but there it is included in the joint income/cash-flow channel.

For the monetary policy shock the results reported are based on a carefully designed common simulation experiment involving a 100 basis point rise in the policy interest rate for two years, accompanied by common assumptions regarding the path of long-term interest rates and the exchange rate. It should also be noted that, for this simulation, unlike the subsequent ones, the results include spillovers between euro-area countries.[11] A detailed description of the design of the experiment is reported in van Els *et al.* (2003).

Table 1.15a summarizes the main findings in terms of real GDP. The 'typical' pattern is that in the first year real GDP falls by around 0.2 per cent relative to baseline. Subsequently the maximum average reduction in real GDP of around 0.4–0.5 per cent is obtained in years 2 and 3 of the simulation. Thereafter, with nominal short-term interest rates returning

Table 1.15a   Monetary policy shock (GDP response)

	1	2	3	4	5
Belgium	−0.15	−0.20	−0.10	−0.05	−0.03
Germany	−0.28	−0.33	−0.09	0.15	0.26
Greece	−0.33	−0.62	−0.52	−0.52	−0.52
Spain	−0.25	−0.38	−0.32	−0.16	−0.06
France	−0.07	−0.15	−0.20	−0.16	−0.08
Ireland	−0.25	−0.48	−0.43	−0.38	−0.32
Italy	−0.26	−0.60	−0.55	−0.21	0.05
Luxembourg	−0.07	−0.24	−0.24	−0.17	−0.09
Netherlands	−0.20	−0.27	−0.25	−0.22	−0.16
Austria	−0.21	−0.29	−0.29	−0.25	−0.20
Portugal	−0.20	−0.57	−0.49	−0.09	+0.10
Finland	−0.34	−0.25	−0.15	−0.22	−0.25
AGG EUR-12	−0.22	−0.35	−0.27	−0.09	0.02
EDGE	−1.97	−0.48	0.21	−0.01	−0.07
EUROMON[2]	−0.12	−0.23	−0.23	−0.21	−0.19
AWM	−0.18	−0.51	−0.65	−0.61	−0.57

immediately to baseline, real GDP also begins to revert to baseline, which in some cases is already reached by year 5.

As can be seen from the table, the impact on real GDP is fairly moderate in the models for Belgium, Germany, France, Luxembourg, Austria, the Netherlands and Finland, with maximum effects of around 0.3 per cent or less. A second group of models with maximum effects on real GDP in the range of −0.3 per cent to −0.6 per cent includes those for Spain, Ireland, Portugal and Italy. Finally the fall in real GDP is largest in the results for Greece. In the majority of the models the negative impact on real GDP is strongest in year 2, although in the model for Finland the impact on output occurs earlier. In the German model real GDP effects are broadly similar in the first two years.

The impacts reported in the AWM and EDGE models tend to be larger than those reported in most of the individual euro-area countries. However the time profile of the effects in the two models is markedly different. The initial impact of the rise in interest rates is much larger in the EDGE model but is very short-lived (the peak effect in the EDGE model is actually reached in the first quarter when output falls by 2.4 per cent). The expected real interest rate increases immediately and cuts domestic demand through the wealth effect. Furthermore an increase in interest rates leads to an immediate appreciation of the real exchange rate, which cuts net trade through foreign trade elasticities. This reflects the highly forward-looking

Table 1.15b   Monetary policy shock (response of consumption deflator)

	1	2	3	4	5
Belgium	−0.10	−0.18	−0.21	−0.17	−0.12
Germany	−0.05	−0.19	−0.38	−0.56	−0.56
Greece	−0.17	−0.24	−0.32	−0.40	−0.45
Spain	−0.10	−0.21	−0.24	−0.22	−0.14
France	−0.07	−0.14	−0.25	−0.43	−0.61
Ireland	−0.09	−0.15	−0.15	−0.17	−0.22
Italy	−0.15	−0.33	−0.47	−0.50	−0.37
Luxembourg	−0.05	−0.13	−0.14	−0.15	−0.18
Netherlands	−0.12	−0.20	−0.22	−0.30	−0.38
Austria	−0.06	−0.17	−0.17	−0.12	−0.10
Portugal	−0.14	−0.27	−0.35	−0.33	−0.25
Finland	−0.54	−0.51	−0.17	−0.03	−0.08
AGG EUR-12	−0.10	−0.22	−0.32	−0.42	−0.42
EDGE	−0.29	−0.63	−0.83	−0.89	−0.89
EUROMON	−0.03	−0.10	−0.21	−0.39	−0.60
AWM	−0.06	−0.19	−0.31	−0.40	−0.49

nature of the EDGE model; as can be seen from Table 1.3, the EDGE model has many more forward-looking elements than the AWM model.[12] EUROMON reports fairly moderate effects of the monetary policy shock for the euro-area.

Table 1.15b gives details of the impact on the consumption deflator. The model for Finland is the only one where a particularly marked impact on prices arises in the first year. In the second and third years the impact on prices is still small in Austria, Ireland and Luxembourg, while the impact is consistently larger in Italy over this period.

Berben *et al.* (2004) examined the reasons for differences in the estimated transmission of monetary policy on the basis of an earlier vintage of these simulations. In particular they considered the extent to which these differences are due to differences in the underlying economies or (possibly unrelated) differences in the modelling strategies adopted for each country. They found that, against most yardsticks, the cross-country variations in the results appeared to be plausible in the sense that they corresponded with other evidence or observed characteristics of the economies in question. Nevertheless the role of differing modelling strategies was also thought likely to play an important role. Important features of the models, for instance in the treatment of expectations or wealth, can have a major bearing on the results that may not necessarily reflect differences in the underlying economies.

Table 1.16a   Fiscal policy shock (GDP response)

	1	2	3	4	5
Belgium	0.99	0.89	0.89	0.86	0.85
Germany	1.20	1.12	0.96	0.81	0.68
Greece	0.71	0.80	0.97	1.16	1.38
Spain	1.15	1.43	1.40	1.16	0.87
France	1.09	1.20	1.11	0.98	0.82
Ireland	1.13	1.22	1.20	1.10	0.92
Italy	1.16	1.30	1.39	1.37	1.21
Luxembourg	0.56	0.51	0.45	0.39	0.33
Netherlands	1.07	0.98	0.95	0.87	0.77
Austria	1.28	1.36	1.38	1.39	1.34
Portugal	1.18	1.20	1.16	1.08	0.99
Finland	1.19	0.86	0.27	0.17	−0.03
AGG EUR-12	1.14	1.18	1.12	1.02	0.88
EDGE	1.16	0.61	0.23	0.00	−0.14
EUROMON	1.07	1.24	1.52	1.74	1.92
AWM	1.31	1.56	1.64	1.63	1.56

The fiscal policy experiment involved a permanent 1 per cent of GDP increase in government consumption and the results are shown in Table 1.16a. Typically the first year effect of the fiscal shock is to raise GDP in the range 0.8 per cent to 1.2 per cent. However some models report lower rises in GDP, notably Luxembourg (0.6 per cent) and Greece (0.7 per cent). Thereafter in most models the impact on GDP rises and reaches a maximum in year 2 or year 3, as there is a loss of competitiveness due to rising prices and wages which leads to a crowding-out of exports.

In the case of Greece this crowding-out mechanism works somewhat more slowly as the impact on GDP, albeit initially small, continues to rise in the first five years. However, as indicated in the chapter on the Greek model, the impact on GDP is moderating by year 10. This slow reaction speed is linked to the fact that its parameters have been derived on the basis of data from 1965 to 2000 and will therefore reflect the important rigidities and regulations prevailing in goods and labour markets over this period. In contrast, in the simulations for Finland, the crowding-out effects are more rapid and there is a return to baseline by year 5. This is likely to be linked to the highly forward-looking nature of these models. As with the monetary policy simulations, including such forward-looking elements tends to raise the speed of adjustment to shocks.[13] Finally some of the smaller, more open economies, for example Luxembourg, tend to have low initial impacts

Table 1.16b   Fiscal policy shock (response of consumption deflator)

	1	2	3	4	5
Belgium	0.05	0.16	0.20	0.22	0.24
Germany	0.03	0.13	0.36	0.65	0.87
Greece	0.00	0.03	0.10	0.19	0.31
Spain	0.19	0.59	0.99	1.26	1.37
France	0.13	0.82	1.78	2.91	4.09
Ireland	0.01	0.07	0.23	0.48	0.79
Italy	0.03	0.23	0.62	1.18	1.89
Luxembourg	0.00	0.03	0.06	0.10	0.14
Netherlands	0.11	0.59	1.32	1.87	2.14
Austria	0.02	0.40	1.10	1.97	2.97
Portugal	0.08	0.21	0.33	0.43	0.51
Finland	0.73	1.32	0.87	0.41	0.17
AGG EUR-12	0.08	0.39	0.83	1.34	1.84
EDGE	0.39	1.00	1.38	1.56	1.66
EUROMON	0.10	0.77	1.91	3.52	5.35
AWM	0.19	0.56	0.92	1.36	1.91

from the fiscal shock as a major share of the rise in demand induced by the fiscal expansion is met through increased imports.

The initial impacts in the area-wide and multi-country models are similar and correspond well with the aggregate of the national model results. Output rises by a little over 1 per cent in the first year (1.3 per cent in the case of the AWM), but thereafter the models start to diverge. In EUROMON and the AWM the effects increase in magnitude, peaking at 1.6 per cent in year 3 using the AWM and reaching 1.9 per cent in year 5 using EUROMON. In the highly forward-looking EDGE model, the initial effect is completely crowded out by year 4. The fiscal impulse leads to a growing demand for goods, which generates an appreciation in the real exchange rate. The positive output effect is crowded out in the medium term as the real exchange rate appreciation cuts net exports through foreign trade elasticities.

These developments in output are also reflected in the developments in consumer prices, as shown in Table 1.16b. In nearly all models prices continue to rise in the first five years as output is above its baseline level. However there is a wide variation in the extent to which prices are above baseline thereafter. For instance, price effects of the fiscal expansion tend to be more moderate in Germany than for the euro area in aggregate. This may be a reflection of the fact that (on average over the estimating periods

Table 1.17a   Foreign demand shock (GDP response)

	1	2	3	4	5
Belgium	0.13	0.08	0.09	0.09	0.10
Germany	0.10	0.17	0.18	0.16	0.14
Greece	0.07	0.13	0.17	0.22	0.27
Spain	0.13	0.30	0.36	0.34	0.27
France	0.06	0.09	0.09	0.09	0.08
Ireland	0.23	0.27	0.28	0.29	0.28
Italy	0.06	0.08	0.09	0.10	0.11
Luxembourg	0.16	0.18	0.19	0.19	0.19
Netherlands	0.10	0.15	0.18	0.19	0.19
Austria	0.08	0.10	0.11	0.11	0.11
Portugal	0.05	0.07	0.08	0.08	0.08
Finland	0.09	0.13	0.08	0.06	0.05
AGG EUR-12	0.09	0.14	0.16	0.15	0.14
EDGE	0.26	0.14	0.06	0.03	0.02
EUROMON	0.07	0.12	0.14	0.16	0.17
AWM	0.11	0.14	0.17	0.18	0.19

for most models) inflation has been somewhat higher in the rest of the euro area than in Germany.

The foreign demand shock involves a permanent 1 per cent increase in the level of real imports of each country's trading partners outside the euro area. The impact of a rise in foreign demand in the first year is to raise GDP in all country models (as indicated in Table 1.17a) but there is some variation in the magnitude of the responses, ranging from 0.05 per cent in Portugal to 0.23 per cent in Ireland. The magnitude of the impact on GDP rises in subsequent years and reaches a maximum in years 3 to 5. The initial impact of the rise in foreign demand on output is comparatively large in the EDGE model, although not very long-lasting. To some extent this is due to the degree of forward-looking behaviour in this model. The impact of the foreign demand shock on prices is given in Table 1.17b. Typically this shows a pattern of steadily rising prices in the first five years.

The exchange rate shock involves the euro strengthening for five years by 1 per cent against all third currencies. The appreciation of the exchange rate generates a fall in output in nearly all models, which typically increases in magnitude and reaches a maximum after two to four years (as shown in Table 1.18a). The exceptions to this are Greece and Ireland, where output is still falling further below baseline in year 5. Once again there is a notable variation in the impact on output in the first year, ranging from nearly zero in Portugal to −0.17 per cent in Austria. The slightly positive effects in

Table 1.17b   Foreign demand shock (response of consumption deflator)

	1	2	3	4	5
Belgium	0.01	0.05	0.04	0.04	0.03
Germany	0.00	0.01	0.04	0.08	0.12
Greece	0.00	0.00	0.01	0.03	0.05
Spain	0.02	0.09	0.19	0.28	0.33
France	0.01	0.05	0.13	0.22	0.33
Ireland	0.00	0.01	0.04	0.09	0.15
Italy	0.00	0.01	0.03	0.05	0.07
Luxembourg	0.00	0.01	0.02	0.03	0.05
Netherlands	0.00	0.02	0.07	0.14	0.21
Austria	0.00	0.02	0.06	0.12	0.19
Portugal	0.00	0.01	0.02	0.03	0.03
Finland	0.05	0.13	0.15	0.10	0.07
AGG EUR-12	0.01	0.03	0.08	0.12	0.17
EDGE	0.09	0.23	0.31	0.34	0.35
EUROMON	0.00	0.00	0.03	0.10	0.20
AWM	0.03	0.06	0.10	0.15	0.20

Luxembourg partly reflect the fact that most of Luxembourg's trade is within the euro area and consequently the effective exchange rate changes by a much smaller amount than in countries with more trade outside the euro area.

The EDGE model reports a large initial effect which rapidly diminishes in size. Once again this pattern of a large initial response followed by a relatively rapid return to baseline reflects the highly forward-looking nature of this model. The initial effects in the AWM and EUROMON are much smaller and tend to increase over time. In nearly all country and euro area models there is a fall in the price level which increases in magnitude over the first five years. There is a fairly wide variation in the impact on prices in both the first and subsequent years (as shown in Table 1.18b).

The effects of the oil price shock, in which oil prices permanently increase by 10 per cent in US dollar terms, are given in Tables 1.19a and 1.19b. The effect of the oil price shock on output is fairly modest in the first year, ranging from zero in Greece to −0.09 per cent in Finland. In most countries a more noticeable adverse impact on output emerges in subsequent years (the largest impacts are seen in Portugal, whose Cobb–Douglas production function includes an explicit oil term, the Netherlands, Greece and Italy).

Consumer prices rise in all models following the oil price hike and in most cases continue to rise in the first three years. In Italy, where the adverse

Table 1.18a   Exchange rate shock (GDP response)

	1	2	3	4	5
Belgium	−0.04	−0.07	−0.07	−0.04	−0.02
Germany	−0.13	−0.23	−0.25	−0.22	−0.19
Greece	−0.09	−0.12	−0.13	−0.14	−0.15
Spain	−0.06	−0.11	−0.12	−0.11	−0.09
France	−0.01	−0.01	0.00	0.00	0.00
Ireland	−0.02	−0.05	−0.09	−0.14	−0.20
Italy	−0.05	−0.09	−0.12	−0.13	−0.12
Luxembourg	0.05	0.04	0.03	0.02	0.02
Netherlands	−0.06	−0.07	−0.07	−0.08	−0.08
Austria	−0.17	−0.21	−0.23	−0.24	−0.23
Portugal	−0.01	−0.02	−0.03	−0.02	−0.02
Finland	−0.12	−0.15	−0.10	−0.09	−0.10
AGG EUR-12	−0.07	−0.12	−0.13	−0.12	−0.11
EDGE	−0.61	−0.32	−0.13	−0.05	−0.04
EUROMON	−0.04	−0.07	−0.09	−0.11	−0.11
AWM	−0.03	−0.06	−0.07	−0.07	−0.07

Table 1.18b   Exchange rate shock (response of consumption deflator)

	1	2	3	4	5
Belgium	−0.06	−0.17	−0.29	−0.37	−0.40
Germany	−0.01	−0.05	−0.09	−0.15	−0.20
Greece	−0.08	−0.16	−0.25	−0.34	−0.43
Spain	−0.05	−0.11	−0.15	−0.18	−0.19
France	−0.04	−0.07	−0.10	−0.13	−0.16
Ireland	−0.05	−0.11	−0.14	−0.17	−0.19
Italy	−0.07	−0.15	−0.21	−0.28	−0.34
Luxembourg	−0.04	−0.12	−0.15	−0.16	−0.16
Netherlands	−0.06	−0.14	−0.19	−0.25	−0.30
Austria	−0.04	−0.12	−0.22	−0.35	−0.49
Portugal	−0.08	−0.17	−0.24	−0.28	−0.30
Finland	−0.19	−0.38	−0.48	−0.48	−0.44
AGG EUR-12	−0.04	−0.10	−0.15	−0.21	−0.25
EDGE	−0.30	−0.64	−0.84	−0.92	−0.94
EUROMON	−0.01	−0.07	−0.16	−0.30	−0.47
AWM	−0.03	−0.09	−0.14	−0.18	−0.21

Table 1.19a   Oil price shock (GDP response)

	1	2	3	4	5
Belgium	−0.01	−0.02	−0.06	−0.10	−0.13
Germany	−0.02	−0.05	−0.08	−0.09	−0.10
Greece	0.00	−0.09	−0.14	−0.17	−0.21
Spain	−0.03	−0.08	−0.11	−0.12	−0.11
France	−0.04	−0.07	−0.07	−0.07	−0.07
Ireland	−0.01	−0.05	−0.08	−0.08	−0.06
Italy	−0.04	−0.16	−0.27	−0.39	−0.50
Luxembourg	−0.01	−0.03	−0.06	−0.07	−0.08
Netherlands	−0.03	−0.10	−0.16	−0.18	−0.19
Austria	0.01	−0.01	−0.02	−0.05	−0.09
Portugal	−0.05	−0.11	−0.17	−0.25	−0.29
Finland	−0.09	−0.25	−0.07	−0.05	−0.11
AGG EUR-12	−0.03	−0.08	−0.12	−0.16	−0.18
EUROMON	−0.01	0.00	0.02	0.04	0.07
AWM	−0.03	−0.07	−0.09	−0.12	−0.13

Table 1.19b   Oil price shock (response of consumption deflator)

	1	2	3	4	5
Belgium	0.19	0.28	0.39	0.46	0.48
Germany	0.06	0.17	0.22	0.22	0.19
Greece	0.14	0.30	0.47	0.50	0.46
Spain	0.12	0.17	0.15	0.11	0.07
France	0.17	0.22	0.24	0.25	0.25
Ireland	0.11	0.25	0.28	0.24	0.17
Italy	0.13	0.13	0.11	0.09	0.03
Luxembourg	0.02	0.23	0.39	0.52	0.65
Netherlands	0.08	0.34	0.44	0.49	0.50
Austria	0.14	0.19	0.20	0.19	0.18
Portugal	0.26	0.31	0.35	0.35	0.32
Finland	0.18	0.09	0.14	0.24	0.15
AGG EUR-12	0.12	0.19	0.22	0.22	0.20
EUROMON	0.08	0.23	0.43	0.69	1.00
AWM	0.10	0.17	0.20	0.20	0.18

Notes:
1.   EUROMON covers the following countries: the euro countries, Austria, Belgium, Finland, France, Germany, Italy, Netherlands and Spain, as well as the USA, the UK, Japan, Sweden and Denmark.
2.   EUROMON results refer to the aggregate outcomes for the euro countries, Austria, Belgium, Finland, France, Germany, Italy, Netherlands and Spain.

impact on output is particularly large, the impact on the price level is smaller and prices show a clear tendency to return towards the baseline in year 5.

5   CONCLUSIONS

This overview chapter has surveyed the main structural econometric models used in the ECB and in the national central banks. It has taken stock of the current macroeconometric model infrastructure available within the Eurosystem, highlighting the purposes, underlying philosophies and structures and main features of the models used. The models generally serve three basic purposes at the national or Eurosystem level: contributing to the preparation of economic projections, updates and risk analysis; scenario analysis; and counterfactual analysis. As discussed, they play a key role in the macroeconomic projections, both in helping to prepare the projections and in subsequent updates and variants.

Not surprisingly it is clear from this overview chapter that there is significant variety in the structure of the macroeconomic models used within the Eurosystem. For example, there is wide variation in the size of models. Each model strikes a different balance between theory consistency and empirical fit. In model building in general there is always some trade-off between these two desirable features. The models used in the Eurosystem span the full range of possibilities, ranging from theoretically based, largely calibrated models to models where a primary role is assigned to 'fitting' the data. Most of the models can be located at an intermediate point along this spectrum, with long-run properties being determined by theory, whereas the short-run dynamics reflect estimated patterns of behaviour. In the same vein, there are notable differences in the way in which expectations and policy rules are treated.

At the same time, there are also many important common features in the models. Nearly all the models are based on an explicit supply side that rests on a Cobb–Douglas or CES production function. Nearly all the models have a single type of output and there is widespread agreement that this is determined by some measures of labour supply, capital and technical progress in the long run. The comparison of key behavioural equations across models reveals many shared characteristics as well as notable differences in both the short-run and long-run determinants. In the vast majority of models, income and wealth constitute the long-run determinants of consumers' expenditure and output and the user cost of capital determine investment in the long run. Nevertheless there are marked differences in the factors which are allowed to influence both these variables in the short run, capturing cyclical factors.

In terms of the channels of transmission of monetary policy, the exchange rate and cost-of-capital channels can be identified in all the models, the substitution-effect-in-consumption in almost all, and the cash-flow/income and wealth channels in most. Except in the case of Germany, there is no direct role for monetary aggregates in determining output and prices.

The simulation exercises illustrate some important similarities and differences in the results. As regards the monetary policy simulation results, Berben *et al.* (2004) show that, against most yardsticks, the cross-country variation in the results is plausible. The results broadly correspond to the differences in business cycle properties across countries and most, but not all, economic, financial and structural statistics. When compared to the VAR evidence, the results were more mixed, with similarities in the pattern of price but not output responses. Nevertheless, despite these signs that the results may also reflect underlying economic differences, the role of differing modelling strategies should not be ignored. Important features of the models (for instance in the treatment of expectations or wealth) can have a major bearing on the results which may not necessarily reflect differences in the underlying economies.

ANNEX: DETAILS OF THE DESIGN OF THE HARMONIZED SIMULATION EXPERIMENTS

The details of the design of the harmonized simulation experiments are as follows.

(1) A temporary *monetary policy shock*, in which the policy interest rate is raised by 1 percentage point for two years. Reflecting the rise in short-term interest rates there is a rise in the long-term interest rate of around 20 basis points in the first quarter. This is steadily eroded by around 2.5 basis points over the subsequent two years and long-term interest rates return to their baseline levels by the start of the third year. There is a corresponding temporary appreciation in the exchange rate which is based on an uncovered interest parity (UIP) condition. This condition requires an appreciation of approximately 2 per cent in the first quarter, followed by a steady depreciation of around 0.25 per cent per quarter for the next two years. From the start of the third year, the exchange rate returns to its baseline level. Full details of this simulation are set out by van Els *et al.* (2003).

(2) A temporary *fiscal policy shock*, in which *real* government consumption would be permanently increased by 1 per cent of initial real GDP for five years. The adjustment should be spread proportionally across all elements of government consumption. Where models have different variables for government employment and government wages, the adjustment should take place in employment rather than wages. For comparability this shock should be fixed at 1 per cent of initial real GDP so that the shock does not increase in magnitude as baseline real GDP rises over the five years.

(3) A *foreign demand shock*, in which the level of real imports of trading partners outside the euro area would be permanently increased relative to baseline by 1 per cent for five years. This would imply that national external demand would expand by less than 1 per cent, depending on the relative weight of intra-euro area trade in each country.

(4) An *exchange rate shock* in which the euro strengthens by 1 per cent against all third currencies for five years. This would imply that the national nominal effective exchange rate would appreciate by less than 1 per cent in line with the share of non-euro area currencies in the index.

(5) An *oil price shock*, in which oil prices permanently increase by 10 per cent in US dollar terms for five years.

Where appropriate it was agreed to utilize a similar set of background assumptions to those in the monetary policy exercise. The following were felt to be relevant to these simulations.

- No monetary policy rules would be implemented and short-term interest rates would hence remain at baseline values for the first five years (except for the path defined in Simulation 1).
- Long-term interest rates would remain unchanged at baseline values for the first five years in all simulations bar the monetary policy shock.
- Except for Simulations 1 and 4, exchange rates would remain unchanged at baseline values for the first five years.
- Except for Simulation 1, models were operated in isolated mode without international spillovers (such as changes in foreign demand, interest rates, wages and equity prices, including spillovers from other euro-area countries). Therefore no (additional) assumptions should be made about any changes in foreign variables due to the simulation that might feed back into the domestic results.
- No fiscal policy rules (like pursuing a specific government budget or debt stock target) should be used in the first five years of the simulation. However, in general terms for fiscal variables, modellers were free to follow their usual practices.
- Standard behavioural equations should be used for either real or nominal wages. In other words, these variables should not be kept exogenous in the simulation.

NOTES

1. Any views expressed are those of the authors and should not be interpreted as those of the ECB or the Eurosystem. The authors are grateful to members of the Working Group of Econometric Modelling for their input into the preparation of this chapter.
2. More information on the approaches to preparing economic projections within the Eurosytem is provided by ECB (2001).
3. In contrast to estimation, calibration involves the selection of parameter values on the basis of other information, such as micro studies, matching moments in the data or other prior information.
4. See, for an early example, Christ (1968).
5. In the Belgian model the unemployment rate also plays a role in the long-run determination of consumption. It has been introduced to account for the countercyclical risking of labour income. Since unemployment appears to be non-stationary it has been included in the long-run rather than short-run determinants to avoid long-lasting swings in consumption growth.
6. While the simulations reported in this chapter are conducted on a largely harmonized basis, some of the individual model chapters results are based on different simulations which illustrate how the models are used in practice.

7. This shock is also reported in van Els *et al.* (2003).
8. One caveat to these results is that these models are not necessarily built to be the main tool that a central bank would use to analyse these specific shocks. Indeed, typically, central banks use a suite of models to answer different shocks. Therefore the simulation results reported here should not be seen as necessarily representing a particular central bank's assessment of the way an economy would respond when faced with such a shock.
9. In the case of the Belgian model the distinction between this channel and the income channel cannot be made very precisely.
10. The change in interest payments sums up to zero, when taking into account the rest of the world.
11. Simulations with the EUROMON, AWM and EDGE models include intra-euro area spillovers.
12. As indicated in McAdam and Morgan (2003) the use of forward-looking elements in monetary policy experiments tends to raise the initial impact of a rise in interest rates but also expedites the return to baseline values.
13. In the case of the Finnish model, additional results were provided with the model operating in a backward-looking mode. These show a much more gradual return to baseline than is the case when the forward-looking elements of the model are allowed to operate.

REFERENCES

Berben, R.P., A. Locarno, J. Morgan and J. Valles (2004), 'Cross-country differences in monetary policy transmission in the euro area', ECB working paper No. 400.

Christ, C.F. (1968), 'A simple macroeconomic model with a government budget constraint', *Journal of Political Economy*, **76**, 53–67.

ECB (2001), *A guide to Eurosystem staff macroeconomic projection exercises*, ECB.

Fagan, G. and J. Henry (1998), 'Long-run money demand in the EU: evidence from area-wide aggregates', *Empirical Economics*, **23**, 483–506.

McAdam, P. and J. Morgan (2003), 'Analysing monetary policy transmission at the euro area level using structural macroeconomic models', in I. Angeloni, A. Kashyap and B. Mojon (eds), *Monetary policy transmission in the euro area*, Cambridge: Cambridge University Press.

van Els, P., A. Locarno, J. Morgan and J.P. Villetelle (2003), 'The effects of monetary policy in the euro-area: evidence from structural macroeconomic models', in I. Angeloni, A. Kashyap and B. Mojon (eds), *Monetary policy transmission in the euro area*, Cambridge: Cambridge University Press.

2. The area-wide model

Alistair Dieppe[1]

1 INTRODUCTION

This chapter summarizes the main features of the area-wide model (AWM). The model was created at the onset of monetary union with the aim of providing insights into economic developments in the euro area as a whole. A more detailed analysis of the model can be found in Fagan *et al.* (2001). Over the past five years some revisions have been made to the model, including updating of some of the equations (see Dieppe and Henry, 2004, for details).

2 THE USES OF THE MODEL

The model is currently used in the context of two different types of tasks: forecasting and policy analysis. *Forecasts* in the ECB are complex exercises in which judgmental and econometric considerations as well as area-wide and country perspectives are all taken into account. Describing the complex interaction underlying these exercises is beyond the scope of this chapter (see ECB, 2001), but this process has an important impact on the way the model is used. The model-based component of the forecast serves two purposes: firstly, as a consistency-checking device, ensuring that the picture as a whole conveyed by the forecast is a coherent one; secondly, as a technical tool able to build (relatively quickly) alternative views of the forecast. *Policy analysis* is performed through shock simulations and the exercises are varied in their implementation owing to the wide-ranging nature of the question that the model is addressing. In addition, the model has been used in research to address various questions relating to euro-area issues. Examples include examining the monetary transmission (McAdam and Morgan, 2003), real exchange rate determination (Detken *et al.*, 2002), labour market dynamics (Dieppe *et al.*, 2004a), forecasting strategies (McAdam and Mestre, 2003), impact of shocks to the euro area (Dieppe and Henry 2004) and optimal monetary policy (Dieppe *et al.*, 2004b). It is important to note that different simulation environments for the model are used for different purposes. For instance, it is usually preferential to treat the model as a whole in simulations, implying that closure rules (such as monetary policy or fiscal rules) are used. In contrast, such rules are normally switched off when the model is used for forecasting, reflecting the fact that the projections are based on a set of exogenous technical assumptions, such as unchanged short-term interest rates. In addition, while the AWM is nearly linear, a fully linearized version has been developed for the analysis of optimal monetary policy in order to facilitate efficient computation. This particular version is documented in Dieppe *et al.* (2004b).

3 AN OUTLINE OF THE THEORETICAL UNDERPINNINGS FOR THE MODEL AND ITS PURPOSE

The AWM is a relatively standard structural macroeconomic model for the euro area. The level of output in the long term is determined by a standard neoclassical equilibrium. However, in the short run, output is determined by demand and deviations of output from potential (and unemployment from the NAIRU) set in motion by a process of wage and price adjustment which, together with the impact of 'policy rules', restores the long-run equilibrium.

The long-run level of output is determined from a whole-economy Cobb–Douglas production function with an exogenous NAIRU and a consistent set of first-order conditions derived from profit maximization under perfect competition. The components of aggregate demand are consistent with this equilibrium via a stock-flow adjustment mechanism involving net foreign assets and the real exchange rate. Regarding prices, the long run is determined by the nominal anchor chosen when running the model (for example, an inflation objective which enters the interest rate setting equation or, in the case of a fixed nominal exchange rate, the 'world' price level).

The model has five key features.

1. It treats the euro area as a single economy. Thus the model contains equations which are expressed in terms of area-wide variables. Area-wide consumption, for example, is modelled as a function of area-wide income and wealth.
2. It is a quarterly model.
3. In comparison with some other structural models covered in this volume, it is a relatively small-scale model. Thus the model comprises around 84 equations of which 15 are estimated behavioural equations.

4. The behavioural equations are estimated on the basis of historical data for the euro area from 1970 onwards, although some key long-run parameters are calibrated. Typically, long-run conditions enter the equations in the form of error correction terms and appropriate dynamic homogeneity conditions are included in the dynamics to ensure the existence of a real equilibrium which is independent of nominal variables.

5. Currently the model is mostly a backward-looking model in which expectations enter implicitly though lagged values of the variables (adaptive expectations).

The key features of the model are elaborated in more detail below.

Production Function and Factor Demand

The model includes a description of technology in which whole-economy potential output is assumed to be given by a constant-returns-to-scale Cobb–Douglas production function with calibrated factor share parameters. The labour share parameter has been set as the average wage income share in the sample and is therefore not estimated.

Trend total factor productivity has been estimated within sample by applying the Hodrick–Prescott filter to the Solow residual derived from this production function. This production function is used to derive theoretically consistent first-order conditions that enter other equations in the model, for example investment. It also provides the measure of potential output which, combined with actual output, determines the output gap.

The factor demand equations of the model (specifically for investment and employment) are specified in such a way as to be consistent in the long run with the underlying theoretical framework of the supply side. This is achieved by means of the inclusion of ECM terms which embody, respectively, the marginal productivity condition for capital and the consistency between employment and the Cobb–Douglas production function. However these relations only hold in the long run: in the short run, investment and employment are driven by short-run dynamic factors such as changes in demand.

The investment equation comprises a long-run component in which capital stock is proportional to output, with the ratio of the two depending on the real user-cost of capital. This variable is defined as the (short-term) nominal interest rate less inflation plus a constant risk premium. The latter is calibrated to match historical averages, that is, ensuring that the average cost of capital thus defined matches the marginal productivity of capital in the sample. The short term of the equation includes a standard accelerator effect.[2] It should be noted that this equation, via the cost of capital term, provides the main channel by which interest rates affect aggregate demand in the model.

Employment growth in the short run depends on real wages and output growth (both adjusted for trend productivity). In the longer term, employment adjusts to a level implied by the inversion of the production function. The constant term in the equation is a parameter which is set equal to steady state labour force growth. Together with the adjustments to the other variables in the dynamics, this implies a long-run solution of the equation in which employment growth equals labour force growth while the ECM term is zero.

Components of Aggregate Demand

Regarding aggregate demand, expenditure on real GDP is split into six components which are modelled separately. Private consumption is a function both of disposable income and of wealth, defined as cumulated savings under the assumption that households own all of the assets in the economy (that is, public debt, net foreign assets and private capital stock). Inventories are modelled in such a way that, in the long run, the ratio between cumulated inventories and final sales remains constant.

Exports and imports comprise both intra and extra area flows, thus equations are not based on consolidated trade; that is, taking into account only trade with the non-euro area countries. This reflects the fact that euro-area national accounts are compiled by summing the accounts of the individual countries. Thus exports and imports in the national accounts include intra-area trade. Trade flows are otherwise modelled in a standard fashion, whereby market shares – in terms of world demand (import-based) and domestic demand, respectively – are a function of a competitiveness indicator involving trade prices, the competitors' index being computed as a weighted average of external and internal prices. In both cases deterministic trends were introduced to ensure cointegration between market shares and the corresponding relative prices. The external indicators for demand and prices as well as the effective exchange rate are based on weighted averages of indicators for the main trade partners of the euro area as a whole (that is, only involving non-euro area countries).[3]

Prices and Costs

On the price side, the current version of the model contains equations for a number of price and cost indicators. This system of prices has been estimated under the assumption that a form of the law of one price should hold; that is to say, imposing static homogeneity on all price equations, which is equivalent to expressing the long-run ECM component of each of those equations in terms of relative prices only.

The key price index used in the model is the deflator for real GDP at factor costs (excluding the effect of indirect taxes and subsidies). This key deflator is modelled as a function of trend unit labour costs. In the short run, import prices also have some effects. The GDP deflator at market prices is in turn derived by using the accounting identity linking market prices to factor costs and indirect taxes net of subsidies through an exogenous ratio in GDP terms. Dynamic homogeneity is strongly rejected by the data, which implies that, in principle, the mark-up in the long run depends on steady state inflation. However the constant term in the above equation ensures that the long-run real equilibrium of the model coincides with the theoretical steady state. In the short run, the mark-up also depends on the output gap, a feature which increases the response of the nominal side of the model to real shocks. In addition, a term in inflation expectations is included in the short run, the coefficient of which has been calibrated following simulation experiments.

Wages are modelled as a Phillips curve which also contains a long-run equilibrium adjustment term, with wage growth depending on productivity, current and lagged inflation (in terms of consumer prices) and the deviation of unemployment from its structural level (NAIRU). This latter variable is exogenous in the model, although it varies over time in sample, having been estimated using the Gordon approach (Gordon, 1997). Since dynamic homogeneity holds, the long-run Phillips curve is vertical in the model. The short-run dynamics include a calibrated term in inflation expectations as in the case for the price equation.

The specification of the wage and the key price equations implies that two independent measures of demand can affect inflation. The first factor is standard and appears in the wage equation through the unemployment gap term. The second factor affects prices and has two aspects. The first is standard, namely the output gap term entering the price equation. The other one is less obvious, stemming from the fact that inflationary pressures are asymmetric because of the differing measures of productivity involved, namely trend productivity in prices and actual productivity in wages. In the reduced form of the price system this last feature would result in the inclusion of a productivity gap as an additional measure of inflationary pressure, besides the unemployment and output gaps. In addition, the long-run equilibrium for both wages and prices is pinned down by the predetermined trend real unit labour costs or, equivalently, by the long-run labour share, in turn equal to the labour elasticity in the production function.

There are two equations for consumption prices: one for the National Account deflator and another for the HICP (Harmonised Index for Consumption Prices). The roles played by the corresponding equations are quite different. While the consumption deflator is a key price indicator within the model's accounting framework and has a strong feedback on the model, it is linked directly to overall HICP, which is split into two components: HICP energy and HICP excluding energy; the latter equation being a function of the GDP and import deflators.

Trade

On the external side, import prices are, on the one hand, a function of export prices of the euro area itself to account for internal trade and, on the other, a function of foreign prices and commodity prices (measured by the HWWA index, which is a weighted average of oil and non-oil commodity prices), both expressed in domestic currency. Export prices similarly have two components, internal and external, depending on the GDP deflator and foreign prices.

Fiscal Policy and Government Sector

The modelling of the fiscal block is relatively simplified, with a limited number of revenue and expenditure categories generally being exogenous, usually ratios to GDP, but real government consumption is exogenous in level terms. However transfers to households (also in GDP percentage points) are modelled as a function of the unemployment rate on the basis of a calibrated equation based on available country estimates. The version used for long-run simulation purposes also incorporates a calibrated fiscal rule in which the direct apparent tax rate, that is to say the ratio between direct taxes paid by households and GDP, is increased in response to the fiscal deficit relative to GDP observed the year before. The rule presumes that apparent direct tax rates are changed with a view to reaching some given deficit ratio: specifically 10 per cent of the deviations of deficit from the target ratio are absorbed in each period. This fiscal reaction is assumed to occur four quarters after the deviation has actually been observed, so as to allow for some inertia in the fiscal response.[4]

As regards the external accounts, the trade balance is given by the equations for the trade volumes and prices discussed above. Net factor income (including international transfers) is determined by a calibrated equation linking it to lagged values of the stock of net foreign assets. The trade balance and net factor income equal the current account balance, which in turn is cumulated to give the stock of net foreign assets.

Monetary and Financial Sector

Two equations are included in the financial sector: money demand and a yield curve. The money demand equation is a fairly standard dynamic ECM equation for the new M3 aggregate[5] which expresses real money balances as a function of real income, short-term and long-term interest rates and inflation. The yield curve expresses the long-term interest rate in terms of the short-term rate. Two versions of the equation are currently available: a purely backward-looking and a purely forward-looking version.[6]

Table 2.1 collects some information on the main equations, summarizing multipliers when key determinants in these equations are permanently shocked.

4   AN OUTLINE OF THE KEY CHARACTERISTICS

Responses to Key Simulations

No description and discussion of the individual equations in a model, no matter how thorough, can convey a proper representation of its overall characteristics, and the AWM is certainly no exception. Barring a lengthy description of all channels included in the model, the only practical way by which this understanding can be gained is by describing the outcome of a number of selected simulations, each emphasizing different mechanisms acting in the model.

Obviously all the shocks are to be considered as stylized devices to study the model, rather than realistic representations of actual shocks that have hit or are expected to hit the euro area. The treatment given to the exchange rate and interest rate in these simulations will differ among them in order to gain some further insights into the properties of the AWM and also for technical reasons. The monetary policy shock has exogenous paths for the interest rate and exchange rate. The design of this shock has been taken from a previous monetary policy exercise (van Els *et al.*, 2001). The other shocks (including the exchange rate shock) do not incorporate a UIP-based jump in the exchange rate.[7] Results for each simulation are collected in Figures 2.1 to 2.5 respectively.

Monetary Policy Shock (see Figures 2.1a and 2.1b)

The shock assumes an upward shift of the short-term interest rate of 100 basis points for eight quarters followed by an immediate return to baseline, together with an exogenous jump of the exchange rate followed by a

Table 2.1   Response of main equations to 10% shock to key determinants

	Multipliers			
	Year 1	Year 2	Year 5	Year 10
Employment				
Output	4.4	8.3	14.2	17.0
Real wages	−1.8	−1.5	−0.6	−0.1
Investment				
Output	10.0	9.9	9.0	6.3
Real user cost of capital[1]	−0.5	−1.7	−5.3	−9.9
Consumption				
Income	5.9	6.7	6.4	6.4
Wealth	0.7	2.0	3.2	3.4
Export volume				
World demand	8.6	8.7	9.9	10.0
Competitiveness	4.8	8.9	8.7	8.0
Import volume				
Domestic demand	14.6	13.2	11.0	10.1
Competitiveness	−0.5	−1.5	−2.9	−3.4
GDP deflator				
Unit labour costs	4.3	6.2	7.8	9.2
Wages				
Consumption deflator	2.5	4.2	0.8	0.0
Unemployment rate	−0.1	−0.3	−0.7	−0.7
GDP deflator	1.4	4.6	9.6	10.0
HICP excluding energy				
GDP deflator	6.7	7.4	8.0	8.2
Import prices	0.4	1.0	1.6	1.7
Export prices				
External prices	1.9	2.9	3.1	3.2
Domestic prices	6.3	7.2	6.7	6.6
Import prices				
External prices	1.0	1.5	1.4	1.4
Domestic prices	4.8	7.4	7.2	7.2

Note: [1]100 basis points to the real interest rate.

smooth return to baseline over the same eight quarters and a common exogenous term structure for the long-term interest rates.

In the short run, that is to say, while the shift in the interest rate is in place, both investment and consumption react negatively to the shock and drive demand down. Output falls by 0.2 per cent in the first year with the

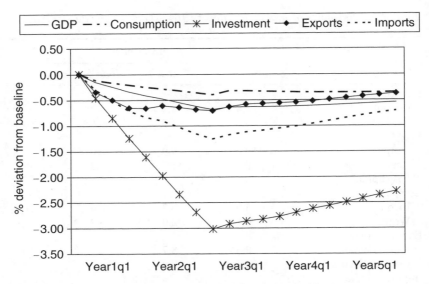

Figure 2.1a   Transitory interest rate shock (real variables)

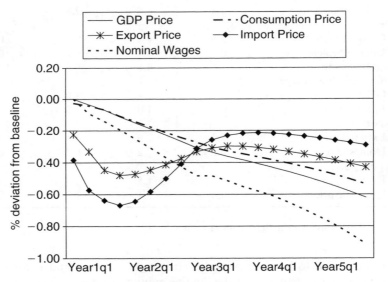

Figure 2.1b   Transitory interest rate shock (nominal)

maximum impact on the GDP level reached after three years. Inflation is affected by the slowdown during this period. Inflation is also affected by the nominal exchange rate which jumps by approximately 2 per cent in the first quarter. The effects are slowly reversed after the interest rate is brought back to base. This reversal also partly reflects the fact that the nominal exchange rate is fixed at its baseline values from the third year onwards. Thus the lower domestic prices mean that there is a depreciation in the real exchange rate, which ultimately boosts output through standard trade channels. Lower domestic activity reduces the demand for imports and lower domestic prices improve both import and export competitiveness. This boost to net trade restores output and prices to the base.

Fiscal Policy Shock (see Figures 2.2a and 2.2b)

It is assumed in the simulation that real government consumption is permanently increased by 1 per cent of GDP ex ante with no fiscal policy rule operating.[8] The shock results in an immediate increase in GDP, which has a direct impact on income and, thereafter, consumption. Investment, via accelerator affects, is also affected. Imports react directly to the increase in government consumption offsetting to some degree the other demand components. In the absence of further policy responses, GDP being higher than potential, the resulting opening of the output gap and unemployment gap drives real wages and prices up, which in turn, through the competitiveness channel, leads to a weakening of the initial impact of the shock on GDP.

Foreign Demand Shock (see Figures 2.3a and 2.3b)

It is assumed that a 1 per cent permanent increase in foreign demand, that is, world demand directed to the euro area, takes place. The resulting slight increase in domestic GDP would force a monetary policy tightening, but for this simulation interest rates are exogenous. Hence, without policy reactions, the increase in GDP leads to an increase in inflation via the output and unemployment gaps. Both exports and imports increase, partly reflecting an increase in intra trade in response to stronger foreign demand. Net trade; however; remains positive throughout the simulation horizon.

Exchange Rate Shock (see Figures 2.4a and 2.4b)

The euro exchange rate is assumed to appreciate immediately and permanently by 1 per cent. This leads to a small drop in GDP and the consumption deflator. Exchange rate movements are passed on to consumer prices mainly via their impact on import prices. The magnitude and timing of

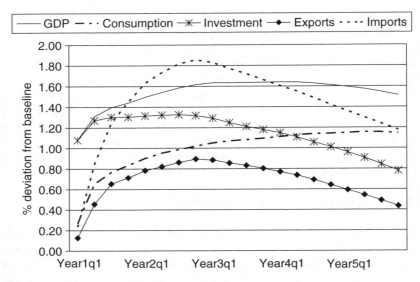

Figure 2.2a   Public consumption shock (real variables)

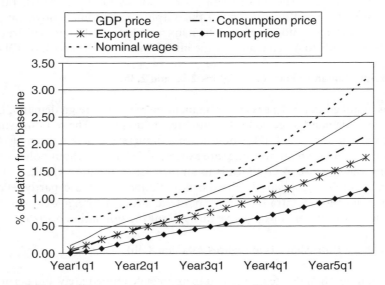

Figure 2.2b   Public consumption shock (nominal)

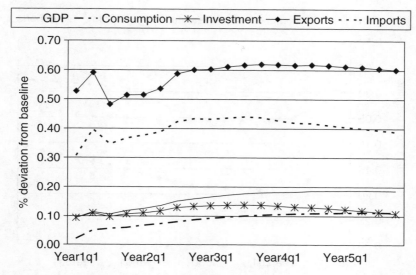

Figure 2.3a   World demand shock (real variables)

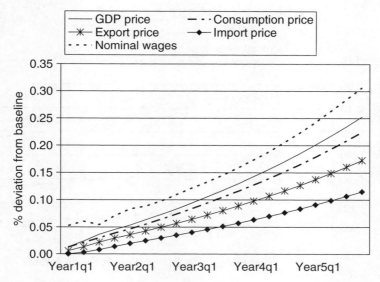

Figure 2.3b   World demand shock (nominal)

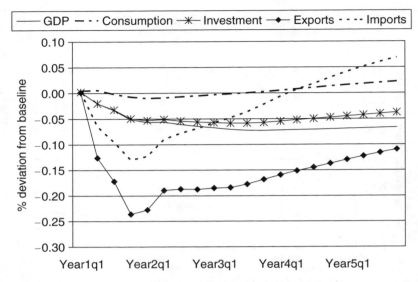

Figure 2.4a   Exchange rate shock (real variables)

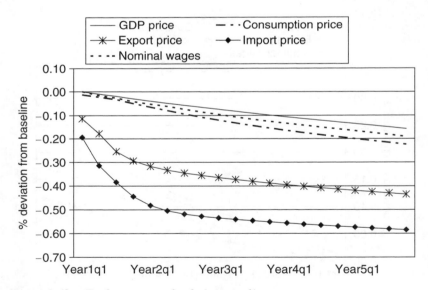

Figure 2.4b   Exchange rate shock (nominal)

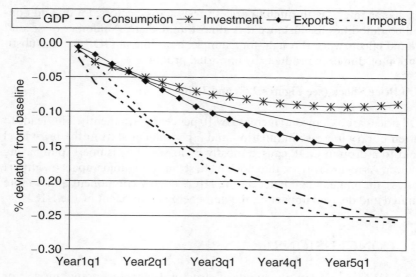

Figure 2.5a   Oil price shock (real variables)

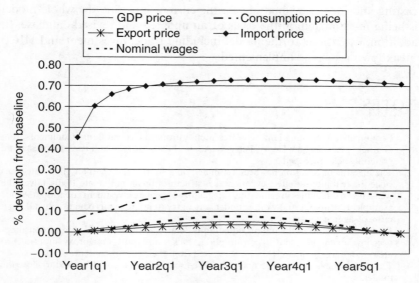

Figure 2.5b   Oil price shock (nominal)

exchange rate pass-through to prices varies across sectors; for oil and non-oil commodities for instance it is almost immediate. A number of second round effects work through, for example, a decline in GDP due to substitution of domestic products by imported products.

Oil Price Shock (see Figures 2.5a and 2.5b)

Oil prices are assumed to increase by 10 per cent permanently. This leads to a temporary increase in inflation and a permanent shift in the price level and to a drop in GDP caused mostly by losses in consumers' purchasing power. As regards prices, the shock has a strong and rapid impact on import prices, an immediate impact on the HICP energy component and a more muted and delayed impact on the non-energy component of the HICP.

5   CONCLUSIONS

The AWM is a relatively standard structural macroeconomic model for the euro area with a well-defined neoclassical steady-state and well-behaved dynamics. It is used extensively within the ECB both for forecasting and for policy analysis. At the current juncture, the whole model is being re-estimated on the basis of an updated and revised database. In addition, extensions to the model including trade, investment and HICP breakdown are being implemented.

NOTES

1. Econometric Modelling Unit, DG Research, European Central Bank. Comments from Gabriel Fagan, Jérôme Henry, Peter McAdam, Julian Morgan and Ricardo Mestre are gratefully acknowledged.
2. The investment equation has been estimated on a shorter sample than other equations since the real interest effect experiences a structural break in the late 1970s. Given the well-known difficulties in estimating satisfactory aggregate investment equations (see, for example, Chirinko, 1993) work is under way to try to improve this equation by taking a more disaggregated approach.
3. Domestic demand in the import equation is defined as the weighted sum of consumption, investment, government consumption, stocks and exports (as a proxy for intra/euro area trade), where the weights are computed from their import content.
4. This fiscal rule is only one of many possible fiscal rules that could be used to close the model.
5. See Coenen and Vega (1999) for further details.
6. For the forward-looking equation, the Fuhrer and Moore (1995) linear approximation has been used.
7. Real interest rates are held exogenous in all other simulations.
8. This implies that receipts as a percentage of GDP remain fixed.

REFERENCES

Chirinko, R.S. (1993), 'Business fixed investment spending: modelling strategies, empirical results and policy implications', *Journal of Economic Literature*, **31** (4), 1874–1911.

Coenen, G. and J.L. Vega (1999), 'The demand for M3 in the euro area', ECB working paper no. 6.

Detken, C., A. Dieppe, J. Henry, C. Marin and F. Smets (2002), 'Determinants of the effective real exchange rate of the synthetic euro', *Australian Economic Papers*, **41** (4), 404–36.

Dieppe, A. and J. Henry (2004), 'The euro area viewed as a single economy: how does it respond to shocks?', *Economic Modelling*, **21** (5), 833–75.

Dieppe, A., J. Henry and P. McAdam (2004a), 'Labour market dynamics in the euro area: a model-based sensitivity analysis', in W. Semmler (ed.), *Monetary Policy and the Labor Market in the US, the Euro area and Japan: A Conference in Honor of James Tobin*, London: Routledge Press.

Dieppe, A., K. Küster and P. McAdam (2004b), 'Optimal monetary policy rules for the euro area: an analysis using the area wide model', ECB working paper no. 360.

ECB (2001), *A Guide to Eurosystem Staff Macroeconomic Projection Exercises* Frankfurt: European Central Bank.

Fagan, G., J. Henry and R. Mestre (2001), 'An area-wide model (AWM) for the euro area', ECB working paper no. 42 (forthcoming in *Economic Modelling*).

Fuhrer, J. and G. Moore (1995), 'Inflation Persistence', *Quarterly Journal of Economics*, **110** (1), February, 127–59.

Gordon R. (1997), 'The time-varying NAIRU and its implications for economic policy', *Journal of Economic Perspectives*, **11** (1), 11–32.

Hernández de Cos, P., J. Henry and S. Momigliano (2003), 'The short-term impact of government budgets on prices: evidence from macroeconometric models', ECB working paper no. 396.

McAdam, P. and R. Mestre (2003), 'Evaluating macro-modelling systems: an application to the area wide model', (http://www.federalreserve.gov/events/cbw/mcadam_mestre_aug 30.pdf).

McAdam, P. and J. Morgan (2003), 'The monetary transmission mechanism at the euro area level: issues and results using structual macroeconomic models', in Angeloni I., A. Koshyap and B. Mojon (eds), *Monetary Policy Transmission in the Euro area*, Cambridge: Cambridge University Press.

van Els, P.J.A., A. Locarno, J. Morgan and J. Villetelle (2001), 'Monetary policy transmission in the euro area: what do aggregate and national structural models tell us?', ECB working paper no. 94.

3. EDGE: the Bank of Finland's macroeconomic model of the euro area

Mika Kortelainen

1 INTRODUCTION

The euro area Dynamic General Equilibrium (EDGE) model is built and used to illustrate the analysis of monetary policy credibility in Europe. The underlying principles of the model are the inclusion of micro-foundations through the optimization behaviour of representative agents and the explicit treatment of expectations. We usually use the assumption of rational expectations, but the model can be used to analyse heterogeneous expectations, too, for example in the context of less than perfect monetary policy credibility. A simplification which has been made in constructing the model is that the derivation of the equations is done under the certainty equivalence assumption, with some risk premia added later ad hoc in the arbitrage equations in the model. The model has nominal rigidities in the short run, which allow monetary policy to have real effects. Hence the model can be characterized as following the New Keynesian approach and it displays many Keynesian short-run properties, but the long run is quite neoclassical, at least in the rational expectations mode, owing to forward-looking expectations and long-run market clearing.

The current version of the EDGE model is calibrated to publicly available euro-area data. EDGE is currently used in policy analysis, but can equally be applied to forecasting. The novel feature of the EDGE model is that it can be used to illustrate the analysis of monetary policy credibility in the face of heterogeneous expectations. Since the model is inherently forward-looking, it may further be used to examine anticipated disturbances in the policy analysis context. EDGE may also be employed either with a monetary policy rule and uncovered exchange rate parity or with a fixed interest rate and fixed exchange rate regime.

EDGE is a quarterly model and is coded and functions in the TROLL simulation software environment. It contains about 40 equations, 11 of which are key behavioural equations, with the rest being technical equations, identities and policy rules. As the model is derived from the optimizing framework there are a considerable number of forward-looking equations in it. Specifically there are seven forward-looking key behavioural equations (labour demand, investment, consumption, nominal value of private assets, prices, wages and inventory demand). Furthermore the exchange rate and long-run interest rates are defined in a forward-looking manner. The model is disaggregated into household, corporate, government and foreign sectors. The fiscal side of the EDGE model contains the budget constraint and two policy rules: an income tax rule for the fiscal authority and a monetary policy rule for the monetary authority. The government sector is treated as a single entity even though the model is intended to describe the euro area.

EDGE has also been calibrated to publicly available US data. Consequently recent model development effort has been devoted to building a two-country model version of the EDGE model. A more detailed analysis of the EDGE model can be found in Kortelainen (2001), Tarkka and Kortelainen (2001), Kortelainen (2002) and Kortelainen and Mayes (2004). The two-country version of the EDGE model is described in Tarkka and Kortelainen (2005) and Kortelainen (2004).

The rest of this chapter is organized as follows: in Section 2 we describe the uses of the model. After that we provide an outline of the theoretical underpinnings of the model. In Section 4 we go through some of the key characteristics via some diagnostic simulation. Section 5 concludes this chapter.

2   USES OF THE MODEL

EDGE is built to illustrate the analysis of monetary policy credibility. As a DGE model its most natural use is in the context of structural policy analysis. In constructing the EDGE model we combined some well-established mainstream economic theories. The advantage of this strategy is that the model should be easy to understand and reasonably well-founded as a policy analysis tool.

EDGE is currently used in policy analysis, but it can equally be applied to forecasting. In order to do this with this type of forward-looking model, new methods need to be developed to generate smooth forecast paths. The rational/model–consistent expectations paradigm is the one that is currently applied in the expectations formation mechanism, but this mechanism can easily be shifted to the other paradigms. As the model is forward-looking, we may easily incorporate anticipated/unanticipated shocks. In addition the EDGE model can be used to assess the effects of different expectations among different agents, especially with regard to monetary policy, which is one of the main challenges of modern monetary analysis.

In addition to the dynamic model, we have also derived a companion steady-state model, which is derived from and is consistent with the dynamic model. This steady-state model is used to obtain the necessary terminal points for the solution of the dynamic model. In principle, the steady-state model could be used separately to analyse the long-run properties of the economy, too. The steady-state model is also helpful in stock-flow considerations since it defines explicitly the stock equilibrium for private financial assets, capital stock, government debt and net foreign assets. The short-run flow equilibria of consumption, investment, government net lending and current account are described by the dynamic model. In this flow equilibrium the stock equilibrium may still be incomplete but in the long-run even stocks of assets will adjust fully to the steady-state stock equilibrium.

3   AN OUTLINE OF THE THEORETICAL UNDERPINNINGS OF THE MODEL

3.1   Production Function and Factor Demands

The EDGE model has a neoclassical supply side with Cobb–Douglas production technology. Capital stock is endogenously accumulated from fixed investments. Labour demand is determined endogenously by the inverted Cobb–Douglas production function in the long run. In the short run, menu cost-type adjustment costs are included in the labour demand. Perfect competition is assumed in the goods market in the long run.

3.2   Components of Aggregate Demand

The consumption is derived from the household maximization problem with no liquidity constraints, myopic behaviour or habit persistence assumption. A closed form solution for the consumption is derived using a logarithmic utility function. The Blanchard approach that we use assumes consumers who face a positive hazard of dying in each period. Also in each period a new cohort is born with zero wealth. An exogenous birth rate determines the population growth rate in the model. The model assumes that there is a competitive life insurance market which distributes in each period the wealth of the dying individuals to the survivors. The financial wealth is calculated by the present value method, applying an exogenous equity premium in addition to the real rate of interest to all capital income incurred by the private sector.

The model includes a forward-looking determination of investment on the basis of expected profits and fixed capital adjustment costs. It also employs a forward-looking determination of inventory demand, including adjustment costs.

3.3 Prices and Costs

Labour supply, NAIRU and population are exogenous in the model. We may, however, allow some exogenous growth rate in the labour supply and population. With respect to the latter, the growth rate is a function of the Blanchard probability of death and some birth rate of newborn generations. EDGE has a forward-looking wage determination with some short-term nominal wage rigidity (modelled as overlapping multi-period wage contracts *à la* Calvo) and a forward-looking price determination with costly price adjustment (*à la* Rotemberg).

3.4 Fiscal Policy and the Government Sector

A fiscal 'closure rule' is used in the model, which ensures that the government debt-to-GDP ratio always converges in the long run to some pre-scribed constant, for example 60 per cent. This is achieved via the gradual adjustment of direct taxes to disequilibria in the debt and deficit. For a wide range of policy and other shocks, the closure rule guarantees that the fiscal solvency constraint holds and that a long-run stock equilibrium exists. The rest of the government sector is described in a very approximate way in the budget constraint; the government consumption, for instance, is fixed to the GDP.

3.5 Trade

Foreign trade is determined on the basis of relative prices and world demand. The associated foreign trade equations follow a simple log-linear formulation including intra area trade.[1] In the euro-area model we also apply some foreign variables, such as commodity prices, foreign price level and foreign interest rates, which are assumed to be exogenous.

3.6 Monetary and Financial Sectors

EDGE is built as a cashless economy and thus the role of money is missing in the model. Monetary policy is described in the model by the Taylor rule.

Thus the short-term interest rate reacts to deviations of inflation from the target rate and to an unemployment gap. In the Taylor rule we apply weights with respect to inflation and the real activity gap, which are close to the 'standard' Taylor rule weights.

EDGE has a floating, fully forward-looking exchange rate, determined by current and expected interest rates on the basis of uncovered interest rate parity. The EDGE model includes a forward-looking determination of long-term interest rates.

4   AN OUTLINE OF THE KEY CHARACTERISTICS

Below we present the responses of the EDGE model in four simulations. The first simulation describes monetary policy reactions by increasing nominal interest rates temporarily. In the other three simulations both monetary and fiscal policy are exogenous for the first five years, after which the policy rules start to work.

The fifth simulation that is suggested is an oil price shock (the results are not reported here). This type of shock is problematic, since EDGE has no direct measure of oil prices. In principle this could be engineered via the assumed portion of oil in the commodity imports. Thus we would have some effects through the import prices. However this has no direct impact on the domestic production and therefore the shock would have only a negligible impact on the euro area.

4.1   Monetary Policy Shock

The results of a temporary (two-year) 1 percentage point increase in the nominal interest rate with floating exchange rates are presented in Figures 3.1a and 3.1b. In this shock the nominal short-term interest rate increases by 1 percentage point above the baseline level for two years and thereafter the Taylor rule determines the path of the nominal interest rate.

An exogenous increase in the nominal interest rate causes both the nominal and the real exchange rates to appreciate immediately. The temporary increase in the nominal interest rate dampens both inflation and real wages by less than half a percentage point in the first two years. This reduction in the inflation rate and increase in the nominal interest rate raises the real interest rate.

The rise in the expected real interest rate causes a sharp but transitory fall in production. Private consumption and private fixed investment fall as the real interest rate increases. Exports fall by almost 2 per cent in the

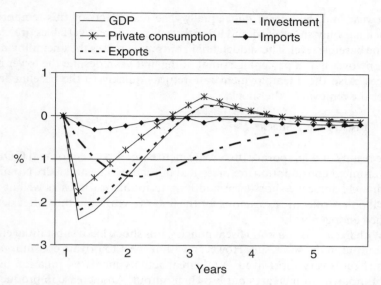

Figure 3.1a   Temporary (two-year) 1 percentage point increase in interest rates, difference from baseline

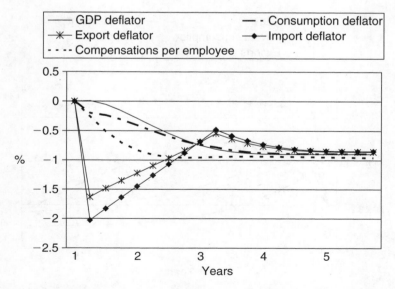

Figure 3.1b   Temporary (two-year) 1 percentage point increase in interest rates, difference from baseline

first year and the output falls equally. The real effects of this temporary shock are only short-lived and after three years all real variables are close to the baseline level. The sudden fall in output increases the unemployment rate by over half a percentage point in the first year, despite the lower real wages. Also the unemployment rate returns quickly to the baseline level after the removal of the shock.

4.2   Fiscal Policy Shock

The results of a temporary (five-year) increase of 1 per cent of real GDP in government consumption are presented in Figures 3.2a and 3.2b. Nominal exchange, domestic short-term and long-term interest rates as well as the fiscal policy rules are exogenous for the first five years and thereafter determined endogenously.

With fixed monetary and fiscal policies, this shock has a substantial effect on output in the short run. However, with respect to private consumption, this effect is very short-lived. As the real activity increases, inflation picks up. Employment increases but less than output. An increase in productivity increases real wages in the short run. The acceleration in the inflation rate in the first year produces a falling real interest rate, which also contributes to the initial pick-up in activity.

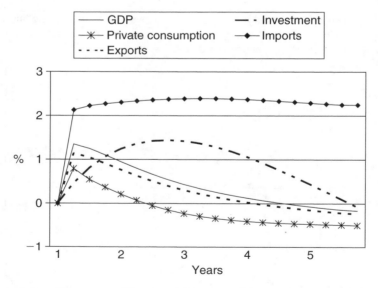

Figure 3.2a   Temporary (five-year) increase of 1 percentage point of real GDP in public consumption, difference from baseline

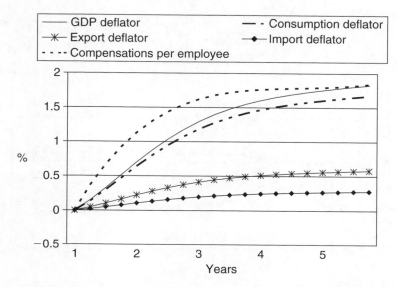

Figure 3.2b   *Temporary (five-year) increase of 1 percentage point of real GDP in public consumption, difference from baseline*

In the second year, private consumption decreases despite the fall in the real interest rate. Private consumption is crowded out by public consumption. The increase in public consumption is funded by bond financing in the short run. This increases the deficit, which accumulates to higher government debt levels.

4.3 Foreign Demand Shock

The results of a temporary (five-year) 1 per cent increase in world demand are presented in Figures 3.3a and 3.3b. Nominal exchange, domestic short-term and long-term interest rates as well as fiscal policy rules and government consumption are exogenous for the first five years and thereafter determined endogenously.

The temporary increase in foreign demand implies an expansion of the euro area's export markets. This leads to an increase in both exports and imports. Inflation increases somewhat during the first two years but stabilizes thereafter. As the nominal rates are fixed and inflation increases somewhat, the real interest rate falls. This development also yields higher private consumption and investment as well as output in the short run. As output and income increase, employment also increases somewhat, but less

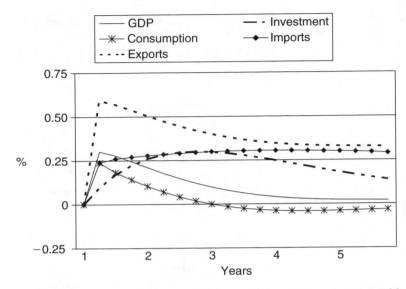

Figure 3.3a   *Temporary (five-year) 1 percentage point increase in world demand, difference from baseline*

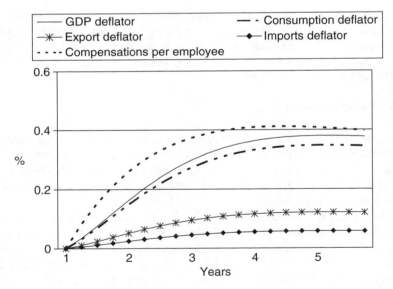

Figure 3.3b   *Temporary (five-year) 1 percentage point increase in world demand, difference from baseline*

than output. Thus productivity and real wages increase in the first year. All in all, the effect of the foreign demand shock is relatively modest.

4.4 Exchange Rate Shock

The results of a temporary (five-year) 1 per cent appreciation of the euro are presented in Figures 3.4a and 3.4b. Domestic short-term and long-term interest rates as well as fiscal policy rules and government consumption are exogenous for the first five years and thereafter determined endogenously.

The appreciation of the euro leads to falling export and import prices. As import prices fall, the price of private consumption and investment also falls, leading to a general fall in prices. Inflation decreases in the first three years but stabilizes thereafter. As the nominal interest rate is then fixed and inflation falls, the real interest rate increases in the short run. Increasing the real interest rate leads to falling private consumption and investment demand. Private consumption recovers back to the baseline level by the end of the second year. As the import prices fall, imports increase somewhat. However exports fall sharply in response to the appreciating euro. These developments generate both falling net trade and domestic demand in the short run.

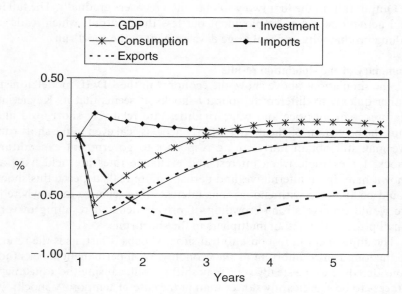

Figure 3.4a   Temporary (five-year) 1 percentage point appreciation of exchange rate, difference from baseline

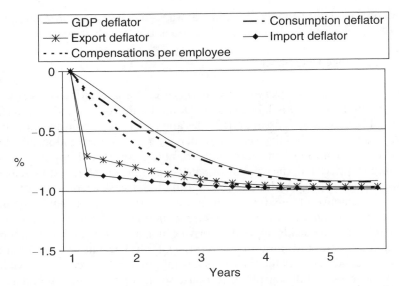

Figure 3.4b   Temporary (five-year) 1 percentage point appreciation of exchange rate, difference from baseline

Output falls in the first two years but then recovers gradually. The fall in real activity decreases employment but less than output, which leads to falling productivity and real wage development in the short run.

Summary of the simulation results
As the simulations above show, the economy in the EDGE model adjusts rather quickly to different temporary shocks. It seems that its Keynesian features, namely price and wage rigidities, are relatively short-lived and thus the behaviour of the model is fairly neoclassical even in the short run. We may still obtain fairly strong responses to government expenditure shock, for example when interest and exchange rates are held fixed as shown here. In an alternative, and perhaps more realistic, case this shock could be analysed with endogenous interest and exchange rates, whereby we would observe strong crowding of private demand resulting in very small positive Keynesian multipliers in the short run.

The adjustment in response to transitory shocks is fast, as is the return to the long-run equilibrium of the economy. With permanent shocks (not considered here) the steady state may shift as well, causing the adjustment process to be significantly slower than in the case of temporary shocks. In particular, the adjustment of different asset balances, especially the adjustment of net foreign assets to their new equilibrium, is slow.

Even though the EDGE model has quite rapid mechanisms for adjusting to equilibrium in most respects, the simulation results are not in conflict with mainstream theory. In particular, the unit root property of the exchange rate, which allows for sudden and persistent movements, accelerates relative price adjustments and thus makes the adjustment processes even faster. When used together with the Taylor rule, which is obviously a very rough description of monetary policy, the simulation results of the model are in most cases plausible both in size and sign.

5   CONCLUSIONS

The EDGE model is a small, open economy, dynamic general equilibrium model calibrated to euro-area data. EDGE is currently applied in policy analysis. The EDGE model can be used to assess the effects of different expectations held by different agents, especially with regard to monetary policy. Assessing such effects is one of the main challenges of modern monetary analysis. Recent development of EDGE has included calibration to US data and combined this with the euro-zone model for a new two-country version of the EDGE model.

NOTE

1. In the two-country version of the EDGE model, we derive trade equations directly from the microeconomic foundations and calibrate euro area to data for extra-euro-area traded goods.

REFERENCES

Kortelainen, Mika (2001), 'Actual and perceived monetary policy rules in a dynamic general equilibrium model of the euro area', Bank of Finland discussion papers 3/2001 (http://www.bof.fi/eng/6_julkaisut/6.1_SPn_julkaisut/6.1.5_keskustelualoitteita/0103mk.pdf)
Kortelainen, Mika (2002), 'EDGE: a Model of the Euro area with Applications to Monetary Policy', Bank of Finland Studies, E:23 (http://www.bof.fi/eng/6_julkaisut/6.1_SPn_julkaisut/6.1.4_tutkimuksia/E23.pdf)
Kortelainen Mika (2004), 'The US current account deficit', *Bank of Finland Bulletin*, **78** (1), 69–75 (http://www.bof.fi/eng/6_julkaisut/6.1_SPn_julkaisut/6.1.2_BOf_bulletin/04b1.pdf)
Kortelainen, Mika and David G. Mayes (2004), 'Using EDGE – a dynamic general equilibrium model of the euro area', in Stephen G. Hall, Ullrich Heilemann and Peter Pauly (eds), *Macroeconometric Models and European Monetary Union*, Berlin: RWI Essen, Dunker & Humblot, pp. 41–78.

Tarkka, Juha and Mika Kortelainen (2001), 'Analysing monetary policy credibility with a model of the euro area', *Bank of Finland Bulletin*, **75** (3), 18–23 (http://www.bof.fi/eng/6_julkaisut/6.1_SPn_julkaisut/6.1.2_BOf_bulletin/01b3.pdf)
Tarkka, Juha and Mika Kortelainen (2005), 'International economic spillovers and the liquidity trap', Bank of Finland Discussion Papers (forthcoming).

4. The Eurosystem's multi-country model and the link block

Tohmas Karlsson and Peter McAdam

1 INTRODUCTION

This chapter briefly describes the main features and uses of the Eurosystem's multi-country model (MCM).[1] The model, the outcome of a joint project coordinated by the WGEM, comprises 'country blocks', one for each country of EMU, linked together with a 'trade block'.[2] The various country blocks have been developed either by the corresponding NCB, the ECB, or jointly, whereas the trade block has been developed at the ECB.

2 THE USES OF THE MCM

The various blocks comprised in the MCM are used for both projections and policy analysis. In central banks where the country blocks of the MCM are employed in forecasting tasks, *projections* are generally arrived at by a combination of judgmental and off-model inputs as well as the simulated output of the models.[3] The trade block of the linked MCM model plays an important role in the so-called 'trade consistency exercise' (TCE), which forms part of the macroeconomic projection exercises of the ECB and ESCB. In these exercises, projections are prepared separately for each individual country. In order for these individual projections to serve as a reliable guide for area-wide conclusions, it is necessary that the country projections of trade volumes and prices are consistent with each other as well as being consistent with the assumptions made about the external environment. In a number of central banks, including the ECB, *policy analysis* is performed with the MCM through simulations reflecting a wide variety of requests and concerns. Such exercises also aid in the validation and evaluation of the model. Indeed, in the context of the WGEM work, regular comparison exercises with NCBs' own models and informational exchanges (on specifications, multiplier profiles, dynamic responses, long-run properties and data definitions) are conducted.

3   AN OUTLINE OF THE THEORETICAL UNDERPINNINGS OF THE MODEL AND ITS PURPOSES

All MCM country blocks are estimated from their respective country databases, which have been constructed by the corresponding NCB and are deposited at the ECB. In all cases the theoretical underpinnings of the models are similar and quite standard. Furthermore the level of disaggregation of components and variable definitions run largely in parallel. In effect, the MCM structure belongs to the same class of model as that of the area-wide model (Fagan *et al.*, 2001).[4] The MCM blocks therefore have a clear common theoretical structure: classical in the long run, 'Keynesian' in the short run. The overall specification is designed to explain the main expenditure categories and production flows in each country, from which employment, investment, prices and financial variables are determined. Aggregate demand is, as usual, built up from private and public consumption, investment, net trade and the change in inventories. Potential output and long-run factor demand are determined by a production function so that capacity utilization (the ratio of actual to potential output) can vary. In the long run, output and factor demands are determined by the supply side. Long-run factor demands are pinned down by standard classical first-order marginal conditions derived from profit maximization and perfect competition in factor markets. Thus potential output is determined from an economy-wide Cobb–Douglas production function with an exogenous 'natural rate' (that is, the NAIRU) and a consistent set of factor demands. The components of aggregate demand are consistent with this equilibrium, via a stock-flow adjustment mechanism involving net foreign assets and the real exchange rate. In the short run, however, output is demand-determined; deviations of output from potential, or of unemployment from the NAIRU, set in train a process of adjustments which, together with the operation of 'policy rules' (where available), drive the model to its long-run equilibrium. Regarding prices, the long run is determined by the nominal anchor chosen in running the model (for example an inflation objective which enters the interest rate-setting equation or, in the case of a fixed nominal exchange rate, the 'world' price level).

Overall the MCM country blocks share the following features:

1.   Apart from the *linked block* (discussed in Section 5), each MCM essentially represents a single, closed economy.
2.   They are of quarterly frequency.
3.   The models are relatively compact and highly aggregated, typically

incorporating around 80–100 equations of which around 15–20 are estimated behavioural ones.

4. The behavioural equations themselves are generally estimated on the basis of national historical data from 1980 onwards. Equations which have been calibrated are (where available) the policy rules and (occasionally) the production function parameters.

5. Typically long-run conditions enter the equations in the form of error correction mechanism (ECM) terms and appropriate homogeneity conditions are generally included in the dynamics to ensure the existence of a real equilibrium, which is independent of nominal variables (that is to say, ensuring a vertical Phillips curve).

6. The models are backward-looking; although expectations are in many cases explicitly modelled, they are based on lagged values of the variables concerned (that is, adaptive expectations).

7. The growth rate of the labour force, the rate of technical progress and the NAIRU are exogenous in the long run.

8. Factor demands are determined by classical marginal optimality conditions.

3.1 The Production Function and Factor Demands

Potential output, for the whole economy, is given by constant-returns Cobb–Douglas technology. The elasticities of this production function are estimated or calibrated (with technical progress typically modelled via a deterministic trend). In general, long-run factor demands and the GDP deflator equations have been jointly estimated. This production function is used to derive theoretically consistent first-order conditions that enter other equations in the model, such as investment. It also provides the measure of potential output which, combined with actual output, determines the output gap. To be more specific, the long-run capital–labour ratio is 'pinned down', through the first-order conditions of a profit-maximizing firm, assuming perfectly competitive factor markets. Potential output is then given by full employment of the labour force (for a given NAIRU) and exogenous technical progress.

Thus the factor demand equations in the model (capital and employment) are specified in such a way as to be consistent in the long run with the underlying theoretical framework of the supply side. This, as mentioned earlier, is achieved by means of the inclusion of ECM terms, which embody, respectively, the marginal productivity condition for capital and the consistency between employment, the production function and the given NAIRU. However, by definition, these relations only hold in the long run: otherwise investment and employment are driven by short-run demand dynamics. In addition, the *investment* (capital stock) equation comprises a long-run component in which capital stock is proportional to output, with the ratio of the two depending on the real user cost of capital: a real interest rate, a depreciation rate and a constant (historically calibrated) risk premium. The short run of the equation includes a standard accelerator effect. *Employment* growth in the short run depends on real wages and output growth (both adjusted for trend productivity). In the longer term, employment (or labour demand) adjusts to a level implied by the inversion of the production function. Together with the adjustments to the other variables in the dynamics, this implies a long-run solution of the equation in which employment growth equals labour force growth.

3.2 Components of Aggregate Demand

Aggregate demand is split into the following components.

- *Private consumption* is a function both of disposable income and of wealth, defined as cumulated savings under the assumption that households own all of the assets in the economy (that is to say, public debt, net foreign assets and private capital stock). In many of the blocks, real interest rates and unemployment rates also determine short-run consumption dynamics.
- *Public consumption*: most government expenditure items are exogenous, either in real terms or in GDP points, with the noticeable exception of transfers to households, which respond countercyclically to activity.
- *Inventories* are modelled in such a way that in the long run the ratio between cumulated inventories and GDP remains constant. In a number of cases, real interest rates also enter the specification.
- *Trade (exports and imports)*: trade flows are modelled in a standard fashion, whereby market shares (in terms of world demand and domestic demand for exports and imports, respectively) are a function of a competitiveness indicator involving trade prices. Furthermore the MCM can be run in linked mode with demand and prices for intra-EU transactions endogenous. (See Section 5 for details on the existing linkages via trade variables.)

3.3 Prices and Costs

Prices have been estimated under the assumption that a form of the law of one price should hold, that is, imposing static homogeneity on all price equations, which is equivalent to expressing the long-run ECM component of each of those equations in terms of relative prices only. The key price index used in the model is the deflator for real GDP at factor costs (that is, excluding the effect of indirect taxes and subsidies). This key deflator is modelled as a function of trend unit labour costs. In the short run, import prices may also have some effects on the resulting mark-up. The GDP deflator at market prices in turn is derived by using the accounting identity linking market prices to factor costs and indirect taxes net of subsidies, through an exogenous ratio in GDP terms.

Wages are modelled as a Phillips curve, with wage growth depending on productivity, current and lagged (consumer price) inflation and the deviation of unemployment from the NAIRU. This latter variable is exogenous. In the case where dynamic homogeneity holds, the long-run Phillips curve is vertical.

The specification of the wage and the key price equations implies that two independent measures of demand can affect inflation, namely unemployment and the output gap. In most cases, however, the only tension affecting the price and wage dynamics is the unemployment term. The long-run equilibrium for both wages and prices is pinned down by the predetermined trend real unit labour costs or, equivalently, by the long-run labour share, in turn equal to the labour elasticity in the production function, given the Cobb–Douglas specification.

There is an equation for the private consumption deflator, sometimes supplemented by another one for the overall harmonized index of consumer prices (HICP). To provide a link between the deflators and the HICP index, (estimated) bridging equations have been introduced into those MCM blocks which also model the HICP. These bridging equations relate the consumption deflator to the overall HICP and its components, namely energy and non-energy. The HICP energy is then a function of oil prices whereas the HICP non-energy depends on unit labour costs and import prices.

3.4 Fiscal Accounts

The modelling of the fiscal accounts is highly aggregated and simplified. In projections, all fiscal variables are exogenous in real terms or in GDP points. Most MCM country blocks, however, embody a standard fiscal reaction function, which is necessary to ensure stability of the model in longer-run simulations. In effect, direct tax rates are set to gradually eliminate the gap between actual and target (that is, baseline) levels for the debt-to-output ratio. Such rules are largely calibrated with the actual parameterization being model-specific and ensuring model stability and plausible dynamics. Furthermore transfers to households are generally modelled as a function of the unemployment rate or level.

3.5 Trade Accounts

Foreign trade is modelled in a traditional fashion, where trade volumes are determined by relative income and relative prices. In the long run, a unit elasticity is imposed on real imports and real exports with respect to domestic and foreign demand. Price competitiveness measures enter the long-run and, in most cases, the short-run equations. Import demand is generally a function of domestic demand components, weighted according to their import content. World demand is based on the given country-specific export market geographical structure, taking into account 23 partner countries/areas for each given country block. The import price is a weighted average of the competitors' prices, the energy prices and the domestic GDP deflator, where the coefficients of these variables sum to one in the long-run equation. The export price is similarly a weighted average of the domestic output price and foreign competitors' prices. Deterministic trends are sometimes introduced to ensure cointegration between market shares and the corresponding relative prices.

Competitors' prices are computed as a weighted average of partners' export prices using a double weighting scheme, that is to say, taking into account third market effects, for exports and a standard simple weighting scheme for imports. In addition both world demand and competitors' prices can be decomposed into intra- and extra-euro area components. Currently there is no available national accounts-based breakdown of aggregate trade flows into intra- and extra-euro area components. Owing to this lack of data, only aggregate trade is modelled. However in some country blocks aggregate trade flows and prices are modelled with different elasticities with respect to intra and extra components.

Net factor income (including international transfers) is determined by a calibrated or estimated equation linking it to lagged values of the stock of net foreign assets. The trade balance and net factor income equal the current account balance, which in turn is cumulated to give the stock of net foreign assets.

3.6 Monetary and Financial Sector

In the monetary sector, the nominal exchange rate is exogenous. Typically in projection exercises, all interest rates are taken to be exogenous. In simulation mode, however, short-term interest rates in the MCM are generally assumed to be exogenous in real terms and long rates are a weighted average of past short and long rates (that is, a simple term structure). In some country blocks, credit rates to households and companies are linked to the short- and long-term rates. There is otherwise no explicit modelling of money demand.

4 DIFFERENCES ACROSS COUNTRY BLOCKS

Although similar in structure, purpose and motivation, the various MCM models have some points of departure. To list all such differences would be a large task and would deflect us from the present purpose of treating the MCM framework as largely unified. Nevertheless it is worth briefly highlighting the following points. First, needless to say, each model is estimated on its own national database. Thus each will embody different point estimates in equations. This may imply differences in the acceptance of static or dynamic homogeneity. It will also clearly imply different polynomial lengths in equations and thus different response times and dynamic behaviour, all of which can have a substantial impact on the respective response to a given shock of the corresponding country blocks. Of particular importance in this respect is the fact that, in some country blocks, an interest rate term enters consumption. Similarly, whether homogeneity is found or imposed in the wage equations clearly matters, since the long-run Phillips curves may not be vertical.

Second, there are other sources of asymmetric responses not related to estimation, such as the fact that each country block embodies different trade weights to determine its overall trade accounts. Different calibration for the policy rules, for example, would also generate differing responses. Finally the measure chosen for a given concept, such as real wages, trend productivity, competitiveness and so on can also vary across models and lead to differences in simulation properties.

5 THE LINKING OF THE MCMS

An important recent development in the MCM is the linking of the separate country models through foreign trade equations. For each given country, all international trade variables related to other country blocks that are part of the linked model should be endogenized in simulations. Some of the international interdependencies among the countries are then explicitly taken into account in the resulting linked model, which now consists of 11 country blocks. The links relate to trade volumes and prices; the exchange rate in relation to the rest of the world remains exogenous.

Table 4.1   Trade variables in isolated and linked mode

	Variable name	Single country	Multi-country
Imports			
Import demand	WER	Endogenous	Endogenous
Intra-euro area competitors' prices	CMD_IN	Exogenous	Endogenous
Extra-euro area competitors' prices	CMD_EX	Exogenous	Exogenous
Nominal effective exchange rate	EEN0	Exogenous	Exogenous
Exports			
Intra-euro area foreign demand	WDR_IN	Exogenous	Endogenous
Extra-euro area foreign demand	WDR_EX	Exogenous	Exogenous
Intra-euro area competitors' prices	CXD_IN	Exogenous	Endogenous
Extra-euro area competitors' prices	CXD_EX	Exogenous	Exogenous
Nominal effective exchange rate	EEN	Exogenous	Exogenous
Trade balance			
Net foreign assets/ current account	NFA/CAN	Endogenous	Endogenous

The linkage variables for each country are (a) domestic import demand (*WER*); (b) competitors' prices on the import side (*CMD*); (c) the nominal effective exchange rate on the import side (*EEN0*); (d) foreign demand (*WDR*); (e) competitors' prices on the export side (*CXD*); (f) the nominal effective exchange rate on the export side (*EEN*); (g) the current account (net foreign assets). Table 4.1 summarizes the effects on the various trade variables of moving from a single to a multi-country framework.

Note that trade variables for countries outside the euro area, such as Switzerland, Japan and the USA, will remain exogenous in the linked model. Thus, even in linked mode, the trade variables will contain an exogenous component. This reflects the distinction between intra- and extra-euro area trade. Intra euro-area trade involves trade between euro-area countries and this is modelled endogenously. Extra euro-area trade is exogenous and relates to those countries not modelled in the linked version.

Those variables (highlighted in Table 4.1) which remain endogenous contain the same specification as in the MCM framework without cross-country linkages but the corresponding equations are now solved simultaneously for all intra-area trade. The endogenized parts are competitors' prices (on both the import and export side) and foreign demand. Country i's competitors' import price index is obtained as a weighted average of competitors' export prices, comprising an endogenous and exogenous component, depending on whether the corresponding competitor is represented by a country block in the linked MCM. The same applies to competitors' export price index. As regards foreign demand, the demand for country i's exports is expressed in the form of a world demand index, WDR, calculated as a weighted average of the import volumes of the trading partners of country i. Again there is a distinction between modelled (intra-euro area) real import demand of countries that are part of the linked model and non-modelled (extra-euro area) import demand from those countries that are not part of the linked model. The trade block of the linked MCM model plays an important role in the so-called 'trade consistency exercise', which forms part of the macroeconomic projection exercises of the ECB and ESCB. In these exercises projections are prepared separately for each individual country. In order for these individual country projections to serve as a reliable guide for area-wide conclusions, it is necessary for them to be consistent with each other. The purpose of the trade consistency exercise is to ensure that individual country projections of trade volumes and prices are mutually consistent with each other as well as being consistent with the assumptions made about the external environment.

There are two aspects of trade consistency which are addressed in the projection rounds. The first, 'cross-trade consistency', ensures that each country's export projection is consistent with the import projections for its trading partners in both volume and price terms. The basic idea behind the 'cross-trade consistency' concept is that each country's export volumes should in principle be determined by its commercial partners' import volumes. For every country we compute the growth in foreign demand that is implied by the projected import growth rate of all its trading partners. This measure of foreign demand growth is then compared with the export growth projections. The difference between projected foreign demand and exports, that is, export market shares, could indicate inconsistencies with regard to changes in competitiveness and thus imply revisions of trade projections.

Secondly, 'ex ante/ex post trade consistency' makes sure that the original assumptions made for each country for external demand variables are consistent with the projections obtained for the imports of other euro-area countries. For ex ante/ex post trade consistency to hold it is required that the measure of world demand (denoted by WDR_IN in Table 4.1 above), which is given as an exogenous variable at the beginning of the forecast exercise, is equal to the projected world demand or aggregate imports at the end of the forecasting round. The same kind of consistency also applies to external competitors' prices.

NOTES

1. Comments from Jérôme Henry, Ricardo Mestre and one anonymous referee are gratefully acknowledged.
2. There is no model available yet for Luxembourg. However Luxembourg is included in the trade matrix, which underlies the computation of competitors' prices and foreign demand in the trade block.
3. For a discussion of the Eurosystem's macroeconomic projection exercises, see ECB (2001).
4. For a more recent listing and simulation analysis of the AWM, see Dieppe and Henry (2004) as well as the AWM chapter in this volume. At the time of writing, only the Spanish MCM block has been formally published: see Willman and Estrada (2002).

REFERENCES

Dieppe, A. and J. Henry (2004), 'The euro area viewed as a single economy: how does it respond to shocks?', *Economic Modelling*, **25** (5), 833–75.
ECB (2001), *A Guide to Eurosystem Staff Macroeconomic Projection Exercises*, Frankfurt: European Central Bank.
Fagan, G., J. Henry and R. Mestre (2001), 'An area-wide model (AWM) for the euro area', ECB working paper no. 42.
Willman, A. and A. Estrada (2002), 'The Spanish Block of the ESCB-Multi-Country-Model', ECB working paper no. 149.

5. EUROMON: a macroeconometric multi-country model of the world economy from the Nederlandsche Bank

Peter van Els

1 INTRODUCTION

EUROMON was originally developed at De Nederlandsche Bank (DNB), in the 1990s but has recently undergone a large number of changes, including an overall respecification and re-estimation of many of the model's equations. This was partly due to the advent of EMU but was also intended to strengthen the long-run simulation properties of the model. Further changes are yet to be implemented. The present version of the model is documented in Demertzis, *et al.* (2003).[1]

2 THE USES OF THE MODEL

EUROMON is used in forecasting, in conducting policy and scenario analyses, and in counterfactual simulation exercises. In the period 1996–8 EUROMON projections for several EU countries were published biannually in DNB's *Quarterly Bulletin* but the publication of such projections was stopped with the start of EMU in 1999. However topical policy and scenario analyses based on simulations with EUROMON are still being presented regularly in the *Quarterly Bulletin*. In the internal process of policy preparation EUROMON projections continue to play their usual role, but the emphasis is gradually shifting towards using the model as a tool for policy analysis and research. Projections are a combination of model-generated and judgmental information. Judgmental sources include available off-model information taken from new releases of cyclical and price indicators or from predictions based on other in-house or external models.

3 A BIRD'S EYE VIEW OF EUROMON

EUROMON is an estimated multi-country model. The current version includes 13 individual country models plus a trade block providing the international linkages. The 13 countries are the EMU participants Germany, France, Italy, Spain, the Netherlands, Belgium, Austria and Finland, the EU countries of the United Kingdom, Sweden and Denmark, plus the United States and Japan. All countries are estimated individually and although not all the euro countries are represented in EUROMON, we approximate the euro area with the eight countries that are modelled. The results presented in the figures that follow refer to this eight-country grouping. The country models all have the same basic structure. Differences mainly relate to distinct values of model parameters and speeds of adjustment and in some cases to slightly different specifications of equations in order to allow for country-specific institutional features. For example, residential investment is affected by short-term interest rates in the UK but by long-term rates in other countries. The same holds for consumption. The current version of the model is backward-looking but forward-looking elements are still being developed and will be incorporated in future versions. The inclusion of forward-looking elements requires well-defined long-run simulation properties, a process that we have tried to strengthen with implementing up-to-date theoretical features. The model is basically New Keynesian, combining a vertical supply curve in the long run with an important role for demand factors in the short-run determination of output. The model incorporates a wage bargaining framework which makes the long-run supply curve dependent on real factors, such as tax policies. EUROMON is an aggregate model, with no further breakdown in sectors or categories of goods and services.

Country models consist of 25 behavioural equations and 50 identities each. In total, EUROMON includes some 1000 equations, of which 330 are estimated. The model is estimated using quarterly data over a sample period starting (if available) in 1970 up to 1999 (2000). In most cases we apply ordinary least squares to estimate the equations and TROLL to simulate the model itself and allow for dummies to capture major institutional developments (for example, German reunification). Detailed information on individual equations and parameters can be found in De Nederlandsche Bank (2000) and in Demertzis *et al.* (2003). Below we give a brief description of the structure of the main features of the model.

Aggregate supply is given by a CES (constant elasticity of substitution) production technology, with capital and labour as inputs. See Bolt and van Els (2000) for a detailed description. In the long run output is determined by the supply of labour (largely exogenous), the equilibrium unemployment rate captured by the NAWRU and technical progress which is measured by the development of total factor productivity. Equations for labour demand and the capital stock (non-residential) are derived from first-order conditions. Labour demand depends on output and real product wages. Non-residential private investment depends on the real user cost of capital and the capital–output ratio, in line with the CES production technology. The dynamics of investment are also affected by short-run changes in total sales and profitability.

Monetary policy and fiscal solvency rules play an important long-run stabilizing role. Here various options are available. In most cases a Taylor rule is used for endogenizing short-term interest rates with feedback from aggregate inflation and the aggregate output gap. Fiscal solvency is implemented by concentrating on the government deficit-to-GDP ratio, using personal income tax rates as instruments.

Turning to aggregate demand, private consumption depends on real disposable household income and real financial and non-financial wealth, with housing and capital stocks measured at market value. The direct substitution effect is captured by the inclusion of the long-term interest rate in the equation. In the short run, private consumption is also affected by changes in the unemployment rate. Residential investment is determined by real disposable household income and by real long- and short-term interest rates. Government investment is largely exogenous or constant in terms of GDP (optional). Inventory formation acts as a buffer for accommodating shocks in the short run. Following the approach suggested by Fair (1984) the inventory stocks-to-sales ratio returns to equilibrium in the long run. In the short run, deviations may also be caused by changes and are affected by the cost of financing which in estimation is best captured by real long-term interest rates. Exports depend on world demand and competitiveness in terms of relative export prices. Likewise imports depend on sales and relative import prices, but also on cyclical conditions. In principle, both exports and imports are affected by cyclical conditions but empirically this is much more easily justified for the latter than for the former. A higher output gap requires producers to raise their imports and vice versa.

The private consumption deflator is the main price variable in EUROMON. In the long run, consumer prices depend on unit labour costs, the mark-up and indirect tax rates. Oil prices have a small separate impact, reflecting the direct consumption of oil-related energy by households. Competitors' prices and cyclical indicators determine the mark-up of prices over the costs of production. Wage formation reflects a bargaining framework according to which equilibrium wages depend on consumer and producer prices, productivity, the unemployment rate and the rates of income tax and social security premiums. Long-run and dynamic homogeneity is imposed to ensure that nominal variables do not affect the equilibrium unemployment rate.

The government sector is treated in some detail. On the revenue side, income taxes, social security premiums, corporate taxes and indirect taxes are modelled separately. Five expenditure categories are distinguished: wages, non-wage government consumption and investment, transfers, interest payments on government debt, and other expenditures.

In the trade block of the model, a relevant world demand variable is modelled for each country as a weighted average of the imports of trading partners. Likewise weighted world export prices and world import prices are constructed (in national currencies), which serve as important determinants of national export prices and import prices, respectively.

The monetary sector of the model consists of behavioural equations for M3 and bank loans to the private sector. Money demand is homogeneous in income and private sector net financial wealth. Furthermore money demands depend on short- and long-term interest rates and inflation. The demand for bank loans is determined in the long run by the condition that interest payments on bank loans develop in line with nominal income. Note that M3 and bank loans are not fully recursive. This implies that changes in both feed back into aggregate demand via the income channel of monetary transmission. This effect turns out, however, to be small in practice.

The transmission of monetary policy operates through various channels. In the short run, prices and output are affected by the responses of the exchange rate. This is the exchange rate channel. In the medium term, cost-of-capital effects and direct substitution effects on the investment categories and on private consumption, respectively, dominate the impact of monetary policy on output. A fourth channel of transmission is the wealth channel, which operates mainly through changes in asset prices (endogenous house and equity prices). Finally the income channel, which has already been mentioned, relates to changes in the net investment income flows received (or paid) by households, triggered by interest rate changes.

3.1 Full Model Simulation Properties

EUROMON's system properties are analysed by conducting five simulation experiments:

1. A two-year 100 basis points increase in the short-term interest rate.
2. A five-year increase in real government consumption by 1 per cent of initial GDP.
3. A five-year 1 per cent increase in non-euro area world demand.

4. A five-year 1 per cent appreciation of the euro in comparison with all other currencies.
5. A permanent 10 per cent increase in oil prices.

A summary of these results can be found in Figures 5.1 to 5.5. The reporting horizon covers a five-year period. The design of the simulation exercises is based on common assumptions regarding the feedback on policy instruments and the responses of long-term interest rates and exchange rates. In Simulations 2 to 5, policy-controlled and market interest rates are exogenous over the reporting horizon and remain unchanged at their baseline values. The absence of endogenous policy feedback mechanisms implies that large inflationary impulses such as the 1 per cent GDP increase in government consumption trigger a very substantial and persistent rise in economic activity and prices. The results shown for Simulation 2 in particular (but also scenarios 3–5) are therefore only indicative of the model's simulation properties under exogenous policy settings and should thus be interpreted with caution. Except for Simulations 1 and 4, exchange rates remain unchanged at their baseline values over the reporting horizon. In Simulation 1 no monetary policy rule is implemented and the responses of long-term interest rates and exchange rates follow from using the (forward-looking) expectations hypothesis and uncovered interest parity condition,

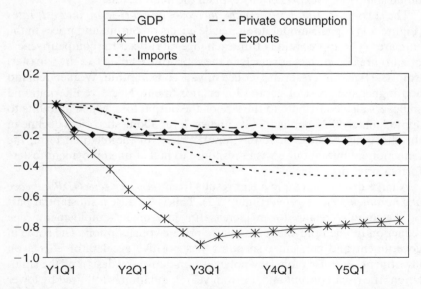

Figure 5.1a   Effects of a two-year 100 bp increase in short-term interest rates (real categories)

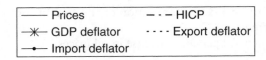

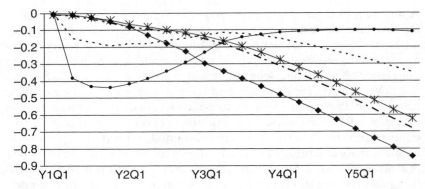

Figure 5.1b   *Effects of a two-year 100 bp increase in short-term interest*
rates (nominal categories)

respectively. We apply no fiscal policy rules. As EUROMON is a world
model, it is operated in linked mode, that is, taking into account international spillovers. Next we briefly explain the main results.

The two-year *100 basis points increase in short-term interest rates*
(Figure 5.1) triggers moderate aggregate effects on output and prices in the
euro area. The appreciation of the exchange rate affects the competitiveness
of euro-area producers adversely in the short run, leading to a drop in (net)
exports. Higher interest rates reduce private consumption. Weaker demand
and higher user cost of capital lower investment. Negative international
spillovers also contribute to the size of the output loss, which amounts to
approximately 0.25 per cent at its highest level. Domestic prices decline in
the short run because of lower import prices. In the medium term, the
reduction in unit labour costs in response to higher unemployment fosters
further price decreases.

A large drop in unemployment results from *the 1 per cent GDP increase
in government consumption* (Figure 5.2). This is because a substantial part
of the impulse relates to an increase in government employment. The
reduction in unemployment stimulates private consumption. The surge in
government and consumer spending has positive accelerator effects on
investment. Because monetary policy is non-active (by design of the simulation) the rise in output and, as from year 2, inflation is followed by lower
real interest rates. This provides an additional stimulus to spending, which
leads to a persistent rise in economic activity and inflation. Because of

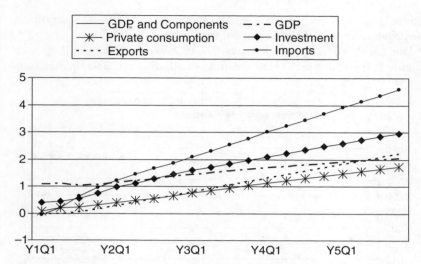

Figure 5.2a   Effects of a 1% increase in government consumption (real categories)

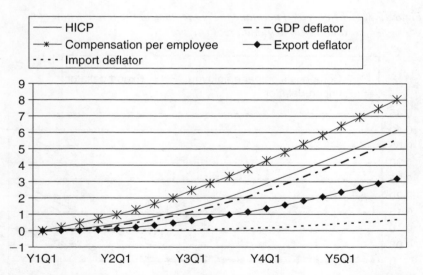

Figure 5.2b   Effects of a 1% increase in government consumption (nominal categories)

international spillovers, world demand increases, which more than offsets the negative impact of the loss in competitiveness on exports.

The effects of a *1 per cent increase in non-euro area world demand* (Figure 5.3) on euro-area GDP are quite small, which reflects the relatively

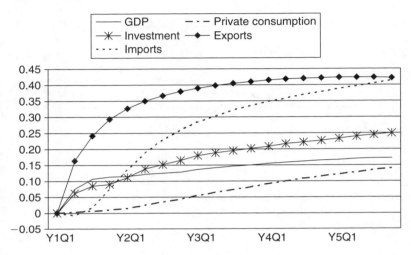

Figure 5.3a   Effects of a permanent 1% increase in the level of non-euro area world demand (real categories)

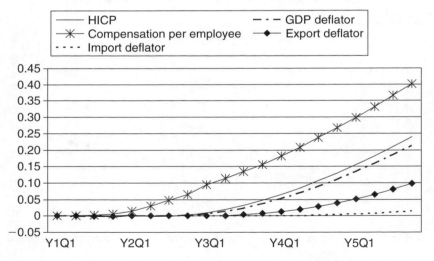

Figure 5.3b   Effects of a permanent 1% increase in the level of non-euro area world demand (nominal categories)

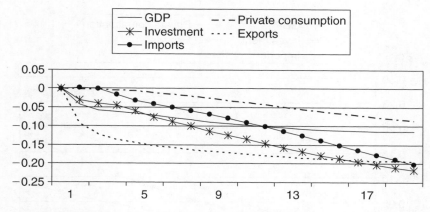

Figure 5.4a   *Effects of a five-year 1% appreciation of the euro* vis-à-vis *all other currencies (real categories)*

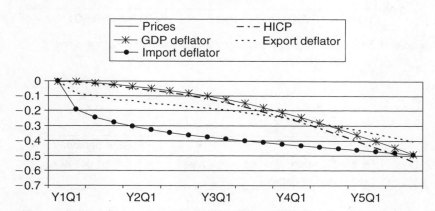

Figure 5.4b   *Effects of a five-year 1% appreciation of the euro* vis-à-vis *all other currencies (nominal categories)*

closed character of the euro-area economy. The shock equates to only a 0.45 per cent increase in total relevant world demand for the euro area. In order to fix the impulse over the entire simulation horizon, world demand is taken to be exogenous in this particular scenario. Wages and prices are somewhat higher, induced by a small decrease in the unemployment rate.

A *1 per cent appreciation of the euro* (Figure 5.4) lowers real GDP by 0.1 per cent. The effects of lower competitiveness on exports trigger the reduction in economic activity. Lower foreign prices feed gradually into domestic prices and wages. After five years, consumer prices are down by about 0.5 per cent.

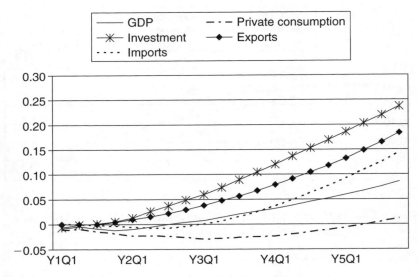

Figure 5.5a   Effects of a permanent 10% increase in oil prices (real categories)

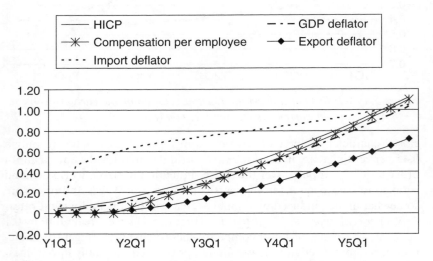

Figure 5.5b   Effects of a permanent 10% increase in oil prices (nominal categories)

A permanent *10 per cent rise in oil prices* (Figure 5.5) leads to higher consumer prices and thus initially to a drop in real disposable income and consumer spending. However, as nominal interest rates are fixed in this simulation, higher inflation is followed by lower real interest rates which in themselves allow for (residential) investment to pick up. As a result, real GDP is slightly above base over the medium term. After five years consumer price levels are 1 per cent higher. This general price response not only reflects the direct effect of higher oil-related energy prices, but also includes indirect second-round effects via wage formation and international spillovers.

4   THE FUTURE OF EUROMON

There are a number of issues that we would like to change in the current structure of EUROMON in order to improve its theoretical cohesiveness but also to make it more appropriate to the ways that the model is currently used. We mention a few below in order to cast some light on the direction we would like to see the model take. First, we would like to strengthen the long-run simulation properties of the model by further improving its theoretical consistency. An important element of this refers to solving the equilibrium unemployment rate explicitly as mentioned in the text and using this variable as an input to the supply side of the model. Second, strengthening the theoretical consistency will provide the basis for including forward-looking elements such as model-consistent expectations regarding future inflation, interest rates and exchange rates, and household income/wealth. Third, we plan to improve the modelling of international linkages by incorporating information on trade linkages with country blocks that are not currently included in the model. A fourth element is to reconsider the modelling of import prices by including pricing to market not only as a short-term phenomenon, as is now the case for most countries, but also in the long-term equilibrium relationship for import prices, and to test for its statistical significance.

Finally, as best modelling practices are currently viewed as moving in the direction of dynamic general equilibrium models, we will, in the future, be required to consider the parallel use of such models alongside EUROMON.

NOTE

1. See Demertzis *et al.* (2002), De Nederlandsche Bank (2000). An earlier version of EUROMON was documented in G.J. de Bondt *et al.* (1997).

REFERENCES

Bolt, W. and P.J.A. van Els (2000), 'Output gap and inflation in the EU', *DNB Staff Reports*, no. 44, De Nederlandsche Bank.

de Bondt, G.J, P.J.A. van Els and A.C.J. Stokman (1997), 'EUROMON: a macro-econometric multi-country model for the EU', *DNB Staff Reports*, no. 17, De Nederlandsche Bank.

Demertzis, Maria, Peter van Els, Sybille Grob and Marga Peeters (2003), 'EUROMON, The Nederlandsche Bank's multi-country model', mimeo, Research Division, De Nederlandsche Bank.

De Nederlandsche Bank (2000), 'EUROMON: The Nederlandsche Bank's multi-country model for policy analysis in Europe', *Monetaire Monografieën*, 19, De Nederlandsche Bank, Amsterdam: NIBE-SVV.

Fair, Ray C. (1984), *Specification, Estimation and Analysis of Macroeconometric Models*, Cambridge MA/London: Harvard University Press.

6. The National Bank of Belgium's quarterly model

Philippe Jeanfils

This chapter briefly describes the main features of the current version[1] of the National Bank of Belgium's quarterly macroeconomic model. This version of the model still needs to be finalized, therefore some results presented here may be revised as new developments take place before the new model is finalized and published.

1 INTRODUCTION

The model we currently use for Belgium was developed in the late 1990s and has replaced a larger multisectoral model which was used previously. It is estimated on quarterly seasonally-adjusted data and has an explicit theoretical structure. Private agents are optimizing over time in the presence of adjustment costs, which leads to an explicit separation of expectations from response lags in many dynamic equations. These costs introduce nominal rigidities leading to Keynesian types of effects in the short run while the steady state growth rate is determined by the labour force and technological progress. The clear delineation of expectations allows the model to answer economic policy-related questions under different expectations formations, from limited information to model-consistent rationality.

The development of this new model of the Belgian economy provided the opportunity to incorporate certain characteristics reflecting recent theoretical and empirical features. One of the main motivations in building our model is our belief that a gap has emerged between traditional econometric macromodels and modern macroeconomic theory. Contrary to many traditional macroeconometric models, the Belgian model is based on formal theories of optimal planning over time and it emphasizes the essential role that market agents' expectations play in the analysis of economic policy; but it also presents equations with statistical properties close to those obtained in traditional econometric macromodels. Our model treats expectations explicitly in estimating dynamic equations and this permits the identification of frictions that impede dynamic adjustments and expectations separately, as is the case in the rational expectations literature. Therefore we believe it is more suitable for a coherent analysis of responses by rational agents reacting to news about future events than traditional econometric models which arbitrarily add *unrestricted* polynomials in the lag operator to deliver a good fit with the data. In order to rationalize the introduction of dynamics in macromodels, the intertemporal optimization problem of households and firms is subjected to costs related to the adjustment of decision variables.

This model, as FRB/US (see Brayton *et al.*, 1997), makes use of a richer dynamic specification than the quadratic cost function encountered in former testing of the rational expectations hypothesis. Such richer dynamics are introduced by means of polynomial adjustment costs (PAC). This generalization of quadratic adjustment costs is due to Tinsley (1993). This approach leads to a decision rule that expands the assumption that it is costly only to adjust the level of the decision variable to include variables in difference. Since the extent of these frictions is estimated rather than imposed by an a priori choice of a particular adjustment cost function, the empirical goodness of fit of the dynamic model equations is far better than those obtained from usual rational expectations models and is comparable to time-series models. In particular, high residual autocorrelation, which is generally present in empirical tests of decision rules based on level adjustment costs, is strongly reduced.

In addition to these frictions, the way in which private agents form their expectations also has important implications for dynamic adjustment. Simulation exercises can be performed under two different assumptions concerning expectation formation. First, the model may be solved under full model-consistent expectations. This option goes some way towards addressing the Lucas critique, but it does not make the model immune to it. However one would admit that the use of fully model-consistent expectations in policy simulations assumes too much knowledge by private agents. Alternatively expectations may be assumed to be based on the small VARs used in estimation, that is, according to some limited information auxiliary forecasting models. In VAR-based expectations simulations, a shock is recognized only when it actually occurs since, by definition, the information set is limited to the predetermined variables. Even in the case of a persistent shock, agents are surprised at each period since they fail to recognize that it will last for some periods. Under forward-looking expectations, when the shock takes place its pattern is known by all agents who can adjust their behaviour, taking into account the future path of the shock. Note that, whatever the option used, the model converges to the same long-run solution.

Since its publication, our model has been continuously re-estimated to account for major data changes such as the transition from ESA-79 to ESA-95. In addition, other important data changes have occurred. These new data, combined with the need to improve its theoretical structure, prompted us to revise the model more fundamentally. In that respect, the accounting framework has been redefined to avoid possible leakages on the income side. In our particular context the CES specification appeared to offer a better characterization of the data than the more traditional Cobb–Douglas form. We introduced flexible mark-up through a model of monopolistically competitive firms that produce internationally tradable and non-tradable goods. This approach has also been extended to exports and imports so that foreign trade is now fully consistent with the rest of demand and supply blocks.

2   USES OF THE MODEL

The model plays a central role in the NBB macroeconomic projections. Additional tools and judgment are also used to assess the recent past and the short-term path for the projections or to introduce policy variables in forecasts, such as wage developments in the private sector or fiscal measures. The Belgian model also contributes to the risk analysis accompanying the Broad Macroeconomic Projection Exercise (BMPE). The model is also regularly used for policy analysis for domestic purposes and for ESCB's sensitivity exercises. Finally it also serves as a supporting device for conducting very comprehensive studies. (See, for example, Burggraeve and Du Caju, 2003.)

3   AN OUTLINE OF THE THEORETICAL UNDERPINNINGS OF THE MODEL

3.1   Households

We use a discrete time version of an overlapping-generations model, which is also tractable with more than two generations (see Blanchard, 1985, for more details). In such a model, the introduction of a probability of death causes future income flows to be discounted at a rate above the market interest rate. As a consequence, Ricardian equivalence does not hold, since the present value of future tax changes does not completely match current adjustments in tax payments.

This life-cycle model determines the desired level of consumption. On the one hand, this depends on financial wealth, which is equal to the market value of financial assets. On the other hand, it also depends on human wealth which corresponds to the present value of expected future labour incomes (defined net of taxes and inclusive of transfer payments). Finally it is a negative function of a real interest rate reflecting intertemporal substitution in consumption, that is to say, the role the interest rate plays on the propensity to consume out of total wealth.

Because of habit formation, consumption does not immediately adjust to changes in the desired level. In addition to taking into account this delayed adjustment, the dynamic consumption equation also depends on unemployment to capture uncertainty in future income.

Households can also invest in housing. The equilibrium ratio of housing investment to consumption is a function of the relative price of consumption to the cost of new houses and on a mortgage interest rate. Stock-flow consistency is ensured through household net financing capacity which is obtained by subtracting consumption and housing investment from disposable income. In turn, this balance is added to previous financial wealth augmented by positive or negative returns to determine a new end-of-period value for financial wealth which subsequently will affect next period's consumption.

3.2 Supply Side

In the initial version of the model we opted, as many other modellers do, for a Cobb–Douglas technology even though the labour factor share did not look constant. This non-constancy was attributed, at that time, to the imperfectly competitive nature of the market for goods and services. Now, with an extended sample, the labour share does not tend to revert to some constant level and a CES technology would appear to offer a better characterization of the data. The estimated elasticity of substitution is below unity.

Monopolistically competitive suppliers produce private[2] value added: this is considered as domestic intermediate goods. The demand curve faced by these firms has an elasticity that depends on their price-setting decision. This feature generates pricing-to-market and hence flexible mark-ups. In a second stage, domestic intermediate goods are combined with imports to generate final consumption, investment and exported goods. In this context domestic suppliers set their price not only in response to changes in their own costs but also in response to the prices set by their competitors. The ratio of foreign prices to own costs, λ, depends on the share of non-traded goods (since a fraction of private value-added is not traded internationally) which determines the proportion of their output facing foreign competition and on the price elasticity of demand. Let us denote p_H the price of home goods sold in the home market, c_t the unit cost and p_F the price of foreign goods sold in the home market. Then the optimal (designated by a circumflex) price may be expressed as

$$\hat{p}_{Ht} = (1 - \lambda)c_t + \lambda p_{Ft}$$

and the dynamics of price evolve according to

$$\Delta p_{Ht} = -A(1)(p_{Ht-1} - \hat{p}_{Ht-1}) + \sum_{i=1}^{m-1} a_i^* \Delta p_{Ht-i}$$
$$+ \sum_{j=0}^{\infty} S_j(\beta, a, m) E_{t-1} \Delta \hat{p}_{Ht+j} + e_t$$

where S_j are the multiple-root discount factors, which are analogous to the inverse of the unstable root in the case of costs affecting only the level. They are non-linear functions of the discount rate β and of the m parameters of the lag polynomial $A(.)$, written compactly as 'a'. Expectations of changes in the target, $E_{t-1} \Delta \hat{p}_{Ht+j}$, are provided by an auxiliary VAR for estimation and for backward-looking simulations but one can also replace this VAR by model-consistent expectations for forward-looking simulations. Optimal adjustment today depends on three factors: (a) the deviation of last period's level from its equilibrium, (b) past changes in p_H,[3] (c) a weighted forecast of future changes in equilibrium levels for which the forecast weights S_i are declining in time since they are functions of the discount factor β (that is, forecasts far in the future are less important than the forecast for tomorrow).

Long-run factor demands depend on output with a unit elasticity, on real factor costs according to the elasticity of substitution, and on the mark-up. Labour productivity is also affected by the rate of technical progress. In the short run there is an additional effect of the rate of growth of output, this effect being more important for investment than for labour. However public investment is exogenous.

Average hours per worker are an increasing function of the extent of full-time working and of conventional working time and are cyclical around a trend.

3.3 Wages

The government regularly intervenes in the wage-bargaining process. In line with the law of July 1996 for the promotion of employment and the safeguarding of firms' competitiveness, the principle of automatic indexation of wages to a 'health' consumption price index is maintained but nominal wages should not grow faster than the weighted average wage growth in France, Germany and the Netherlands. Nevertheless, despite its discretionary nature, wage formation seems to be adequately characterized as the result of bargaining between unions and firms. Following a 'right to manage' model, unions and firms bargain over the wage level, taking the labour demand curve into account. Thereafter firms set prices and employment. Consequently equilibrium wage setting depends on the tax wedge, the relative price of output in terms of the consumption price level, the unemployment rate and trend labour productivity. Note that oil, tobacco and alcohol are excluded from the basket used to calculate the 'health' consumption price index. This feature may be important in understanding the transmission of oil price shocks. Labour supply is currently exogenous in the model.

3.4 Prices

Since final goods result from the combination of domestic products and imported goods, price indices for consumption, investment by companies and the cost of producing exported goods are weighted functions of the price set by domestic suppliers (value-added deflator) and the price of imported goods. Note that, in line with available input–output tables, housing investment is produced from domestic materials only.

Given that the value-added deflator is defined at factor costs, the consumption deflator is modelled by adding indirect tax rates to a weighted average of the value-added, import deflators and the energy price (to account for the direct effect of this latter price on fuel). It is possible to break down the consumption deflator into its three underlying components: unprocessed food, energy and core inflation.

Energy prices and competitors' prices excluding energy are, of course, exogenous factors herein. Static and dynamic homogeneity are imposed throughout.

3.5 Government Sector

Many variables in this sector are either exogenous in real terms or defined through identities. Current expenditure is divided into interest payments on government debt and different types of primary expenditure categories. The allocation of the outstanding debt over the long term in euros, the short term in euros and foreign currency debt is taken as given and representative interest rates are applied to each corresponding debt category. The weighted sum of these representative rates is in turn used to estimate the implicit rate on government debt. In modelling primary expenditure, the following main items are distinguished:

- government wages and pensions are indexed on the 'health' CPI;
- government purchases of goods and services and public investment are exogenous in real terms and their deflators are linked to the private consumption deflator and to the investment deflator;
- most transfers to households are exogenous in real terms but are indexed to the 'health' CPI. Unemployment benefits are the only business cycle sensitive component. In the long run, total transfer payments to households are sufficiently adjusted, according to a fiscal policy feedback rule, to ensure that the debt to GDP ratio settles down to its steady-state value.

General government receipts have been split into direct taxes on households' earned income, taking into account their progressiveness and the (possibly irregular) indexation of the tax brackets, direct taxes on companies, capital income tax, employers' and employees' social security contributions and indirect taxes. In most cases, implied tax rates are determined by official rates.

3.6 Foreign Trade

The specification of foreign trade is based on an imperfect substitution approach: neither real imports nor real exports are perfect substitutes for domestic and international goods, respectively. Here total goods and services are modelled together: there is no disaggregation by products or by destination.

Exporters combine traded domestic intermediate goods and imported brands to produce export goods. The minimum cost of producing such goods is thus a weighted function of domestic goods and imported goods prices. Exports are sold in monopolistically competitive markets. Profit maximization yields a static pricing rule relating the export deflator to a weighted average of the cost of producing exported goods and of competitors' prices on export markets. The weight depends on the price elasticity of demand. Then the share of home goods in the export market is related to the export deflator relative to competitors' export prices. These latter prices contain an energy and non-energy component.

To obtain aggregate import volume we add up the conditional import demands stemming from private consumption, investment by companies, government purchases of goods and services, and exports. Each conditional demand relates the price of the expenditure categories under consideration to the import deflator. Since there is also imperfect competition in the market for intermediate imported goods, the nominal price of imports responds, not only to the price of foreign competitors on import markets (which once again are decomposed into an energy and non-energy component), but also to the price of domestic producers. Both importers and exporters are then subject to polynomial adjustment costs in changing their prices.

3.7 Monetary and Financial Sector

Monetary policy is exogenous to the model so that, whatever the outcome of shocks in terms of inflation, the monetary policy stance will remain unchanged. There is no role for monetary aggregates in determining prices and output. Monetary policy affects model results through the interplay of interest rates. The model includes a three-month interest rate, a long-term bond rate, a mortgage rate and a rate for credit to companies.

3.8 Steady State

The focus on model-consistent expectations necessitates that more attention be given to equilibrium properties than is the case in traditional macromodels. Solving forward-looking models requires the imposition of terminal conditions that pin down agents' expectations beyond the simulation horizon. The natural way to determine such end points is to make use of the model's steady-state growth rates. The latter can be summarized as follows. Along a balanced growth path and given that technical progress is purely labour-augmenting, the real growth rate of the economy equals the growth rate of labour in efficiency unit, provided that the capital stock also grows at that rate. Exogenous variables and their growth factors are as follows:

- working age population and labour supply: $1+n$;
- technical progress increases with the labour efficiency index: $1+\xi$;
- all foreign prices inflate at the rate of steady-state inflation in the euro zone: $1+\pi^*$.

Corresponding details for endogenous variables are as follows:

- various ratios, rates of growth, and rates of return are constant: 1;
- all 'real' variables increase at the same rate as the working population measured in efficiency units: $(1+n)(1+\xi)$;
- domestic and foreign inflation rates converge: $(1+\pi^*)$.

In order to determine the rate of international growth and the adjustment of euro area inflation towards π^*, we use a stochastic dynamic general equilibrium model for the euro area (see Wouters and Dombrecht, 2000) and/or NiGEM.

4 HARMONIZED SIMULATION RESULTS

The purpose of these simulations is limited to illustrating model properties. For the sake of comparison and for simplicity, all the simulations have been run in backward-looking mode.[4] In order to reflect the functioning of the model as it is used most of the time, that is, for forecasting and the accompanying scenarios, the fiscal rule has been switched off and there is no bargaining over real consumption wages.

Simulation 1: a Rise in the Short-term Interest Rate for Two Years

For a small open economy member of a monetary union it is of crucial importance to know how foreign variables, including those inside the union, react to an interest rate change. In fact, if one ignores the effects on the exchange rate and on the euro-zone variables the monetary multiplier is rather limited, provided that there is no accompanying fiscal policy change. Therefore, in order to assess how inflation and output will behave if the short rate is 'exogenously' modified, exchange rate and spillover effects are taken into account. Broadly speaking, following these external effects, one observes first a deceleration in output and in inflation accompanied by the appreciation of the exchange rate. Then these price and volume effects are reinforced by movements in the same direction of our euro-area trading partners caused by the interest rate increase and exchange rate appreciation.

On the real side, in the first year, GDP falls by around 0.2 per cent relative to baseline. Thereafter the reduction of real GDP is around 0.5 per cent and 0.4 per cent in years 2 and 3, respectively. Purely domestic factors, that is, abstracting from exchange rate and spillover effects, account for around one-third of these results. As is clear from Figure 6.1a, the drop in real exports is the major driving force in years 1 and 2. Our export markets inside the euro zone reflect the impact of monetary policy tightening on economic activity in the monetary union and, in addition, Belgium experiences a loss of market share outside the euro-area accompanying the deterioration of euro-area competitiveness following the appreciation. When nominal interest and exchange rates return to baseline, real GDP also begins to revert to baseline and this reversion is achieved in year 5. The simulation has been run without a fiscal policy rule

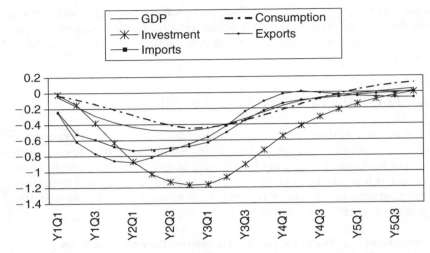

Figure 6.1a   *Simulation of a two-year shock to short-term interest rates by 100 bp*

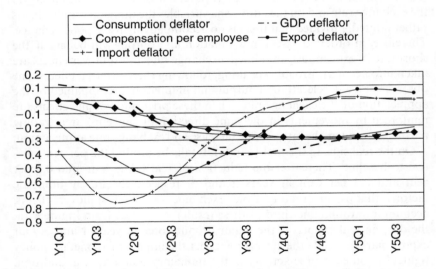

Figure 6.1b   *Simulation of a two-year shock to short-term interest rates by 100 bp*

so that no measures are taken when the budget balance deteriorates. It is worth noting that, in the past, this mechanism has appeared to be an important transmission channel of interest rate changes.

Deflators are mainly affected by changes in foreign prices. These enter the model through two main channels. First, prices of competitors both inside and outside the euro area directly influence the mark-up of Belgian producers. The second channel reflects the effects on import and export competitors' prices as well as the price of imported energy components of an appreciation of the domestic currency. The impact on the consumption deflator is about 0.1 per cent in the first year. The effect is at a maximum, at 0.3 per cent, after three years and subsequently there is a slow tendency to return to base.

Simulation 2: Fiscal Policy Shock

This fiscal policy shock is a temporary increase in government spending by 1 per cent of GDP in real terms, for a period of five years. The adjustment is spread proportionally across all elements of government consumption (that is to say, purchases of goods and services, civil servants' wages and pensions and health care).

On impact there is a positive accelerator effect on investment, but GDP initially increases by only a little more than 1 per cent owing to the deterioration in the net exports caused by a decline in Belgian price competitiveness which compensates for the increase in domestic demand. Since foreign prices, including those of our trade partners inside the euro area, are exogenous and assumed to be unchanged, the modification in export and import deflators only reflects the change in domestic prices. For the duration of the shock the fiscal rule has been 'switched off' so that households get more disposable income and increase their consumption. However human wealth only increases gradually as households observe the increase in their current income (they fail to recognize immediately the size and the persistence of the easing in fiscal policy) so consumption follows the same path and we observe an increase in the savings ratio. The bell-shape impulse response of consumption stems from the additional effect that changes in employment exert on consumption in the short term. Once additional job creation stops, there is no extra boost to consumption expenditures.

The increase in production combined with some labour hoarding[5] raises apparent labour productivity in the first year. Productivity gains do not compensate for the pressure on capacity utilization so that a slight increase in inflation is observed.

After five years this temporary fiscal expansion leads to an increase in the level of real GDP by 1.05 per cent, but at the cost of an increase in the public debt-to-GDP ratio. Note that the risk premium on long-term interest rates is assumed to be unchanged despite the steady increase in the ratio of public debt to GDP.

It is worth mentioning at this stage some monetary arithmetic for keeping interest rates fixed at base level. The increase in the budget deficit,

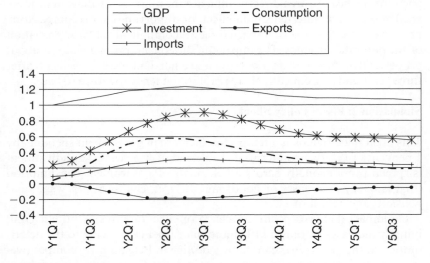

Figure 6.2a   Simulation of a rise over five years in real government consumption by 1% of GDP

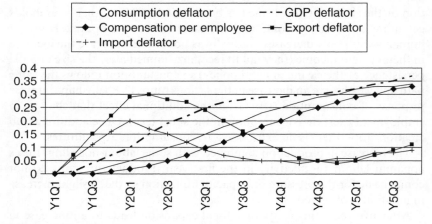

Figure 6.2b   Simulation of a rise over five years in real government consumption by 1% of GDP

by diminishing the open economy's aggregate rate of saving, creates a current account deficit. However if, at the same time, this expansionary policy is pursued in all euro-area countries, the decrease in aggregate saving will raise the equilibrium interest rate, as in a largely closed economy. On the contrary, in this simulation, by keeping nominal interest rates constant, we observe a reduction in real rates at all maturities in the first two or three years following the increase in inflation. In our model, as inflation accelerates without the reaction of interest rates, there is a positive impact on both residential and business investment. This initial impact is magnified as demand faced by firms increases, meaning they also increase their demand for labour and capital.

Simulation 3: Foreign Demand Shock

The 1 per cent increase in real export markets has been simulated by increasing both extra- and intra-euro area markets. This increase in foreign demand is assumed to leave prices inside and outside the euro zone unaffected.

In response, Belgian exports increase by almost 1 per cent, which raises GDP by a quarter of a per cent on impact and by around 0.15 per cent in the medium run. The improvement in the trade balance is limited through the large import content of exported goods. The major domestic change concerns investment while, owing to the sluggish response of employment and hence of disposable income, the effects on private consumption are

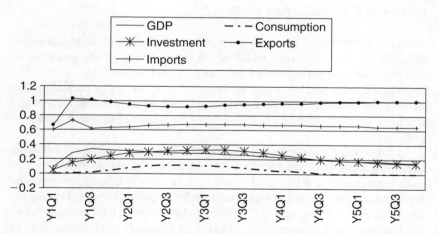

Figure 6.3a   Simulation of an increase in export market volumes by 1% for 5 years

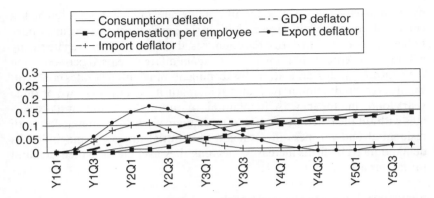

*Figure 6.3b   Simulation of an increase in export market volumes by 1%
                for five years*

rather weak. The magnitude of the impact on GDP is at its maximum in
the second and third years. Finally there is a small increase in prices due to
increased demand. This rate of increase decelerates at the end of the simulation so that ex post real interest rates increase after an initial decline. This,
in addition to the simulation impact on *real* disposable income, explains the
response of consumption and investment. Note that this increase in prices
and the associated deterioration in competitiveness are responsible for the
fact that, on impact, exports grow more slowly than export markets.

Simulation 4: Exchange Rate Shock

We have implemented the analysis as a 1 percentage point appreciation in
the effective exchange rate, which alters competitors' prices (taking into
consideration the percentage of intra as opposed to extra-euro area trade)
and the oil price. Such a scenario, however, gives us a very partial picture
of what happens (actually only first-round price effects are considered) and
does not take account of possible effects on trade volume and monetary
policy reactions.

   As expected, real exports fall by around 0.1 per cent on impact following
the loss of competitiveness. Real imports also slightly decrease because
they react more quickly to the contraction of absorption (export and
investment in the present case) than to relative price changes. During the
five years of the shock, real GDP is somewhat less than 0.05 per cent below
the baseline, but it recovers afterwards. This relatively mild impact may be
explained by the large proportion of intra-euro area trade in Belgian
foreign trade.

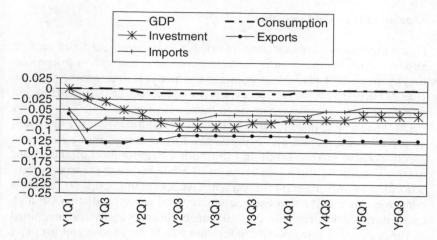

Figure 6.4a Simulation of a rise by 1% for five years of the euro effective exhange rate

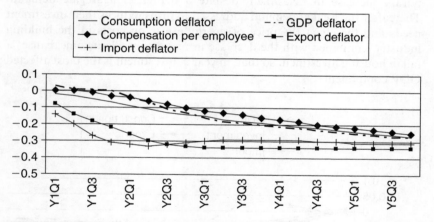

Figure 6.4b Simulation of a rise by 1% for five years of the euro effective exhange rate

Once marginal costs are also reduced through wage indexation, export and import deflators tend to move almost in line with foreign competitors' prices. Reduced imported inflation allows a 0.5 percentage point improvement in consumption price inflation which decelerates slightly after three years.

Simulation 5: an Oil Price Shock

Following this price shock, import prices rise by almost 0.5 per cent on impact, which results in an increase in domestic consumption price inflation by around 0.1 percentage points in the first year and somewhat less in year 2. Thereafter it also affects export prices but to a lesser extent, so that one observes a slight deterioration in the terms of trade.

On the real side, there is some loss of GDP resulting from the reduction of private consumption and exports. The former stems from a decline in real disposable income resulting from both a deterioration of the labour market conditions and a loss of terms of trade for wage earners. Indeed, according to institutional arrangements, wages are indexed according to a consumer price index that excludes energy and other products with high excise duties. This decline in the real 'consumption' wage is also magnified by the presence of retrospective indexation which makes wages adjust more slowly than prices.

In the absence of changes in the nominal interest rate in the light of accelerating inflation, the reduction in real rates leads to a small and temporary increase in investment despite a depressed aggregate demand. Thereafter the weaker demand addressed to firms reduces their investment needs and the effect the price of energy exerts on costs in the building industry, combined with the decrease in real disposable income, causes a fall in housing investment so that, in year 3, investment is the most affected GDP component.

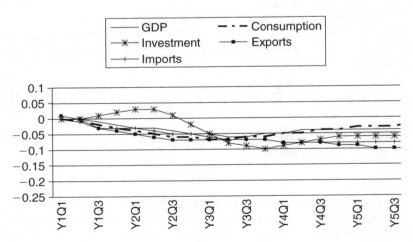

Figure 6.5a   Simulation of a rise by 10% for five years in the price of oil

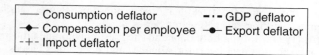

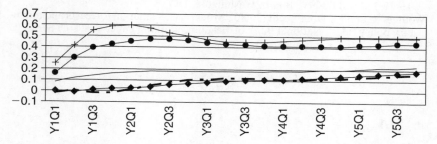

Figure 6.5b   Simulation of a rise by 10% for five years in the price of oil

NOTES

1. The first version was published in March 2000: Ph. Jeanfils, 'A model with explicit expectations for Belgium', National Bank of Belgium, Working Paper Research Series, 4.
2. The reason for using private sector value added rather than GDP lies in the importance of identifying as accurately as possible the rate of technical progress and the elasticity of substitution, which are essential parameters determining the steady-state properties of the model. Since GDP contains public wages and pensions, working with GDP may bias these parameters.
3. These lagged terms are not present if agents minimize only the costs associated with changing the level of y, which was the assumption made in earlier applications of rational expectations models.
4. Forward-looking simulation would have required a complete specification of the shocks after year 5 and also an assessment of their (un)anticipated nature.
5. As labour is not a totally flexible factor, it exhibits some sluggishness so that when output changes, labour demand does not change in the same proportion due to adjustment costs, such as hiring, firing and training.

REFERENCES

Blanchard O.J. (1985), 'Debt, deficit, and finite horizons', *Journal of Political Economy*, **93**, 223–47.

Brayton F., A. Levin, R. Tyron and J.C. Williams (1997), 'The evolution of macro models at the Federal Reserve Board', Federal Reserve Board FEDS working paper 1997–29.

Burggraeve K. and Ph. Du Caju (2003), 'The labour market and fiscal impact of labour tax reductions: the case of reduction of employers' social security contributions under a wage norm regime with automatic price indexing of wages', National Bank of Belgium, Working Paper Research Series, 36.

Jeanfils P. (2000), 'A model with explicit expectations for Belgium', National Bank of Belgium, Working Paper Research Series, 4.

Tinsley P.A. (1993), 'Fitting both data and theories: polynomial adjustment costs and error correction decision rules', Finance and Economics Discussions Series 93–21, Federal Reserve Board, Washington, DC.

Wouters R. and M. Dombrecht (2000), 'Model-based inflation forecasts and monetary policy rules', National Bank of Belgium, Working Paper Research Series, 1.

7. The macroeconometric multi-country model of the Deutsche Bundesbank

Britta Hamburg and Karl-Heinz Tödter

1 INTRODUCTION

The macroeconometric model of the Deutsche Bundesbank has been used continuously for policy analysis and forecasting since about 1970.[1] It was one of the first macroeconometric models for the German economy. Since its initial setting up, the model of the Bundesbank has undergone several stages of development which have led to considerable changes in the model's structure over time.

In line with macroeconomic theory of the 1970s, the Bundesbank's model started as a Keynesian system in which output was driven by demand and relative prices played a small role in the goods and labour market, even in the long run. However a strong emphasis was placed on the financial sector of the economy, albeit with exogenous instruments of monetary policy.

In the 1980s the model was respecified along neoclassical lines. Behavioural equations were derived from assuming optimizing firms and households. A supply side based on a production function was introduced and the labour market was modelled in more detail. Moreover a portfolio demand system for the financial assets and liabilities of the private sector was added. The estimated equations were increasingly formulated in terms of error corrections mechanisms, allowing the long run to be separated from the dynamics of the adjustment process.

The need to respecify the model arose after German reunification and the introduction of the D-Mark in eastern Germany in 1990. For a short time, two separate western and eastern German blocks were modelled. However, owing to data limitations, the model now covers unified Germany as a whole since 1990, and the West German economy before. The resulting statistical jumps in the data are accounted for by dummy variables.

Up to the mid-1990s, the Bundesbank model was a single-country model for the German economy. However the increasing international economic integration of Germany following the removal of foreign trade barriers and the liberalization of capital transactions made it necessary to attach more importance to international economic interdependencies in the model. Therefore the Bundesbank macroeconometric model became a multi-country system which now includes blocks for the eight most important trading partners of Germany, especially the G-7 member countries. The trade linkages are modelled in a separate block.

Another extension of the model was motivated by European monetary union and the introduction of the euro. In order to consider the consequences of the single monetary policy, a separate monetary and financial block at the aggregate euro-area level was added. This block especially determines short- and long-term interest rates, the aggregate money stock and the euro exchange rate.

The model is constantly updated to account for developments in economic theory, empirical data and institutional changes.

2   THE USES OF THE MODEL

At present the Bundesbank model is used both for policy analysis and in the forecasting process. Policy analysis is carried out through shock simulations of various types and under different sets of restrictions, depending on the requests received. These mostly come from the economics department of the Bundesbank, but also from the ECB or other national and international economic institutions. Similarly the model is applied in the forecasting process for scenario analysis as well as for the generation of projection update elasticities.

It is important to note that, depending on the task, changes to the model's structure are required, which basically imply generating different versions of the model: for example, the isolation of the German block of the model by exogenizing foreign trade and price variables that are responsible for the spillover effects from the rest of the world. Other simulations may need to be carried out under the restriction of constant interest rates, meaning that the monetary policy rules are not activated.

3 AN OUTLINE OF THE THEORETICAL UNDERPINNINGS FOR THE MODEL AND ITS PURPOSE

3.1 General Characteristics

The long-run properties of the country models can be described as neoclassical. Potential GDP has been estimated on the basis of a Cobb–Douglas production function with constant returns to scale. In the long run, actual production approaches potential GDP, which implies full capacity utilization. This is achieved by optimizing the behaviour of economic agents in the central behavioural equations of the model. The expectation formation process of economic agents when modelling financial variables is partly assumed to be backward-looking, that is, adaptive, and partly forward-looking, that is, model-consistent. Economic growth in the long run is determined by population growth and productivity progress. Price and wage rigidities affect the short-run properties of the model. The rather slow adjustment of prices and wages to their equilibrium levels leads to persistent market disequilibria and cyclical fluctuations around the path of potential gross domestic product.

The model covers the European Union member states of Belgium, France, Germany, Italy, the Netherlands and the United Kingdom. Each of the country models has a similar structure, except for Germany which is specified with more detail. The German block contains approximately twice as many equations as those for the other countries. In addition, country models for the USA, Canada and Japan have been included, which means that the model contains all G-7 countries, Germany's most important trading partners. The remaining countries have been aggregated into four regions which contain other EU countries, other OECD countries, OPEC countries and the rest of the world. The linkages between countries via international trade flows and prices are modelled in a separate trade block. The common monetary policy in the euro area is incorporated through the specification of a euro-area financial sector.

The Bundesbank model is a quarterly model and currently consists of 691 equations, approximately 290 of which are estimated behavioural equations. The data are taken from different OECD sources, such as the main economic indicators, quarterly national accounts and the economic outlook as well as from the Bank for International Settlements (BIS). For Germany, national data sources are used. Some data series go back to 1970, while the introduction of the new system of national accounts (ESA-95) required a considerably shorter estimation period for the European economies. In many behavioural equations, the dynamic adjustment process has been specified to follow an error-correction mechanism in order to ensure that both short-run dynamics and long-run equilibrium aspects of the behaviour of economic agents are taken into account. The model is coded and simulations are performed in the Windows version of TROLL.

3.2   A Description of the Structure of a Country Submodel and its Key Features

3.2.1   The production function and factor demand

Technology is modelled through a specification of potential gross domestic product in the form of a Cobb–Douglas production function, containing labour and capital as well as an autonomous rate of technical growth. Factor share parameters are calibrated on the basis of labour income shares, while the rate of technical progress is estimated. The discrepancy between actual and potential gross domestic product, that is, aggregate demand and aggregate supply, is expressed through the rate of capacity utilization.

With a Cobb–Douglas production technology investment expenditure is assumed to adjust the real capital stock to its optimal long-run level. Given existing technologies and endowments and a constant real capital stock in the short run, firms determine the profit-maximizing allocation of their factors of production, such that the optimal stock of capital increases with higher production or sales and decreases with higher user cost of capital. The real long-term interest rate, which is used as a proxy for the user costs of capital in the investment equation, enter the short-run adjustment process of real investment expenditure. Real inventory investments are modelled to depend dynamically on the quarter-by-quarter changes in real final demand.

In accordance with the profit-maximizing behaviour of firms, the optimal demand for labour results from the marginal productivity condition. In the long run, labour demand is determined by real final demand as well as the ratio of sales prices, corrected by the indirect tax rate, to the wage rate.

3.2.2   Components of aggregate demand

Real private consumption is modelled by an error-correction mechanism, which ensures that it is proportional to the real gross domestic product in the long run. Long-run real per capita consumption is determined by the real gross domestic product as well as the real expected long-term interest rate, which implies a constant consumption ratio in the steady state. The consumption equation for Germany follows a two-step error-correction specification. It takes into account two components of disposable income: (a) the sum of net wage income and government transfers to households, and (b) income from withdrawn profits and property of households and the adjustment for the change in net equity of households in pension funds reserves, which are reduced by transfers to foreign countries. Furthermore real private consumption is affected by the level of real net financial wealth of households. In the short run it is also influenced by the real long-term interest rate.

The modelling of imports for each country results from the assumed production technology and the optimizing behaviour of firms. This implies that the marginal product of imported inputs has to be equal to its marginal costs. The restriction of a unit long-run elasticity of imports with respect to final demand had to be imposed for many countries in order to ensure feasible long-run solutions.

3.2.3 Prices and costs

The central price index used in the Bundesbank model for each country is the price deflator of domestic demand. In the short run, changes in production costs and the level of capacity utilization have an effect on prices. The rate of inflation is anchored to an explicit target rate of inflation. The effect of the target rate on current inflation is realized through an expectation formation process, which incorporates both backward-looking and forward-looking expectations, where the forward-looking part is formed through a weighted average of expected actual inflation rates and the inflation target. The inflation determination process is modelled differently between non-euro area countries and the euro-area countries, where the P-Star approach is implemented. The area-wide equilibrium price level P-Star is derived from European money demand.[2] Therefore inflation rates in the participating countries are influenced in the short run by national cost and demand factors. In the long run, however, inflation rates are determined by the common monetary policy, with the steady-state inflation rate being the same for all participating countries.

Changes in the price deflators for other GDP components are modelled to be determined by the price deflator of domestic demand, such that there will be no changes in the relative domestic price deflators in the long run. Export prices are influenced additionally by the price deflator of foreign competitors, which is determined in the foreign trade block. Furthermore, in the German block, capital costs and production costs are additional determinants of various investment deflators.

The index of production costs is defined as a weighted average of labour and import costs, which are represented by wages and import prices, respectively. In the German block capital costs are specified as a separate component. Wages are modelled to take into account the adaptive expectation on consumer price inflation and the gap between the actual unemployment rate and the trend rate of unemployment.

3.2.4   The government sector

The activities of the government in the country blocks of the model include direct and indirect taxes, expenditures for consumer goods, investment goods and services and transfer payments to private households. In the long run, the ratio of real government demand to real GDP is assumed to be constant. In the short run, however, anticyclical reactions to the output gap are accounted for, functioning as built-in stabilizers within the model. The ratio of transfer payments to private households and GDP is assumed to be constant in the long run. The deviation of the unemployment rate from its long-run trend is a further determinant of the ratio of transfer payments to GDP and acts as a built-in stabilizer. The adjustment processes of transfer payments to households as well as government consumption to their long-run ratios are found to be very slow.

The fiscal block in the country submodel for Germany is more detailed, disaggregating the categories of direct and indirect taxes into wage taxes and others and into value-added taxes and others. The specification of the German government consumption expenditure incorporates a fiscal policy reaction function such that a higher deficit to GNP ratio leads to lower nominal government consumption expenditure. Social security contributions are divided into those provided by employees and those provided by employers. Government debt and interest payments as well as government subsidies to private firms are additionally included in the German submodel.

3.2.5   The monetary sector

For the common monetary sector of the euro-area countries, measures of area-wide domestic demand, real GDP and potential output are generated. Behavioural equations determine the money stock, based on the theory of money demand. Represented by a two-stage error-correction model, long-term real money demand depends on the real gross domestic product and on the long-term interest rate as a measure of the opportunity cost of holding money. In order to obtain an area-wide indicator for inflationary pressures, the P-Star approach is applied. The euro-area equilibrium price level (P-Star) is derived from the long-term money demand function. The resulting price gap, that is, the deviation of the actual price level from P-Star, combines inflationary pressure from the goods market (output gap) and the money market (liquidity gap) and helps to explain inflation dynamics (Tödter, 2002).

A reaction function of the European central bank determines the short-term interest rate, which is the monetary policy instrument. The short-term interest rate responds to the gap between expected money growth and the money growth target, thereby implicitly aiming at reaching the inflation target. In addition the policy rule contains a strong smoothing component. Parameter values of the policy reaction functions are calibrated.

The government bond yield is established by an expectation formation process, incorporating a combination of forward-looking and backward-looking expectations, on short-term rates over a time horizon of ten years and a term premium. The exchange rate of the euro against the dollar is determined through a combination of uncovered interest rate parity and purchasing power parity. Purchasing power differences affect the exchange rate only slowly, whereas interest rate differentials have an immediate impact on the exchange rate.

3.3 The Foreign Trade Block

In conjunction with the EMU block and the exchange rate equations, the foreign trade block constitutes the main link between individual country submodels. Within the trade block nominal export volumes of individual countries are determined in a manner that guarantees a consistent relationship between imports and exports between individual countries, as import volumes are determined domestically. Furthermore the relationships between import prices and the domestically determined export prices as well as between the price index of foreign competitors and domestic price indices are determined. In addition to the countries described in the model, the foreign trade block contains nominal import volumes and export prices for the rest of the EU countries and the rest of the OECD, as well as export prices for the OPEC countries and for the rest of the world in line with the categorizations in the OECD's 'Monthly Statistics of Foreign Trade'. The trade relationships are modelled on the basis of a static trade matrix. The oil price as well as non-energy commodity prices are exogenous. Future values of both indices are determined through autoregressive processes.

In order to determine each country's nominal exports an auxiliary variable is calculated, specifying the weighted average of all other countries' nominal import volumes in the exporting country's domestic currency, with the weights being equivalent to the respective country's export shares. As export volumes for the rest of the world are unknown, the auxiliary variable needs to be normalized. Each country's nominal exports are then determined through a dynamic adjustment process. The import price deflator of every country is determined in a similar way. First, a weighted average of the country's trading partners' export prices are calculated, denominated in the importing country's domestic currency, with the weights being equivalent to the respective import shares. The export price index of the group of OPEC countries is represented by the oil price, while the export price index of the rest of the world is represented by the non-energy commodity price index. The German import price equation includes, not only the auxiliary variable of weighted export prices, but also the index of oil prices and the importing country's GDP deflator in order to take into account pricing-to-market effects. In order to incorporate competition effects into the determination of each country's export price index, a competitors' price deflator is calculated in the foreign trade block as a weighted average of the trading partners' domestic prices, converted into the local currency, where the weights correspond to the export shares. Domestic prices for OPEC countries and for the rest of the world do not enter the equation, so that a normalization of the competitors' price index is carried out as it is for the export volumes.

4   AN OUTLINE OF THE KEY CHARACTERISTICS

A set of five simulations is used to illustrate the key characteristics and the functioning of the model.

4.1   Monetary Policy Shock

Simulation results here are taken from the WGEM monetary policy transmission exercise. The short-term interest rate increases over a period of two years by 100 basis points. Afterwards it returns to its baseline value. The monetary policy variable is, therefore, exogenously set and the policy rule is not in operation. Furthermore the experiment required predetermined reactions of the long-term interest rate in line with a simple interest parity condition and an appreciation of the euro exchange rate against all non-euro area currencies in line with a simple uncovered interest rate parity condition. Both reactions were also exogenously imposed. Furthermore fiscal policy reaction rules were required to be switched off, so that real government consumption was kept at baseline levels. The results include spillover effects from other euro-area economies. The reaction of world demand and the foreign competitors' export and import prices were exogenously imposed according to calculations undertaken by the ECB that ensure trade consistency.

Figure 7.1a illustrates in a stylized way the monetary transmission process in the Bundesbank's model. The policy shock to be simulated for this experiment implied an exogenously given development of the short-term interest rate, therefore the monetary policy reaction function is not illustrated in the figure. Reactions of the long-term interest rate and the exchange rate were also exogenous in the experiment. These variables trigger adjustments of the real demand components and lead to changes of potential output via labour market and capital stock adjustments.

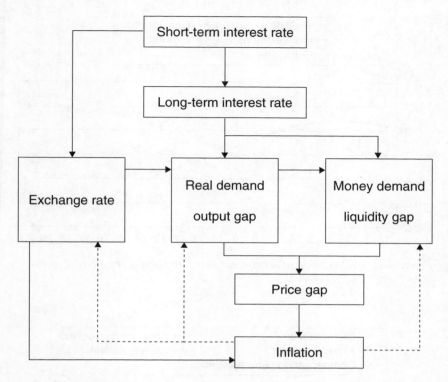

Figure 7.1a   Monetary transmission in the Bundesbank model

The long-term interest rate, as well as real GDP, influences money demand and results in changes of the liquidity gap. The output gap and the liquidity gap determine the size of the price gap, which leads to the adjustment of inflation and thus various price deflators. Through its impact on import prices the exchange rate has an additional direct effect on inflation. There are feedback effects from inflation to money demand and via changes in relative prices to real demand components. In simulations with endogenous exchange rates, changes in the inflation rate would also lead to adjustments of the exchange rate as purchasing power parity is the long-run determinant of the exchange rate.

The results of the WGEM monetary policy transmission exercise illustrate the reduction in prices as a result of the temporary monetary tightening (Figures 7.1b and 7.1c). Consumer prices lie 0.56 per cent below baseline in the second and third years after the end of the shock. We observe a fast transmission of price effects in import prices due to the euro appreciation.

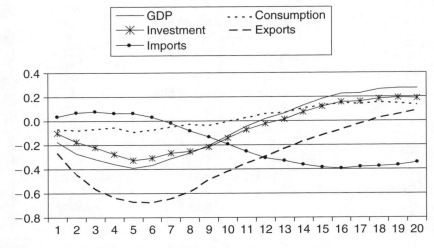

Figure 7.1b   Simulation of a two-year shock to short-term interest rates by 100 bp

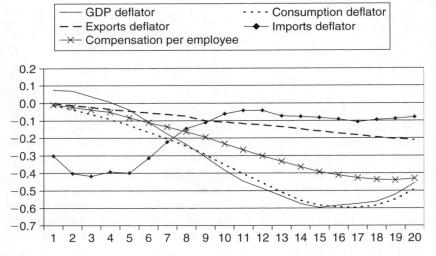

Figure 7.1c   Simulation of a two-year shock to short-term interest rates by 100 bp

German export prices react more sluggishly and only dominate the import price effects in the medium term.

The short-run effects of the interest rate rise on real GDP are -0.28 per cent in the first year and -0.33 per cent in the second year, driven by the reduction in investments, exports and, to a smaller extent, private consumption. In the medium run, owing to the strong fall in prices, real disposable income rises, which results in a positive deviation of real private consumption from its baseline values. The subsequent increase in final demand in turn leads to a rise in real investment. Overall this results in a positive real GDP effect from the second year after the end of the shock. If a longer horizon of ten years were considered, however, the effects of the temporary interest rate rise on real GDP would vanish in the long run. Real imports increase in the first year because of the reduction in import prices. In the subsequent two years, the decrease of the deflator of final demand dominates the behaviour of real imports. Because of the sluggishness of real imports, their decline continues until the end of the fourth year.

The initial reduction in output has a negative effect on the labour market with a fall in employment and a rise in the unemployment rate. In the longer run both return to their baseline values. On the fiscal side, government expenditure as a percentage of GDP temporarily rises by more than the receipts do, so that the government debt increases.

The following four simulation experiments were carried out according to a harmonized design described in 'Details of the design of harmonised simulation experiments to be included in the technical annexes' (ECB, 19 March 2002). Each shock was set over a period of five years. Short-term interest rates, long-term interest rates and the exchange rate were kept at baseline levels over this five-year period. No fiscal rule was in operation during the shock period; with the exception of the simulation of the fiscal policy shock, real government consumption expenditure was set to baseline levels. The Bundesbank model was operated in an isolated mode, that is to say, any effects spilling over from abroad via the foreign trade block or the common monetary policy block owing to changes in foreign demand or price variables were eliminated.

4.2   Fiscal Policy Shock

Real government consumption expenditure was increased by 1 per cent of initial real GDP over a period of five years. Real government consumption therefore rises by more than 5 per cent above baseline levels over the first three years. Real GDP lies 1.20 per cent above baseline in year 1, with the positive effect gradually decreasing to 0.68 per cent in year 5 (Figures 7.2a and 7.2b). Real investments react to the strong rise of real final demand

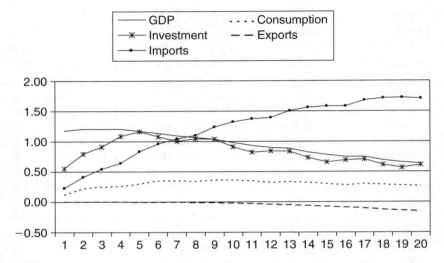

*Figure 7.2a   Simulation of a five-year increase of real government
consumption by 1% of initial real GDP*

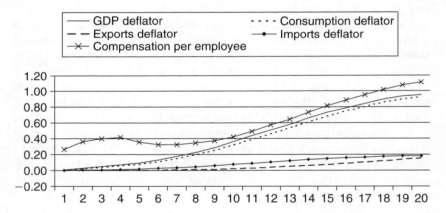

*Figure 7.2b   Simulation of a five-year increase of real government
consumption by 1% of initial real GDP*

and move up by a maximum of 1.07 per cent in year 2. Real private consumption expenditure reacts positively to higher real disposable income. Part of the higher final demand is served from abroad with real imports lying 1.71 per cent above baseline in the long run.

Labour demand increases thanks to higher real final demand.

Employment rises to 0.40 per cent above baseline levels. The fall in the unemployment rate results in an increase in the wage rate, which exerts an upward pressure on domestic prices. The effects on the private consumption deflator amount to 0.87 per cent in year 5. With the strong increase in productivity levels over the first three years of the shock, unit labour costs fall before rising above baseline levels in years 4 and 5 as wages keep on increasing. Higher direct and indirect tax income counterbalances the higher government expenditure to a certain extent, nevertheless the fiscal budget deficit in relation to GDP is around 0.7 percentage points higher compared to baseline throughout the simulation.

4.3 Foreign Demand Shock

Real import demand of the trading partners outside the euro area increases by 1 per cent over a period of five years. This means that the world import demand for German exports rises by 0.56 per cent, in accordance with the share of German extra-euro area exports. The adjustment of German exports takes place gradually, with a rise of 0.23 per cent in the first year, increasing to 0.54 per cent in year 5 (Figures 7.3a and 7.3b). Real investments grow by up to 0.17 per cent thanks to the higher real final demand, which also has a positive effect on real imports. The rise in real disposable income leads to an increase in real private consumption expenditure.

The higher real final demand is also the reason for the slight rise in labour demand. Employment lies at 0.06 per cent above its baseline levels towards the end of the reporting period. The slight fall in the unemployment rate

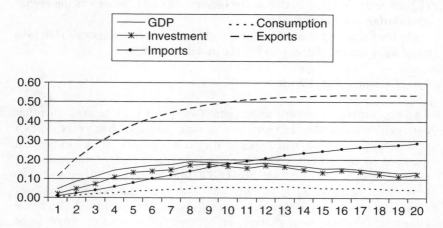

Figure 7.3a   Simulation of a five-year increase of non-euro area 'trading partners' real imports by 1%

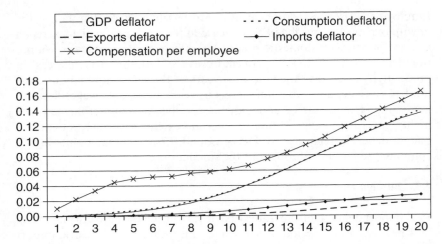

Figure 7.3b   Simulation of a five-year increase of non-euro area 'trading partners' real imports by 1%

results in a slightly higher negotiated wage rate. As the rise in the compensation per employee is initially below the increase in productivity, due to higher output, unit labour costs fall before showing a slight rise towards the end of the reporting period. The upward movement of the domestic price level compared to baseline is very slow and moderate, with the consumer price index lying 0.12 per cent above baseline level only in year 5. Higher prices are mainly due to the increase in wages as well as the higher equilibrium price level P-Star.

On the fiscal side, government expenditure as a percentage of GDP falls more than receipts do, improving the budget deficit.

4.4   Exchange Rate Shock

The experiment of a euro appreciation of 1 per cent against all other currencies outside the euro area over a time period of five years yields a very strong effect on real exports, for which model results indicate a decrease by more than 0.5 per cent in the second half of the reporting period (Figures 7.4a and 7.4b). Real GDP falls by up to 0.25 per cent. The lower final demand leads to reduced investment expenditure and consumption reacts to the decrease in real disposable income. A moderate adjustment on the labour market can be observed with an unemployment rate 0.07 percentage points above baseline. Although the compensation per employee falls, the productivity decrease is more pronounced over the first

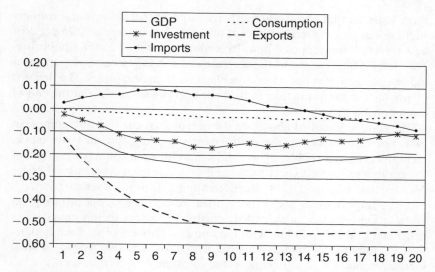

Figure 7.4a   Simulation of a five-year appreciation of the euro against all third currencies by 1%

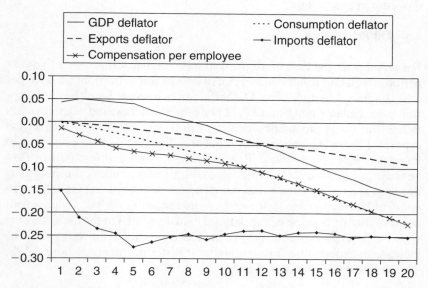

Figure 7.4b   Simulation of a five-year appreciation of the euro against all third currencies by 1%

three years, so that unit labour costs rise over this period before showing a slight fall in year 5. German import prices decline by around 0.25 per cent as a result of euro appreciation. In conjunction with a lower equilibrium price level P-Star, caused by the decrease in the money stock owing to lower money demand, this has a negative effect on domestic prices. The deflator of private consumption falls to 0.20 per cent below baseline at the end of the reporting period.

The results described above are the outcome of the transmission of an exchange rate shock via the multi-country model's foreign trade block. Here the activity variables of world demand for each country's exports, of the trading partners' export prices and of the foreign competitors' prices are defined, which in turn are determining factors of each country's exports, import price and export price, respectively. Concentrating on German exports after an estimated adjustment process, their nominal value is defined to develop in line with the nominal imports of its trading partners in domestic currency, weighted with the respective weight in total German exports. If foreign imports are constant, exports adjust fully in the long run to the euro appreciation in line with the weight of non-monetary union members among its exports. In a forecasting context, residual adjustment (add factoring) would be applied in order to dampen the real effects of a euro appreciation.

4.5   Oil Price Shock

For an oil price increase of 10 per cent in US dollar terms over a five-year period simulation results show a rise in import prices by more than 0.6 per cent (Figures 7.5a and 7.5b). Domestic prices increase with the consumption price deflator lying up to 0.22 per cent above baseline. Export prices follow the development of domestic prices and result in a fall in real exports. The trade balance effect is positive, however, as the decline in real imports is more pronounced. Real consumption expenditure falls by 0.14 per cent owing to the lower real disposable income, while real investments decrease as a result of the reduced final demand. Overall real GDP lies 0.10 per cent below baseline at the end of the reporting period. Employment declines slightly because of the reduced final demand. On the fiscal side, the higher government income from value-added taxation is outweighed by the increase in expenditure through higher transfer payments to households. The budget deficit declines slightly.

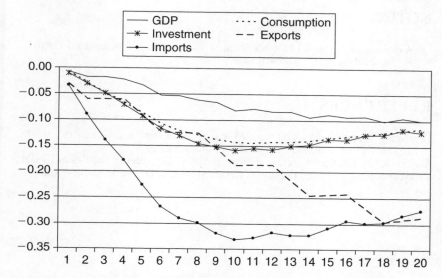

Figure 7.5a   Simulation of a five-year rise of oil prices in US$ terms by 10%

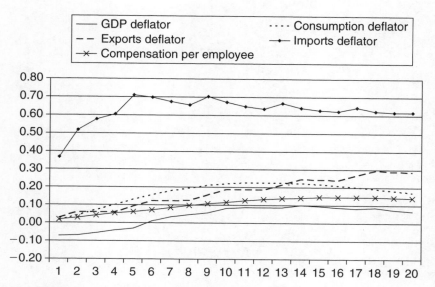

Figure 7.5b   Simulation of a five-year rise of oil prices in US$ terms by 10%

NOTES

1. A more detailed analysis of the model can be found in Deutsche Bundesbank (2000).
2. For more details please see section 3.2.5.

REFERENCES

Deutsche Bundesbank (2000), 'Macro-econometric multi-country model: MEMMOD' (available at http://www.bundesbank.de).
Tödter, K.-H. (2002) 'Monetary indicators and policy rules in the P-Star model', discussion paper 18/02, Economic Research Centre, Deutsche Bundesbank.

8. Model of the Banco de España

Pablo Burriel, Ángel Estrada and Javier Vallés

1 INTRODUCTION

This chapter describes the main characteristics of the Spanish macro-econometric model of the Banco de España. The structure of this model is similar to the ones developed for other countries with the objective of constructing a multi-country model (MCM) for the euro area, although it has some specificities that are linked to the properties of the Spanish economy. The first version was jointly developed by the staff of the European Central Bank and the Banco de España (see Willman and Estrada, 2002). The latest version was fully developed by the Banco itself (see Estrada *et al.*, 2004) and was estimated under the new ESA-95 data set.

2 USES OF THE MODEL

The model is used at the Banco de España with two main goals: to obtain medium-term forecasts of the Spanish economy (two to three years) and to integrate the results provided by the other forecasting tools in a more general framework. The model can incorporate the forecasts from other models and, especially, the judgments of analysts through the use of 'add factors', which make the projections a combination of model-generated forecasts and judgmental information. These projections are done quarterly and, although they are not made public, they are used to elaborate the quarterly report of the Spanish economy, published in the *Boletín Económico*. They also represent the Banco de España's contribution to the ESCB's broad macroeconomic projection exercises.

The new version of the model (Estrada *et al.*, 2004) has been improved in several ways. Firstly, the dynamic properties of the model, in particular the structure of the lagged coefficients, have been simplified since the model is now estimated with seasonally and working days-adjusted ESA-95 data. Secondly, the accounting framework is much richer, incorporating two institutional sectors (the private and the government sector) and a disaggregation of taxation and government expenditure. Finally, total imports and exports are divided into goods and services and the foreign trade of goods has been further disaggregated into euro-area and non-euro area trade components.

This model includes two specific elements that are not present in other country blocks of the MCM: the treatment of the labour rate participation and the housing sector. The participation rate is affected by demographic factors as well as the NAIRU. The housing equilibrium condition is obtained from a demand for housing services derived from utility maximization and a fixed supply of services derived from the housing stock.

In addition the model is used to conduct policy and scenario analysis and in counterfactual simulation exercises; however, given the nature of the model, these simulations have important limitations. Scenario analyses usually address topics such as the transmission of monetary policy, the implications of fiscal and budgetary policies for output and inflation, and labour market policy, social security regulation and wage formation.

3   THEORETICAL UNDERPINNINGS OF THE MODEL

The Spanish block of the MCM is a quite traditional macroeconometric model in which short-run behaviour is determined by the demand side, but there is a vertical supply curve determining the level of long-run output. This level of long-run output is driven by a Cobb–Douglas production function with constant returns to scale on two productive factors (labour and capital) and exogenous technological progress (captured by a time trend). Besides this the supply side endogenously determines a NAIRU and the level of the mark-ups. Thus, in the short run, the level of demand (and therefore production) may differ from the level of long-run output, but this generates a process of price and wages adjustments that drive the model to the long-run equilibrium.

In this model, both the exchange rate and the short-term interest rate are exogenously determined, so the response of the external sector and the public sector (through a fiscal rule) is crucial to return to the long-run equilibrium. In this equilibrium, domestic prices are determined by world prices, this being consistent with the size of the Spanish economy in the world economy.

This quarterly model may be considered small by international standards. It has over 150 equations of which only 23 can be considered behavioural. This means that the model is not very detailed. Nevertheless the model includes a breakdown by sector (government and private sectors), by external trade (euro area and rest of the world) and by type of investment (residential and productive). Finally, it is worth mentioning that the model includes some financial variables, such as wealth, which are evaluated at market prices.

These behavioural equations have been estimated using cointegration methodology in two steps. First, the relations in levels were estimated imposing all the constraints needed to ensure the existence of the long-run equilibrium described earlier; secondly, these relations in levels were included in the dynamic specification of the equations as error correction terms. This last dynamic specification also required some constraints in order to achieve the nominal independence of the real equilibrium. The model is backward-looking; that is, expectations enter implicitly through the lags in the dynamic specifications.

The model can be seen to include four main blocks: the supply side, the behaviour of households, the trade block and the public sector.

3.1 The Supply Side

The supply side of the model includes ten behavioural equations defining the demand for factors (labour and capital), the value-added deflator (net of indirect taxation), the nominal wage and other demand deflators.

The representative firm produces goods and services combining capital and labour through a Cobb–Douglas production function with constant returns to scale and exogenous technological progress (modelled as a time trend). The demand for factors in the long run is derived from the first-order conditions of the optimization problem of the firm. Under this hypothesis, from the first-order condition for capital (productivity of capital equal to the real user cost of capital) and for labour one can see that the ratio of capital to output moves one-to-one with its real user cost. This condition is met in the long term by including it as the error correction model (ECM) of the equation for the growth of investment. In order to satisfy the production function in the long run, the condition for labour is derived from the inversion of the production function. As in the previous case, in order to ensure this condition in the long term, it enters into the equation for the growth rate of labour as the ECM. This equation in the short run also includes real wage developments.

The representative firm is assumed to retain a certain market power, so it sets the price (value-added deflator net of indirect taxation) as a mark-up over marginal costs. Marginal costs correspond in this context to unit labour costs and the mark-up is specified as a function of the degree of competitiveness, in order to capture the size and the degree of openness of the Spanish economy. This implies that increases in external prices allow domestic firms to expand their mark-ups since they face fewer pressures from external competitors. Therefore domestic prices in the model are seen to be a weighted average of domestic and external factors. In addition this equation incorporates a static nominal homogeneity condition to guarantee that prices are independent of quantities in the long run.

The nominal wage (labour cost) equation can be rationalized as the result of a bargaining process where trade unions and the representative firm negotiate the wage the workers are going to receive, leaving the firms to decide the level of employment they hire. Assuming that trade unions maximize the utility of their members, real wages in the long run will depend on productivity, the unemployment rate, the replacement ratio, indirect taxation and the gap between domestic and consumption prices. This equation, along with the equation for the value-added deflator, determines the level of unemployment that holds inflation stable, and it is the main mechanism linking prices and quantities in the short term. Finally, it is assumed that the decision of the working age population to participate in the labour market depends positively on the gap between the market and the reservation wages, while other cultural and demographic factors affecting this decision are captured through dummy variables. Reservation wages are defined as a weighted average of actual wages and unemployment benefits, with the weight depending on the unemployment rate.

The potential output in this model is defined as the output that would be reached if all the factors were used at their constant inflation values. This is obtained by substituting the potential values of its components in the production function. In particular, the potential values of the capital stock are assumed to be equivalent to the observed values, potential total factor productivity (TFP) is captured through a trend and potential private employment is defined as the product of the working age population and the participation rate multiplied by one minus the NAIRU.

The deflators of private consumption and productive investment (net of indirect taxes), and the two harmonized index of consumer prices (HICP) components (non-energy and energy) are modelled in the long run as a weighted average of the private value-added deflator and the three components of the import deflator (goods from the euro area, goods from the rest of the world and services),[1] it being imposed that the corresponding parameters add up to one to incorporate the nominal homogeneity condition. This captures the notion that these demand components are a mixture of domestically produced and imported goods.

3.2   The Demand Side

The demand side of the model is divided into three blocks: first, the block describing private consumption and residential investment, including all the identities that enable disposable income and wealth to be calculated; secondly, the equation for inventory investment; finally, the trade block, which includes equations of imports, exports and their corresponding deflators, plus all the identities that determine the net borrowing or lending of the nation.

3.2.1 The behaviour of households

This block includes three behavioural equations (private consumption, residential investment and the residential investment deflator) which, according to the life cycle hypothesis, are derived from the first-order conditions of the optimization problem of a representative household that obtains utility from consumption and housing services when the utility function is separable (both intertemporally and between goods) and isoelastic.

The level of private consumption is given by permanent income and the real interest rate, while the level of residential investment depends on private consumption plus the user cost of capital. In the empirical model, permanent income is proxied by a weighted average of wealth and disposable income, both in real terms, while the real interest rate is defined expost. Disposable income includes employees' compensation and labour income of non-wage earners, the imputed income of house owners, transfers from government, other income (which incorporates the income from financial assets), minus social contributions and direct taxes.

The wealth variable is defined as the sum of nominal financial and residential wealth, deflated by the private consumption deflator. The financial wealth is that of the private sector; thus, in nominal terms, it includes the private productive capital stock times the Madrid stock exchange index, public debt and net foreign assets. The non-financial component of wealth in nominal terms is the product of the residential capital stock and the residential investment deflator. From this point of view, the model is not 'Ricardian', since a rise in public debt increases financial wealth and consumption.

Finally, in order to obtain an empirical expression of the residential investment deflator, it is assumed that new residential investment represents a very small fraction of the total housing stock, meaning that the supply of housing services is given by the residential stock of the previous year. In this context, the residential investment deflator is the price that balances the supply and demand of housing services. Therefore it depends negatively on the housing financing cost and positively on the gap between the demand for housing services and their supply.

This block models some of the most powerful mechanisms to stabilize the model after a shock. The consumption equation in combination with a fiscal rule (which will be described later) implies that, when the public debt grows, direct taxes increase, which has a negative effect on disposable income and private consumption. At the same time, any disequilibrium in the external sector, for example a reduction in net foreign assets, is translated into reduced wealth, depressing consumption again and helping to stabilize the model.

3.2.2 Inventory investment

Inventory investment is modelled in the long run assuming that the ratio of the desired level of inventories to private potential output is a negative function of the real interest rate, while in the short run there are quadratic increasing costs associated with deviations of actual production from the potential level and with deviations of actual inventories from the desired level.

3.2.3 The trade block

This block is disaggregated into trade in goods with the euro area, trade in goods with the rest of the world and trade in services. The separation of trade with the euro area from that with the rest of the world is advisable because the exchange rate regime is different. Unfortunately, owing to statistical limitations, it is not possible to isolate the euro-area exports and imports of services, so a third block is considered.

The equations for real exports and real imports of the three categories of goods and of services are quite standard: they depend only on a scale variable and on relative prices, to assess the impact of competitiveness. In the case of real exports, the scale variable captures the changes in the relevant Spanish world markets. This involves weighting the other country indicators of external purchases by their importance in Spanish trade. Competitiveness is measured by subtracting from domestic export prices an external competitor price constructed as a weighted average of other countries' export prices measured in the same currency, where the weights are calculated using a double weighting method. This means that the weights represent both the relevance of Spanish exports to a particular country and the importance of that country in total world trade, taking into account the competition coming from that country via third markets.

In the case of real imports the scale variable is defined as the weighted sum of the different components of final demand, the weights capturing their import content. With respect to relative prices, competitiveness is proxied by the difference between import prices and the private sector value-added deflator.

The export prices of the three categories of goods and services are modelled as a function of private domestic prices and the previously defined external competitor prices, subject to a nominal homogeneity condition. These equations can be rationalized by regarding the export prices as a mark-up over domestic marginal costs, where the mark-up is variable and depends on the relative competitor export prices.

As in the case of export prices, import deflators are modelled as a function of private domestic prices and foreign prices, subject to the nominal homogeneity condition. Domestic prices capture pricing-to-market effects. Foreign prices are defined as a weighted average of the export prices of the respective trade partners, the weights being the share of total imports from the country in question.

Apart from the trade balance, the balance of payments includes the net compensation of employees from the rest of the world and net interest payments, modelled using the long-term US interest rate multiplied by net foreign assets.

3.3 The Government Sector

The role played by the public sector in the model is comparatively modest, in that most of the variables considered are exogenous, or the result of 'pseudo-identities'. This block is separated from the private sector, although this does not mean they are independent. In fact, some public variables enter the determination of the long-run equilibrium of the model even though they are exogenous, while the behaviour of certain private sector variables determines the receipts and expenditures of the public sector. Furthermore the inclusion of a fiscal rule is crucial for the sustainable trend of government debt and thus of household wealth.

This block considers four different price equations: the public investment deflator, public wages, the public value-added deflator and the public consumption deflator. In the long run, the public investment deflator depends on the private sector value-added deflator and the different components of the import deflator (excluding energy prices), since these goods can be produced domestically or imported. As with the other deflators, the nominal homogeneity condition is imposed. The equation for public wages implies that real wages (deflated by the consumer price index) in the public sector are around half of those of the private sector (the growth rate of productivity in the public sector is about half of that of the private sector). The public value-added deflator depends on public wages and the public investment deflator. Finally, the government consumption deflator is modelled as a function of the public sector value-added, the private sector value-added deflator and the imported goods (excluding energy) and services deflator.

The other equations in this block capture the behaviour of receipts and expenditures in the government accounts. Beginning with the expenditures, consumption, investment and employment of the public sector are considered exogenous; transfers to households are modelled as a ratio to GDP, this ratio depending on unemployment; finally, net interest payments depend on interest rates and the level of public debt. From the income side, direct taxes – levied on households and firms, plus net taxes from the rest of the world – indirect taxes and social contributions (paid by wage earners, firms, non-wage earners, the unemployed and imputed contributions) are modelled using a similar strategy: an effective tax rate is calculated and considered exogenous, so the resulting receipt will vary with the tax base, which is an endogenous variable.

The model includes a fiscal rule that prevents the continuous accumulation or depletion of public debt following a shock, guaranteeing that the consumption-to-GDP ratio remains constant in the long run. This rule is specified so that the effective direct tax rate on households adjusts to maintain the public debt-to-nominal GDP ratio on a predetermined path.

4 MEDIUM-TERM SIMULATION PROPERTIES OF THE MODEL

In this section we perform several exercises to analyse the simulation properties of the empirical model. These simulations can be considered medium-term as they cover five years. We consider five different shocks: a contractionary monetary policy shock, an expansionary fiscal policy shock (both without an active fiscal rule), an expansionary extra-euro area demand shock, an appreciation of the euro exchange rate and an increase in the oil price. In the last three simulations the model is configured in the forecasting mode, which means that some endogenous variables are considered exogenous, the reason being that either these variables are set well in advance (for example, public sector variables) or markets provide a path for them that is considered a better projection than that obtained from the model (for example, financial prices).

4.1 A Monetary Policy Shock

This monetary simulation consists of an increase in the short-term nominal interest rate of 100 basis points over two years. Using an estimated term structure, we consider that long-term interest rates also increase, but by a smaller amount (0.16 percentage points in the first year and 0.06 percentage points in the second). Moreover, since this increase in interest rates should be implemented at the area level, the uncovered interest rate parity condition implies that the euro/US dollar exchange rate appreciates temporarily by 1.6 percentage points in the first year and by 0.6 percentage points in the second.[2] This translates into an appreciation of the Spanish effective exchange rate of 0.7 percentage points in the first year and 0.3 percentage points in the second.

Given the structure of the model, this shock feeds into the endogenous variables through five channels. First, the appreciation of the currency damages competitiveness and, therefore, the trade balance (exchange-rate channel). Second, the increase in interest rates raises the user cost of productive and residential capital, inducing a downward adjustment in both components of investment (user-cost-of-capital channel). Third, the increase in interest rates makes saving more attractive for households who postpone consumption (substitution-effect channel). Fourth, as households and firms have fixed-yield assets and liabilities, their net interest payments are also affected (income/cash-flow channel). Finally, the increase in interest rates reduces the market value of firms and houses, reducing household wealth (wealth effect).

As can be seen in Figure 8.1, following the shock there is an immediate drop in domestic demand, mainly arising from the user-cost-of-capital channel, and in exports, associated with the worsening of competitiveness induced by the appreciation of the exchange rate. This downward adjustment of final demand causes firms to reduce output and, thus, the demand for productive factors. In particular, lower employment creation reduces

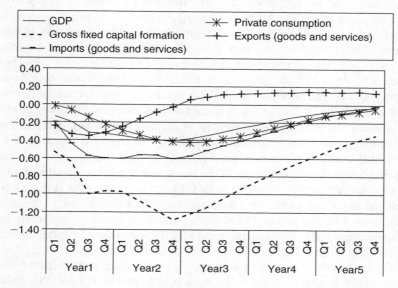

Figure 8.1a   Monetary shock: economic activity (constant prices)

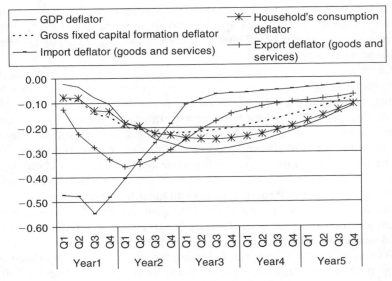

Figure 8.1b   Monetary shock: price and cost developments
(annual change)

household disposable income, which is also adversely affected by the increase in net interest payments.[3] In addition, the market value of their wealth declines, resulting in a downward adjustment of private consumption, although the saving ratio initially declines. The correction of final demand depresses imports, even though there is a worsening of competitiveness, alleviating somewhat the downward pressures on GDP. These channels, along with the substitution effect, also operate in the second year, when the maximum impact on GDP is reached (−0.4 percentage points). Afterwards, the impact of the exchange-rate channel substantially moderates when the exchange rate returns to its baseline values, disappearing thereafter. In fact, exports become positive by the third year because of the recorded competitiveness gains. The wealth and the income/cash-flow channels still show some effect in the third year, even though interest rates have returned to their baseline values. In the first case, this is due to the delayed impact of wealth on consumption and, in the second, to the stock nature of debt and assets. The substitution effect, which is very small, has also disappeared by the fourth year. Only the user-cost-of-capital channel shows certain persistence.

On the nominal side, the excess supply makes firms reduce their prices, although this effect begins to be sizable only one year after the shock. More relevant and rapid is the reduction in imported inflation (due to the appreciation of the exchange rate) which, first through the private consumption deflator and then through wage claims, reduces nominal costs and inflation. The maximum effect on prices is reached three years after the shock (−0.28 percentage points) and on inflation one year earlier (−0.1 percentage points).

The budget balance deteriorates over the five years, though it returns to the baseline after reaching a peak two years after the shock (−0.34 percentage points). Initially the worsening is the result of the increase in net interest payments; when the interest rates return to the baseline values, only the reduction in GDP and the subsequent working of the automatic stabilizers explain the negative deviations.

4.2 A Fiscal Policy Shock

This shock consists of an increase in government consumption, amounting to 1 per cent of GDP. Defining public consumption as the sum of net government purchases of goods and services, the compensation of public sector employees and the gross operating surplus, we have shocked the first two components (the other is endogenous).

This expansionary fiscal policy has an impact on domestic demand through two channels. On the one hand, increases in the compensation of public sector employees stimulate the real disposable income of households and, thus, private consumption and residential investment. On the other, net government purchases of goods and services directly increase the demand for firms' output. In order to meet this excess demand, firms try to expand their production, so they demand more capital and employment, expanding household disposable income once again. The increase in domestic demand partly leaks out to the external markets so imports deviate positively from their baseline values; also exports decline because of the competitiveness losses associated with inflationary pressures. As a result, GDP increases by more than one percentage point above the baseline (see Figure 8.2), reaching its maximum effect two years after the shock (1.4 percentage points).

As regards inflation, the increase in domestic demand and the decline in the unemployment rate initiate a price–wage spiral, which remains present five years after the shock, because GDP is still well above its baseline values. This increase in prices is especially harmful to the trade balance as it substantially worsens Spain's competitiveness.

The budget balance also deteriorates, but by much less than the initial impact of the shock, because the strong correction of unemployment reduces transfers from government and the expansion of activity increases tax receipts.

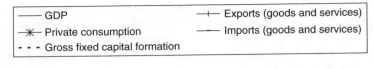

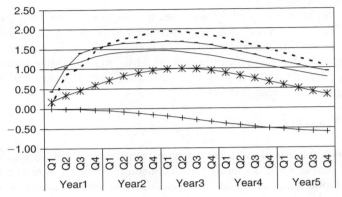

Figure 8.2a   An increase in real government consumption of 1%: economic activity (constant prices)

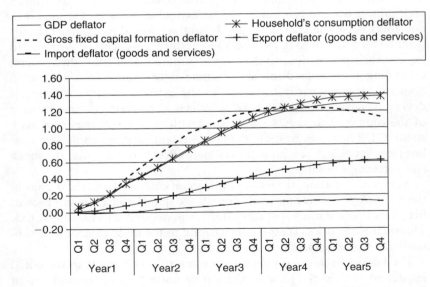

Figure 8.2b   An increase in real government consumption of 1%: price and cost developments (annual change)

4.3   An Extra-euro Area Demand Shock

In this exercise we have simulated a shock consisting of a 1 percentage point increase in the imports of the countries inside and outside the euro area. This means that the scale variables determining the exports of goods and services increase permanently by 1 per cent. In this exercise the model is configured in the forecasting mode, which means that all the asset prices and most of the fiscal variables are left exogenous.

As can be seen in Figure 8.3, this shock implies an increase of 1 percentage point in Spanish export markets, which generates an increase in exports of 0.7 percentage points in the first year. As domestic firms perceive this increase in demand they adjust output upwards by hiring more labour and buying more machinery. The increase in employment stimulates disposable income and thus private consumption and residential investment. Although part of this upward adjustment in domestic demand leaks out to the external market through imports, GDP increases, the maximum impact (0.4 percentage points) being reached three years after the shock.

The effect on prices, associated with demand pressures, is small but positive. The budget balance improves very moderately thanks to the working of the automatic stabilizers.

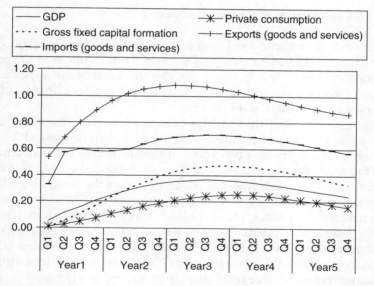

Figure 8.3a   An increase in world trade volume of 1%: economic activity (constant prices)

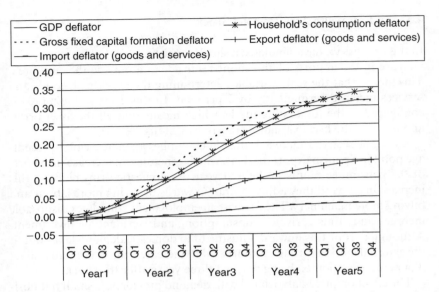

Figure 8.3b   An increase in world trade volumes of 1%: price and cost
developments (annual change)

4.4   An Appreciation of the Euro Exchange Rate

In this case the exercise consists of a 1 per cent appreciation of the euro exchange rate. The configuration of the model is the same as in the previous case. As can be seen in Figure 8.4, this shock implies an appreciation of our effective exchange rate of around 0.4 per cent, consistent with an extra-area export share of 40 per cent.

The appreciation of the exchange rate implies a worsening of competitiveness that is reflected in a marked decline of exports (by around 0.2 percentage points in the first two years). The reduction in external demand leads to a downward adjustment in domestic production, so firms reduce their demand for productive factors. In particular the downward adjustment of employment squeezes the real disposable income of households, who reduce their spending plans, although there is a temporary contraction of the saving ratio. Initially imports decline following the adjustment in final demand, but afterwards they increase, when competitiveness effects begin to dominate. Thus the impact on GDP is negative and the maximum deviation is reached three years after the shock (-0.12 percentage points).

On the nominal side, the decline in external prices in euros induces a downward adjustment in both export and import prices, which is higher in

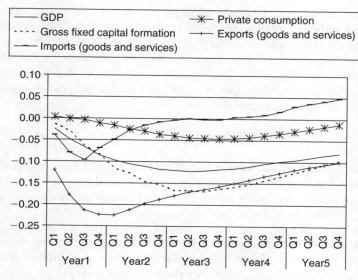

Figure 8.4a An appreciation of the euro by 1%: economic activity (constant prices)

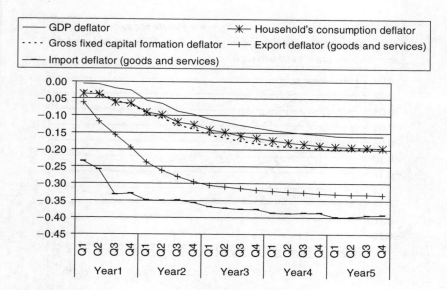

Figure 8.4b An appreciation of the euro by 1%: price and cost developments (annual change)

the latter case. Import price reductions feed into the prices of domestic demand, inducing smaller inflationary pressures and reducing wage claims. In addition the downward correction in activity and the decline of markups also contribute to reducing prices, which still deviate from the baseline five years after the shock. The balance of the public sector worsens by around 0.07 percentage points of GDP after the second year owing to the working of the automatic stabilizers.

4.5   An Increase in the Oil Price

The last simulation exercise consists of an increase of 10 per cent in the oil price in US dollars using the same configuration of the model as in the previous two cases. As shown below, the model treats this shock as a supply shock, specifically as a cost-push shock.

The immediate effect of the increase in the oil price is a quick and sustained reaction by import prices, which rise 0.8 percentage points above the baseline values (see Figure 8.5). Insofar as private consumption includes these imported products, its deflator also increases, reaching a maximum of 0.2 percentage points two years after the shock. The worsening of workers' inflationary expectations induces higher wage claims, pushing up firms'

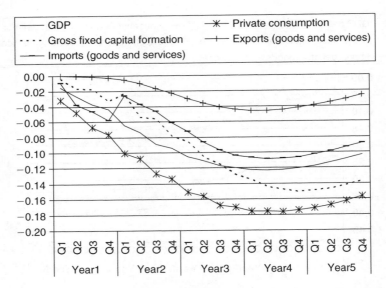

Figure 8.5a   An increase of 10% in the crude oil price: economic activity (constant price)

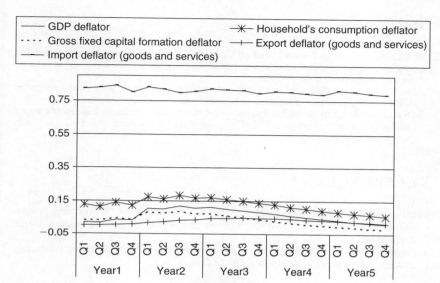

Figure 8.5b   An increase in the crude oil price: price and cost developments (annual change)

nominal costs. Although firms temporarily reduce their mark-ups, they increase the prices of domestically produced products, initiating a price–cost spiral. At the same time, the rise in the consumption deflator reduces the real disposable income of households; this induces a downward revision in private consumption (smaller than the initial reduction in disposable income due to the temporary decline in the saving ratio) and in residential investment. This reduction in domestic demand causes firms to cut production (the maximum impact on GDP, of −0.12 percentage points, is reached four years after the shock) and thus private investment and employment, thereby increasing the unemployment rate. Obviously this correction in demand helps to reduce inflationary pressures.

On the external front, exports decline as a result of the competitiveness losses (note that the prices of our competitors remain unchanged) and the same happens with imports, because the impact of the losses of competitiveness is counteracted by the downward adjustment in final demand. It is interesting to note that the trade balance improves in real terms while it worsens in nominal terms, owing to the increase in the energy bill. With respect to the public sector, the budget balance, as a percentage of GDP, worsens, increasing government debt. This is the result of an increase in expenditure associated with the working of the automatic stabilizers.

NOTES

1. This import deflator is constructed excluding the oil price from the investment deflator, since oil is not considered an investment good. The oil price is also excluded from the non-energy component of the HICP.
2. Note that, although the interest rate is set at the euro-area level, we do not consider its impact on the growth and inflation of the other members of the Monetary Union.
3. Note that the sign of this effect depends on net indebtedness. In Spain, households are net creditors, but they are net payers of interest, because of the different returns of fixed-yield assets and liabilities.

REFERENCES

Estrada, A., J.L. Fernández, E. Moral and A.V. Regil (2004), 'A quarterly macro-econometric model of the Spanish economy', *Banco de España Documento de Trabajo 0413*.
Willman, A. and A. Estrada (2002), 'The Spanish block of the ESCB-multi-country model', *Banco de España Documento de Trabajo 0212*.

9. Mascotte: the Banque de France forecasting model

Jean-Pierre Villetelle, Olivier de Bandt and Véronique Brunhes-Lesage

1 INTRODUCTION: HISTORY OF THE MODEL AND INFORMATION ON ITS DEVELOPMENT

The project of the first macroeconometric model developed at the Banque de France was launched in the early 1970s (Plihon, 1979; Maarek and Thoraval, 1980). This model, called at that time 'Monnaie–Crédit–Change' (MC2), was finalized in the mid-1980s. It was explicitly designed as a tool for performing detailed macroeconomic projections, highlighting the consequences of macroeconomic policy decisions (especially monetary policy decisions) and analysing the current macroeconomic developments. Since then, the main objectives of this type of model at the Banque de France have hardly changed and the macroeconometric model described in this section is, in this sense, one of the successors of MC2.

Many reasons led to the revision of the model. Among them, the regular change in the database due to the rebasing of the National Accounts is always a natural time for an in-depth reconsideration of the specifications and the estimation of the model as a whole. The release of ESA-79 data thus gave rise to the specification of a model called the 'Modèle de la Banque de France' (referred to as the 'BdF model', *Economie et Prévision*, 1998; Irac and Jacquinot, 1999). The release of ESA-95 data was a chance to improve further the BdF model. This led to the estimation of the Mascotte model 'Modèle d'analyse et de prévision de la conjoncture trimestrielle' ('quarterly analysis and forecasting model') in 2003 and this model is currently operational (Baghli, Brunhes-Lesage, De Bandt, Fraisse and Villetelle, 2004a, 2004b).

Like many other projection models, Mascotte is what is commonly called a neo-Keynesian model, in which prices are almost fixed in the short run and output is determined by the demand side. In the longer run, pressures on goods and labour markets materialize in the model via the impact of capacity utilization and unemployment on wages and prices. These changes in nominal variables then exert a feedback effect of the supply conditions on demand. The model is quarterly, with around 280 equations, of which 60 are estimated. The latter are specified with error-correction mechanisms that explicitly take into account the long-run relationships among economic variables and ensure the stability of the model after temporary shocks. The model is entirely backward-looking and expectations cannot be distinguished from adjustment costs and the other sources of lags.

These features were already present in the BdF model, although the role of the supply side was not as rigorously stressed as in Mascotte. The BdF model was also more detailed, especially as regards the external side. In the BdF model, for instance, exports and imports were broken down into six types of goods and services. In Mascotte, the distinction is only made between goods and services, energy also being isolated on the import side. The former degree of detail in making the model less tractable has not proved to improve significantly the forecasting performance. This type of simplification helps to focus on the macroeconomic variables to be projected and the current degree of details being chosen, either in order to provide a better understanding of some phenomena or to improve the forecasting performance of the model.

In parallel, econometric modelling at the Banque de France has undergone many changes since MC2, especially in recent years. As in many other institutions, it became obvious that the quantitative approach to economic developments could no longer rely on a single model (see, inter alia, Adenot *et al.*, 2001; Boutillier and Cordier, 1996; Baude, 1999; Jondeau *et al.*, 1999; ISMA, 2000; Jacquinot and Mihoubi, 2000, 2003; Irac and Sédillot, 2002).

2   USES OF THE MODEL

This model is primarily used for forecasting and this imposes two main requirements. First, since the forecast has to be made within a short period of time, the size of the model has to be relatively small. Second, the behavioural equations have to provide as much useful information as possible in explaining the recent past and must prove reasonably robust to be used with some confidence out-of-sample. In some cases there may be a trade-off between sound theoretical foundations, on the one hand, and goodness-of-fit and stability of the behavioural equations, on the other. In such cases, the latter has been favoured.

The aim of the projection exercises (ECB, 2001) is to project the main aggregates over a two-to-three year horizon: the GDP and its components, the related deflators, employment in the business sector, the unemployment rate and the main elements of appropriation accounts. The short-term assessment of GDP and its components is provided by other models (ISMA, 2000, and the OPTIM model: see Irac and Sédillot, 2002). The fiscal side is basically exogenous in this model, the annual data being forecast with a specific model (Adenot *et al.*, 2001), nevertheless using some variables of the macro model. Finally, the inflation forecast is also based on the use of a specific model. In this context the 'add-factors' of the equations (the discrepancy terms between what the estimated equations explain and reality) show to what extent the various elements given by the other models can be made consistent with Mascotte. Given the short-run assessment, the main role of the model is then to build a consistent scenario over the rest of the forecast horizon.

The model is also used for simulation purposes. An obvious reason for simulating the model in the context of the projection exercises is to assess the risks to the baseline scenario. Alternative options relating to the projected path of some exogenous variables, as well as the choice made by the forecasters regarding the path of some add-factors, have an impact on the overall projection and such simulations give the magnitude of the consequences of the various options.

The simulation of counterfactual situations is another use of the model. For example, the contribution of inflation to the rise in the price of oil, together with the appreciation of the euro over the years 2002–3, has been assessed in Baghli *et al.* (2004b). The model was simulated under the assumption of an unchanged value of a barrel of oil and of the euro exchange rate over that period. The difference between the actual level of inflation and the counterfactual level (taking into account the international spillover effect) thus gave the contribution of the two shocks under review.

Policy shocks are also frequently simulated in order to assess their likely implications for macroeconomic developments. These types of shocks are typically the area in which a central bank cannot rely on a single model. Indeed the validity of the results has to be evaluated case by case. In general the impact of demand shocks is correctly replicated by the model. This feature stems from its neo-Keynesian structure, which emphasizes the role of demand. Supply shocks have to be analysed more cautiously. In particular the competitive structure of the markets and its implications for pricing behaviours, or the role of expectations, are some of the features that are difficult to take into account with this type of model. Nevertheless the information they convey has to be considered.

3   AN OUTLINE OF THE THEORETICAL UNDERPINNINGS OF THE MASCOTTE MODEL

Four agents are identified: the business sector (unincorporated enterprises, financial and non-financial corporations[1]), households, the public sector and the rest of the world.

3.1   Production Function and Factor Demands

Firms have a price-setting power corresponding to a 'monopolistic competition regime', which is an intermediate situation between perfect competition and monopoly. The degree of competition is measured by the mark-up that firms add to their production costs to set their prices. This theoretical specification is derived from the maximization of profits by a representative firm, subject to the double constraint of its market power and its production function. The characteristics of the latter depend on assumptions about return to scale, technological progress, the number of factors of production and their substitutability. Three factors have been considered: employment, machinery and buildings. The latter two are assumed to be complementary and, in examining the elasticity of substitution between capital and labour, the conclusion was reached that a Cobb–Douglas function could be adopted.

In this framework the exogenous labour productivity trend, together with the exogenous long-run growth rate of the population, defines the growth rate of the economy in the long run. The factor demands are derived accordingly, namely by the first-order conditions linking their marginal productivity to their real cost and to the mark-up. In the short run, besides adjustment lags, the capacity utilization rate has an impact on both employment and investment. Profitability exclusively affects capital formation.

Total employment is broken down into several components, of which only employment in the business sector is modelled as above. The other components (public sector, non-profit institutions serving households (NPISH), households and the self-employed) are exogenous.

3.2   Components of Aggregate Demand

The consumption equation specifies the way households divide their disposable income into consumption and savings. A long-run unit income elasticity of consumption makes the saving ratio a function of the rate of growth of the real disposable income in the long run and of inflation (the inflation tax). In addition an exogenous credit variable (together with a dummy variable) also plays a prominent role over the period 1986–90: this period corresponds to a phase of financial liberalization during which the outstanding number of loans to households increased quite substantially, leading to a fall in the saving ratio (Sicsic and Villetelle, 1995). A direct impact of the real short-term interest rate ('substitution effect') in the presence of the credit variable is not significant and hence not present in Mascotte.

The equation regarding stockbuilding makes the change in inventories a function of the change in demand (which involves total consumption, total investment and exports), the cost of holding stocks (the real short-term interest rate) and the cost of production (the unit labour cost). The demand term plays a prominent role in this equation.

Housing investment is a function of real disposable income and real long-term interest rate. This provides an additional channel for the monetary policy transmission mechanism.

3.3   Price and Costs

As in most macroeconometric models, this block constitutes the core of the mechanism for stabilizing the nominal and the real spheres in the model. The theoretical specification of the supply side should lead to adopting a long-term target for the value-added deflator in the form of a factor price frontier for labour and capital costs. Nevertheless this specification delivers a poor goodness-of-fit, which is detrimental to the inflation projections. The actual equation is therefore a mark-up over unit labour cost only. In addition to adjustment lags, the capacity utilization rate in the equation accounts for the fluctuations in the mark-up in the short run. As regards unit labour costs, the value-added deflator adjusts more rapidly to changes in wages than to changes in productivity. Hence the trend productivity of labour enters the equation, not the apparent productivity.

Mascotte's estimation of the wage equation has benefited from special attention. Indeed it is crucial in assessing what price drives the wage formation and how productivity gains, social contributions and previous imbalances affect wage developments. The wage equation has a specification that reconciles the Phillips curve (where all variables, except the unemployment rate, are expressed in growth rate) and the WS–PS model (where the variables are expressed in levels and the specification is derived from more elaborated microfoundations). The error correction term includes the consumption deflator, the apparent productivity of labour (per head) and the unemployment rate. The estimation strategy led to the conclusion that wage earners bargain in terms of net wage, and in terms neither of gross wage (that is, including employees' social contributions), nor of total labour cost (that is, the gross wage plus employers' social contributions).

In Mascotte, dynamic homogeneity that makes the long-run value of the variables independent of their growth rate is imposed in both the price and wage equations. The equilibrium rate of unemployment that comes out is hence a NAIRU, but it is subject to a 'term of trade effect': the discrepancy due to the import prices between the value-added deflator (important for firms) and the consumption deflator (important for households) is one of the determinants of the level of the unemployment rate in the long run.

The other deflators are a weighted average of the value-added deflator and the import deflator. Nevertheless the consumption deflator plays a specific role since it feeds back into the wage equation.

3.4   Fiscal Policy and the Government Sector

As regards the public sector, employment is exogenous. Public consumption and investment are also exogenous at constant price. The deflators are endogenous, as described above. The other components of the fiscal side are defined in a different way, depending on whether the model is used for forecasting or for simulating shocks. In forecasting mode, the model delivers a conditional forecast. Some elements are therefore exogenous. In addition information regarding the budget is specified in relation to annual data that may differ substantially from annualized quarterly data. Some bridge equations are thus used to reconcile the two sources of data as much as possible. In simulation mode, tax receipts and social transfers are the result of the product of apparent rates by the appropriate tax base. These rates are exogenous and no fiscal rule is used routinely in the model; changes in the fiscal variables are hence the result of changes in the various elements of the tax bases.

3.5   Trade

In the trade block, it must be emphasized first that the nominal exchange rates are exogenous. Because of marked differences in the trends of the variables, it is essential to distinguish between various products. As regards exports, a distinction is made between exports of goods and exports of services. France produces mainly services (around 70 per cent of the value-added at constant price, excluding construction) but exports mainly goods (around 80 per cent of total exports at constant price). A deflator illustrative of internal developments as a whole cannot explain external developments, and vice versa. The main export equation is therefore the export of goods, modelled as a function of a world demand variable (weighted average of imports of the main trade partners) and price competitiveness.

The export deflator is a function of a production price index and a competitors' price index.

As regards imports, a distinction is made between energy and non-energy goods and services. The latter are a function of a weighted sum of the components of total demand; this index therefore includes exports. The largest weights are given to stockbuilding and investment. The import deflator (excluding energy) is a function of a competitors' price index and a production price index, modified in the short run by the capacity utilization rate. Imports of energy are linked to the overall level of activity and the relative price of imported energy. The latter is a function of the price of oil.

3.6 Monetary and Financial Sector

Mascotte is a model without money. The monetary channel is given by the role of interest rates in the model. Hence the main financial channels are given by the flows of interest payments. Interest payments are specified for all institutional sectors (except the rest of the world which ensures the equilibrium) as a function of net lending and the level of the interest rates. This way, the accumulation of debts or assets and the interest rates have an impact on interest payments. These in turn affect the disposable income and, more specifically as regards firms, their profitability. Before this block was finalized, the connection of these flows with outstanding levels of assets and liabilities came from a specific model (Baude, 1999). In addition loans to households, used in the consumption function, are also endogenous.

4   AN OUTLINE OF THE KEY CHARACTERISTICS

Consistent with economic theory, only relative prices matter in Mascotte. If all nominal variables are changed in the same proportion after a shock, relative prices are unchanged; hence the real equilibrium is unaffected in the long run. In the short run, prices are almost fixed and output is determined by the components of demand. With exogenous exchange rates, and in the absence of any reaction function, the mechanism that stabilizes the model after a shock comes primarily from the adjustment in prices. A change in the price level affects competitiveness and determines market shares on both the export and the import sides and hence the level of activity. The way value added is broken down between wages and profits also affects investment and activity. A change in the level of activity in turn modifies the level of employment, alters the unemployment rate and then affects wages and prices in return. In the long run, the absence of monetary illusion in the model ensures the stability of relative prices and, as long as relative prices are unchanged, the nominal side has no impact on real activity. In this respect, a feature of this model is that the wage–price equations are slow to adjust fully after a shock. This stems from the strength of the wage bargaining process. This feature is specified in the equation through the presence of a terms of trade effect: a rise in prices leads to upward pressures on wages on the basis of the consumption deflator on the part of workers, which firms tend to oppose in order to preserve their earnings (on the basis of the value-added deflator). This conflict results in a partial adjustment of wages in the short run and a protracted adjustment thereafter. An additional feature of the response functions of the model is that a nearly homogeneous response in prices is reached well before the full adjustment in the price level. As a consequence, since relative prices are close to what they will be in the long run, even though price levels are not, volumes that respond to relative prices only can be close to baseline even if the adjustment in the price level is not completed.

These mechanisms can be illustrated by a set of simulations for which the consumption and stock building equations incorporating a direct impact of interest rates have been used.

4.1   A Monetary Policy Shock (Figure 9.1)

This shock has been designed in the context of a general study of the monetary transmission mechanism, coordinated by the ECB (van Els *et al.*, 2001). The shock is a two-year increase of 100 basis points in the short-term interest rate. In addition, some exogenous hypotheses regarding the adjustment of the long-term interest rate and the exchange rates have been made. The long-term interest rate responds to this change according to the expectation theory and the exchange rate of the euro appreciates according to an uncovered interest rate parity condition, so these variables progressively return and stay at their baseline value. In addition no fiscal rule is taken into account, while international spillover is included: all external variables (foreign prices, foreign demand, price of oil and so on) are changed according to the consequences of the shock in the other countries of the euro zone. The total impact of the shock is to reduce both prices and activity over the short to medium term, the whole system progressively returning to baseline.

The interest shock reduces households' consumption (to the extent that the substitution effect offsets the income effect) and firms' investment and stockbuilding, hence activity. This has an impact on employment and the rise in the unemployment rate induces an adjustment in wages and prices in order to reach a new equilibrium. The process through which interest rates

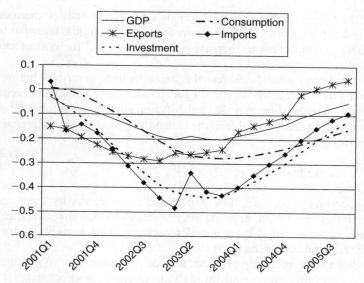

Figure 9.1a   Monetary policy shock (volume response)

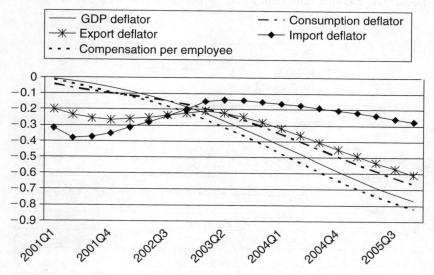

Figure 9.1b   Monetary policy shock (price response)

affect the aggregate demand can be analysed in terms of two 'channels' in the model: the income channel (however, for households, higher interest income is not sufficient to increase consumption) and the cost of capital channel.

The exchange rate shock has the consequences described below (see Section 4.4). On the whole, the biggest impact comes from the exchange rate channel in the short run. The substitution effect is not significant in the presence of the credit variable in the consumption function and is absent in Mascotte.

4.2   A Fiscal Shock (Figure 9.2)

Real government consumption is increased permanently by 1 per cent of GDP. In this simulation, nominal interest rates and exchange rates are kept exogenous. It illustrates the multiplier–accelerator properties and the role of prices in stabilizing the model.

Higher public spending provides a direct stimulus, first to production, then to corporate investment through an acceleration effect. Higher production causes employment to rise and unemployment to fall. Labour market pressures induce wages to rise. Higher employment and wages cause household incomes, and hence consumption, to rise. The rise in demand

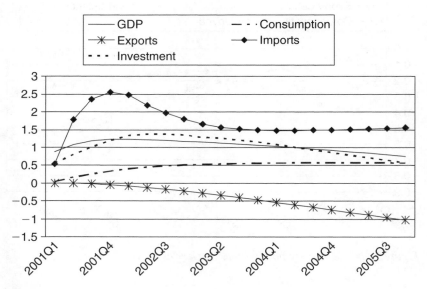

Figure 9.2a   Fiscal shock (volume response)

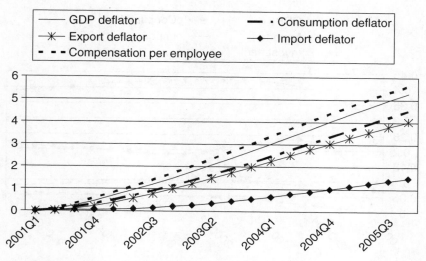

Figure 9.2b   Fiscal shock (price response)

leads to higher imports in the short term. Imports continue to rise in the medium term because of declining price competitiveness. Exports fall. This deterioration in foreign trade gradually attenuates the beneficial effect of higher public spending on GDP, so that the multiplier is below one in the fourth year. Foreign prices and nominal exchange rates being exogenous, the change in export and import deflators only reflects the change in domestic prices and explains, together with the absence of any reaction function, the slow adjustment to the shock.

4.3   A Foreign Demand Shock (Figure 9.3)

The level of real imports by countries outside the euro area is permanently increased by 1 per cent. The weight of these countries in world demand for French exports is about 48 per cent. The effect of this shock and the response of the model are close to those of the fiscal shock described above, with a magnitude of one-tenth of the previous shock. The behaviour of the model is initiated by an increase in demand addressed to firms. Unlike the fiscal shock, the foreign demand shock does not deteriorate the budget balance. On the contrary, the increase in activity leads to an expansion of the tax base which reduces the borrowing requirement of the public sector.

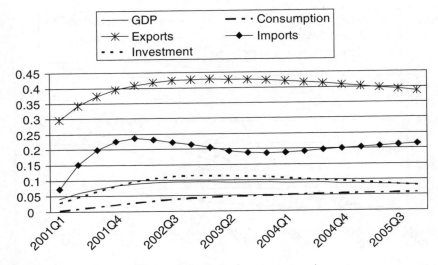

Figure 9.3a　Foreign demand shock (volume response)

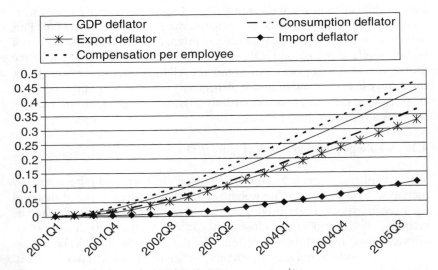

Figure 9.3b　Fiscal demand shock (price response)

4.4 An Exchange Rate Shock (Figure 9.4)

The exchange rate of the euro appreciates against all currencies for five years by 1 per cent. The weights of the non-euro currencies used in the model represent one-third of the indexes. The appreciation of the euro leads to losses in price competitiveness and hence in market shares on both the export and the import side. This reduces the level of activity. The level of domestic prices falls gradually, first following the fall in import prices and then with the adjustment in wages due to the rise in the unemployment rate. This simulation illustrates the absence of monetary illusions in the model in the long run and its role in the adjustment process: the mechanism just described continues until all domestic prices have fallen by the amount of the exchange rate shock, so that the initial equilibrium is restored.

4.5 An Oil Price Shock (Figure 9.5)

The price of oil permanently increases by 10 per cent in US dollar terms. Since oil is both an element of final demand and an intermediate good, this shock reduces both demand and supply. As a result, domestic agents try to compensate for it: firms raise their prices and households ask for higher wages. The new equilibrium is reached when all prices and wages have changed by approximately 1 per cent (that is to say, the 10 per cent rise in

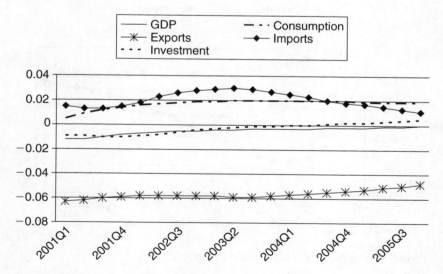

Figure 9.4a   Exchange rate shock (volume response)

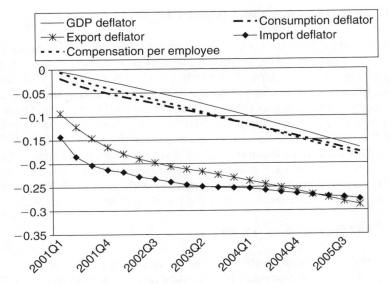

Figure 9.4b   Exchange rate shock (volume response)

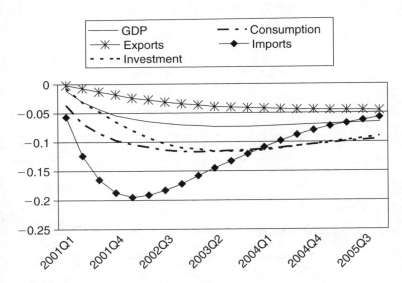

Figure 9.5a   Oil price shock (volume response)

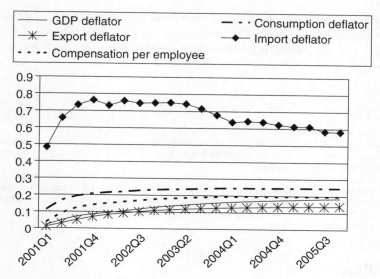

Figure 9.5b   Oil price shock (price response)

the oil prices, multiplied by the share of energy imports at current price).[2] This shock clearly highlights the role of the domestic terms of trade, namely the difference between the value-added deflator and consumption prices, in the definition of the equilibrium rate of unemployment. The value-added deflator has no direct content in oil, contrary to the consumption deflator. Thus the former increases by less than the latter. Wages being negotiated on the basis of the consumption deflator, a permanent discrepancy shows up between the firms' revenue (the value-added deflator) and their costs (the wages). They react by permanently reducing the supply of jobs, and the equilibrium rate of unemployment rises. The new equilibrium is reached at a higher level of prices and a lower level of economic activity with a higher unemployment rate.

5   CONCLUSIONS

Models like Mascotte are still the cornerstone of projection exercises, to the extent that they give the large set of variables required for projections with a goodness-of-fit that allows one to think that the estimated parameters, despite severe problems of identification, convey information about the actual behaviour of the economy. The next step after Mascotte will aim at providing the model with stronger microeconomic foundations, at the same time preserving its forecasting abilities and its capacity to deliver a sound analysis of the current macroeconomic developments: in other words, the prerequisite of MC2.

NOTES

1. Financial corporations are included in the business sector insofar as financial services are not separated from the other services in the model. Nevertheless they are isolated as regards financial transfers.
2. Since the 1970s, the share of imports of energy in total imports has followed a downward trend and is now less than 4 per cent at constant price and 10 per cent at current price). As a consequence, the initial impact of the shock is fairly limited. In addition, given the overall slow reaction of the wage–price equations of the model to shocks, adjustment is protracted.

REFERENCES

Adenot C., C. Bouthevillain and G. Moëc (2001), 'Présentation de MEADE (méthode d' évaluation avancée du déficit de l' état)', note Banque de France, f01-096, September.
Baghli M., V. Brunhes-Lesage, O. de Bandt, H. Fraisse and J.-P. Villetelle (2004a), 'MASCOTTE, modèle d'analyse et de prévision de la conjoncture trimestrielle', NER no. 106, Banque de France, February.
Baghli M., V. Brunhes-Lesage, O. de Bandt, H. Fraisse and J.-P. Villetelle (2004b), 'The Mascotte forecasting model for the French economy: main features and results from variants', *Banque de France Bulletin Digest*, no. 124, April.
Baude J. (1999), 'Modalisa: un modèle annuel de flux d'intérêts', Banque de France, note SEMEF no. m99-079, May.
Boutillier M. and J. Cordier (eds) (1996), *Economic Modelling at the Banque de France*, New International Studies in Economic Modelling, New York and London: Routledge.
Economie et Prévision (1998), 'Structures et propriétés de cinq modèles macro-économiques français', **134** (3), April–June.
van Els P., A. Locarno, J. Morgan and J.-P. Villetelle (2001), 'Monetary policy transmission in the euro area. What do aggregate and national models tell us?', European Central Bank Working Paper Series, no. 94.
European Central Bank (2001), 'A guide to staff macro-economic projection exercises'.
Irac D. and P. Jacquinot (1999), 'L'investissement en France depuis le début des années 1980', NER no. 63, Banque de France, April.
Irac D. and F. Sédillot (2002), 'Short run assessment of economic activity: using OPTIM', NER no. 88, January, Banque de France.
ISMA (Indicateur Synthétique Mensuel d'Activité (2000), 'La situation économique de la France', Bulletin mensuel de la Banque de France, no. 73, January, pp. 7–21.

Jacquinot P. and F. Mihoubi (2000), 'Modèle à anticipations rationnelles de la conjoncture simulée: MARCOS', NER no. 78, November, Banque de France.

Jacquinot P. and F. Mihoubi (2003), 'L'apport des modèles de la nouvelle génération à l'analyse économique, l'exemple de MARCOS', Bulletin mensuel de la Banque de France, no. 117, September, pp. 63–84.

Jondeau E., H. Le Bihan and F. Sédillot (1999), 'Modélisation et prévision des indices de prix sectoriels', NER no. 68, September, Banque de France.

Maarek G. and P.-Y. Thoraval (1980), 'Le modèle MC2 Monnaie–Crédit–Change (Cadre théorique et premiers résultats économétriques)', note Banque de France, SEER, March.

Plihon D. (1979), 'Un modèle d'ensemble de l'économie: "Monnaie–Crédit–Change" (MC2)', note Banque de France, SEER, December.

Sicsic P. and J.-P. Villetelle (1995), 'Du nouveau sur le taux d'épargne', *Economie et Prévision*, **121** (5), 59–64.

10. The econometric model of the Bank of Greece

Nicholas Zonzilos

1 INTRODUCTION: A BRIEF HISTORICAL OVERVIEW

Econometric modelling at the Bank of Greece started in 1975 when the first model of the Greek economy was developed in the Econometric Forecasting Unit, then headed by Nicholas Garganas, now Governor of the Bank.[1] In its initial version, the model was relatively small and limited in many respects, but it has been substantially extended and elaborated over the years. Since the late 1970s, the macro model has been the Bank's primary formal model of the Greek economy. The model is used in a wide variety of activities, but mainly in forecasting and, to a lesser extent, for policy analysis.

A comprehensive presentation of the model, as it stood in 1991, is included in a book written by Garganas (1992) entitled *The Bank of Greece Econometric Model of the Greek Economy*. At that time, the model contained 507 variables, 84 of which were determined by behavioural equations. Technical equations, accounting as well as reporting identities, completed the model, while 202 variables were exogenous.

This earlier version of the model was deeply rooted in the Keynesian tradition: output was determined by aggregate demand, while the supply side was rather passive. Aggregate demand was built up by a series of equations describing the spending behaviour of different agents in a detailed disaggregated manner. The particular focus of the specification on aggregate demand reflected the main use of the model, that is, short-term forecasting.

The accounts of the public sector were modelled in substantial detail, reflecting the interest of the Bank in a judicious monitoring of public sector aggregates as well as the possibility of examining the quantitative influence on the economy of different discretionary measures (changes in a wide spectrum of tax rates, for example). The monetary sector of the economy was also modelled in considerable detail and the empirical specification focused especially on the modelling of the availability of credit. The underlying theoretical structure of the monetary sector was the 'high-powered money multiplier' model developed by Brunner and Meltzer (1972, 1974) where the monetary base was endogenously determined through a set of identities by the net position of the foreign and public sector of the model. A salient feature of the model was that monetary influences were transmitted to the real sector and prices, mainly through the availability of credit for invest-ment via a rationing scheme, while the direct interest rate effect on demand was modest and limited only to some specific components of aggregate demand.

The earlier formulation was dictated by the particular institutional framework operating in Greece until the mid-1980s, when financial liberal-ization started gradually to take place.[2] Until that time, monetary policy was conducted in a rather direct manner by controlling the monetary aggre-gates, particularly through the availability of credit via a complex set of regulations. Interest rates were maintained relatively fixed for long periods of time and well below the rate of inflation. Moreover the large public sector deficit was financed at preferential rates by commercial banks, which held a large part of the outstanding debt. At the same time, secondary markets for securities were practically non-existent. Under these circum-stances, an excess demand for credit was the prevailing situation in a wide range of sectors of the Greek economy.

It is worth noting that this model has been the only large-scale oper-ational econometric model in Greece for many years, providing assistance to the members of the Monetary Policy Committee of the Bank of Greece over a broad spectrum of issues related to their economic policy objectives. However, given the extensive structural and institutional changes that the Greek economy has undergone in recent years, especially in the financial sector, it was decided that the model should be rebuilt by revising its struc-ture in a number of directions. Of course, one of the main motivations in rebuilding the model was to embed in its structure features that reflect the new regulatory and institutional setting prevailing in Greece. Moreover, given that economic forecasts are usually carried out under strict and rather restricted time constraints, it was judged more appropriate to develop a medium-sized model (requiring a less time-consuming data-updating process), better able to support forecasting and, more generally, the eco-nomic policy-making process within the Bank. Last but not least, the ambi-tion was to update the theoretical structure of the model using some recent modelling advances.

The whole project of model respecification was undertaken at the econo-metric forecasting section of the Bank of Greece. The new model, specified to include equilibrium conditions, is more aligned with the 'neoclassical synthesis' and explicitly takes into account the long-run supply side of the economy. By its very aggregative nature, the revised model omits useful information provided in forecasting by the previous large-scale Bank of Greece econometric model. On the other hand, the new structure has the advantage over the previous one of being a more flexible and manageable tool. In addition its medium size, together with the theoretical restrictions imposed on the long-run relations, allows a more sensible interpretation of its properties and the possibility of communicating the forecast and simulation results in fully understandable economic terms. In the following section, the revised model and its uses are described as they stood in its late 2001 version.

2   USES OF THE MODEL: AN OUTLINE OF THE ROLE OF THE MODEL IN FORECASTING AND POLICY ANALYSIS

The main use of the model is in forecasting and scenario analysis and it is used at the Bank in its regular forecasting rounds and also in the European System of Central Banks (ESCB) forecasting exercise. Moreover the new model is designed to simulate the economy in terms of the main aggregates and to produce quantitative information for a variety of purposes (for example, the evaluation of the effects of inflows from EU structural funds). Without describing the forecasting process itself, we now turn to a more detailed exposition of the use of the model in the Bank of Greece.

2.1   The Use of the Model as a Forecasting Device

The use of the model in the internal forecasting rounds of the Bank of Greece

At least twice a year, the staff of the econometric forecasting section of the Research Department of the Bank prepare for internal purposes annual projections for the main macroeconomic aggregates and inflation up to one or two years ahead. These forecasts are generated in order to facilitate discussion, as well as to shape the views of the members of the Monetary Policy Committee (MPC) about the prospects of the Greek economy before the regular (mandatory) submission of the Monetary Policy Report of the Bank to the Parliament. While the econometric model of the Bank has always been the main vehicle in the forecasting process, the nature of the forecasts can be qualified as judgmental. Indeed the forecasts combine pure model-based information with off-model information and judgments provided by the MPC members as well as by the experts monitoring particular sectors of the Greek economy. The combination of model and off-model information is carried out by an iterative procedure allowing full interaction between the views of the econometric forecasting section staff and the views and suggestions of the members of the MPC as well as of the experts monitoring particular sectors of the Greek economy. For example, conditioning assumptions about the future path of exogenous variables are the results of a consensus view of the members of the MPC. Moreover information about future policies that also play a central role in shaping the forecast is also a valuable input from the MPC members.

The confrontation of model-based information with the experts' judgments about developments in particular sectors of the economy is another key element of the forecasting process. The revelation of discrepancies between the two approaches constitutes the fundamental ingredient for a non-trivial, judgmental intervention in the forecast based on past error adjustments and expected future shocks. Furthermore, by providing a fully articulated national accounting framework, the model is a useful platform for an evaluation of the overall coherency of views, projections and judgments emanating from a broad spectrum of different sources. In this way the model is used as a cross-checking device of the heterogeneous assessments about the economy made by specific sector experts, possibly using a common set of initial assumptions but processing information using different analytical tools and having different feelings and perceptions about the future.

The use of the model in the ESCB broad macroeconomic projection exercises

As already mentioned, the model is also used in the ESCB broad macroeconomic projection exercises (BMPE). The BMPE projection differs in at least two important respects from our internal forecast. The BMPE forecast covers three years ahead instead of one or two years, as covered by the Bank of Greece's internal forecast; more importantly, the BMPE projection is strictly considered as a staff forecast and not as a forecast necessarily reflecting the Bank of Greece's views. This has important implications for the way in which the BMPE forecasting process is carried out within the Bank, but does not alter the role and the use of the model in the forecasting process itself.[3] The way in which the Bank's model is used in the context of the BMPE is practically identical to its internal use described above. As in our internal forecast exercise, the model has an important role as a tool for checking the internal consistency of the forecast. Moreover, in the BMPE, the forecast for the outlook of the economy is yet again carried out in a decentralized manner blending model information with experts' knowledge from specific sectors of the economy. In addition the model helps in the communication of the forecast results as well as in the formulation of the underlying economic analysis supporting the projections and the accompanying reports.

2.2 The Use of the Model in other Activities of the Bank

Aside from forecasting, the model is also used to run simulations and policy scenarios under a variety of policy interventions. In this context, the model can provide useful insights into the way the effects of policy interventions are transmitted to the economy and how these interventions affect the baseline forecast. Moreover, given that at the Bank of Greece these has not yet been developed a formal probabilistic framework to analyse the risks surrounding the projections, the formulation of model-based alternative scenarios is a useful guide to evaluate the quantitative impact of different shocks and assumptions on the central projection.

Furthermore it is worth noting that a previous version of this model was used for an ex ante evaluation of the impact on the Greek economy of the third Community Support Framework.

3 AN OUTLINE OF THE THEORETICAL UNDERPINNINGS OF THE MODEL

The new Bank of Greece model is a standard aggregate demand and supply structural econometric model developed by the Econometric Forecasting Section. The model shares many features with the ECB area-wide model (Fagan *et al.*, 2001) and the multi-country model (MCM) project.

At present, the model contains over 90 equations, 17 of which are behavioural, the remainder being technical relations, identities and reporting identities. The model is dynamic and uses the error correction formulation and cointegration techniques in the specification and estimation of the behavioural equations. The model is built around national income and product accounts and has been fitted to annual observations covering the period 1964 to 2000, using the ESA-95 system. Shorter periods were used, mainly in investment equations, in order to preserve financial regime homogeneity. The structural equations were estimated by the two-step Granger–Engle procedure. The computer implementation of the model is given in portable TROLL. The estimation and the simulation exercises are all carried out in the TROLL system.

Current work on this model focuses mainly on a further development of its theoretical foundations and the respecification of the main behavioural equations. The model is continuously simulated and tested in order to examine its properties. In this respect the model should be viewed more as work in progress and a platform for empirical research within the Bank, rather than as a finished product.

In the new version of the Bank of Greece model, real interest rates are endogenous and directly affect domestic demand. However the main policy variable, that is, the short-term nominal interest rate, is left exogenous while the nominal exchange rate follows an agreed predetermined path. This is in accordance with the ECB forecasting practice. Hence there are no equations for the short-term interest rate and the exchange rate.

In what follows, a more complete description of the equations of the model is presented.

3.1 Aggregate Demand

Aggregate demand is determined by individual equations for each expenditure component of demand including consumption, fixed investment, inventory investment, exports, imports and government expenditure. Inventories, public consumption and public investment are exogenous in real terms.

Private consumer expenditure constitutes a large part, about 55 per cent, of total final expenditure and it is modelled in an aggregative manner including both durables and non-durables. In the long run, private consumption is determined by real disposable income and the real interest rate. In this version of the model, wealth variables are not introduced explicitly in the long-run consumption function and therefore any type of stock accumulation effects on consumer behaviour is not taken into account. However, in the short-run dynamic equation, which is of the error correction type, an inflation surprise term measured as a deviation of the private consumption deflator from its trend (calculated by the Hodrick–Prescott filter) is included. This variable reflects the erosion of the real value of nominal assets in the face of an unexpected inflation increase and therefore indirectly and partially captures wealth effects in consumers' behaviour.

The optimal capital stock is determined by the marginal conditions as a function of the user cost of capital. In other words, and given the assumed Cobb–Douglas technology, in equilibrium the productivity of capital should be equal to the real capital cost. From an econometric viewpoint this long-run function is estimated in order to overcome scaling problems and then reintroduced in an error correction formulation for private business investment. The dynamic specification of the investment equation incorporates an acceleration (activity) term and some profitability effects measured by the gross operating surplus.

3.2   The Supply Side of the Model

Output is given by a constant return to scale Cobb–Douglas production technology in labour and capital. The coefficients of the equation are calibrated according to the average sample share of labour income in value-added. Potential output is derived by inserting in the calibrated function the actual capital stock and the trend in total factor productivity, and by replacing actual employment with its full employment level (derived from the exogenous labour force and the calculated NAWRU). The output gap is the difference between potential and actual output.

The long-run employment equation is derived by inverting the production function. In the short run, total employment adjusts towards its long-run level by an adjustment equation in which short-run influences from changes in final demand and real product wages are taken into account. Self-employment is treated as exogenous and demand for dependent employment is determined residually.

3.3   Prices and Wages

With respect to the determination of prices, the GDP deflator at factor cost is considered to be the general inflation indicator. Modelling the GDP deflator reflects our interest in the domestic origins of inflation. All other prices, except import prices, are related to this indicator, with specific additional context-dependent adjustments. Import prices are linked to foreign prices via the exchange rate.

The formulation of the price equation is given by monopolistic price setting. As already mentioned, firms operate under a Cobb–Douglas constant-return-to-scale production technology. Assuming a degree of monopoly power, the representative firm sets prices in the market for its diversified product with a constant mark-up on marginal cost. In this set-up, the profit-maximizing price level is determined by the unit labour cost and the mark-up subject to the demand function faced by firms and the production function.

This price equation can also be viewed as a short-run supply curve of the economy, which has the usual positive slope. However the mark-up is not constant and varies with the elasticity of demand. The mark-up can be affected by economic activity and also, given the openness of the Greek economy, by the real exchange rate. Moreover, given the considerable structural changes that have taken place in Greece in the last few years, the ratio of value-added in the services sector to total value-added is included in the long-run supply function. These variables also help the cointegration properties of the respective equations. With this consideration in mind, the long-run price equation is a function of unit labour cost (based on a measure of average productivity), import prices and the services-to-GDP ratio. Long-run homogeneity is imposed on the equation.

The residuals of the long-run equation are incorporated in a dynamic ECM price equation. Some short-run influences from the unit labour cost and import prices have also been introduced.[4] The consumption deflator and the CPI are modelled as a function of the GDP deflator and import prices. Wages are modelled via a bargaining-type equation and the dynamic specification displays dynamic homogeneity. In the long run, real product wages are determined by average productivity and the exogenously determined NAWRU. Moreover, in the short run, nominal wages respond to the deviation of actual unemployment from the NAWRU level and to the changes of productivity.

3.4 Foreign Trade

Exports of goods and services are determined in the long run by world demand, which enters the equation with a unit elasticity, and relative prices. The unit elasticity restriction is accepted by the data. In the short run, real export growth is affected by the growth in relative prices, the growth in foreign demand and the lagged long-run relationship, which enters as an error correction term and, thus, ensures adjustment to equilibrium.

Imports of goods and services are determined in the long run by total final expenditure and relative prices. A unit elasticity is imposed on the demand variable and a logistic trend is also included in the long-run specification. The logistic trend captures the gradual but significant import penetration observed in Greece over the sample period which cannot only be explained by the increase in final expenditure. The dynamic adjustment of real imports of goods and services towards long-run equilibrium is given by a standard ECM in which the growth of domestic demand and relative prices influence imports' growth.

Import prices as measured by the deflator of imports of goods and services are mainly determined by foreign prices and the exchange rate. However a pricing-to-market effect is also captured by the GDP deflator in the long-run equation. The dynamic adjustment equation takes the traditional ECM form.

The export deflator of goods and services is determined by the GDP deflator and competitors' prices. In the long-run equation the coefficient of domestic prices is rather small. As a result, domestic inflation has a low impact on exports prices and ultimately on exports, while domestic exporters' profit margins are significantly affected. The adjustment of export prices to their long-run equilibrium is described by a standard ECM.

The fiscal block has no behavioural equations, but is modelled by accounting identities. Direct and indirect taxes are the product of exogenous tax rates and the corresponding nominal aggregates. Interest payments by the government to the private sector are not yet linked to the debt stock but are estimated by off-model calculations. In some simulations a fiscal reaction function for direct taxation is in operation. In the fiscal reaction function, the change in the direct tax rate reacts smoothly to the deviations of the public debt, expressed as a ratio to GDP, from its baseline values or a target level.

Long-term interest rates are linked to short-term rates by a backward-looking term structure scheme.

4   AN OUTLINE OF THE KEY CHARACTERISTICS OF THE MODEL

In this section, the characteristics and the functioning of the model are described through a set of standard simulation results. At first it should be stressed that the simulation results, as expected, are strongly dependent on the underlying assumptions made. Therefore the results should be evaluated against the background of these assumptions. That said, it is worth noting that all simulations are carried out without any policy rule in operation (monetary or fiscal) and in addition the exchange rate is held fixed (except for the monetary policy shock). Under these circumstances the only mechanism at work to equilibrate the model in case of an exogenous shock is prices through their effect on aggregate demand and supply and in particular on foreign trade. However, given the low price elasticity of foreign trade as well as the rather low and slow responsiveness of prices to aggregate demand, the adjustment process of the real side of the model after a shock is sluggish and generally could not be completed within the five-year simulation period. The low and slow price responsiveness to demand changes is a salient feature of the Greek economy and it is mainly due to prevailing rigidities and regulations in the goods and labour markets.

4.1   A Monetary Policy Shock

This is a standardized monetary policy simulation carried out in the context of the monetary transmission exercise undertaken by the WGEM. Results (intra-euro area spillover effects are included) refer to a temporary (two-year) shock of 100 basis points in short-term nominal interest rates and an immediate return to base for the rest of the simulation period. Long rates are adjusted according to a term structure scheme and the exchange rate appreciates according to an area-wide uncovered interest parity (UIP) condition. The simulation was originally designed to be conducted over a ten-year period and therefore numerical results are available for this horizon. A graphical exposition of the main results for the first five years of the simulation is given in Figure 10.1.

The temporary monetary policy shock sets off a cyclical response from all the endogenous variables of the model. Output and prices remain below base throughout the simulation period. The maximum effect on output is reached in the second year, while the maximum for prices is reached in period 5. By the end of the simulation period (ten years) the effect on output and prices is reduced considerably and practically eliminated.

The fast inflationary impact of the shock comes more from the exchange rate channel (the exchange rate follows the predetermined UIP path) than from the change in demand. Prices respond with a lag to lower demand and higher unemployment. There are two real channels that affect prices and operate through the effect of unemployment on wage bargaining and through the effect of the capital stock on average productivity. The weak responsiveness of employment to output reflects the prevailing rigidities in the Greek labour market.

The domestic demand components move in line with GDP and are below base throughout the ten-year simulation period. Investment starts to recover slowly after six years, reflecting the long-lasting effect of the

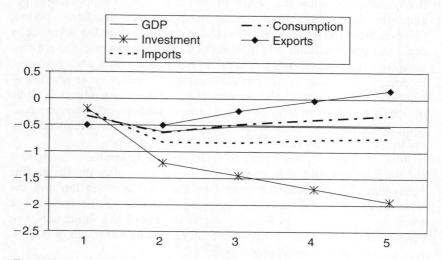

Figure 10.1a   Simulation of a two-year shock to short-term interest rates by 100 bp

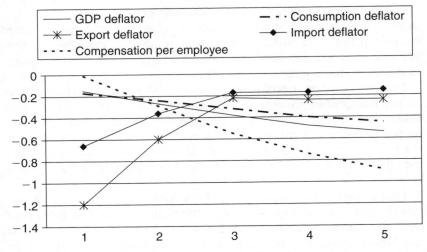

Figure 10.1b   Simulation of a two-year shock to short-term interest rates by 100 bp

monetary policy shock. The accelerator term dominates investment, which is much stronger than the cost of capital effect. The recovery of investment has a stabilizing impact on the capital stock, improves the supply conditions and undermines the return of prices to base. Compensation per employee drops throughout the reported five-year simulation period; however, from the seventh year, it starts recovering under the influence of consumer prices and the reduction in the unemployment rate. Private consumption reacts vigorously to the fall in real interest rates and disposable income. The maximum effect is attained in the second year when consumption falls by around 0.65 per cent. As there is no monetary policy rule in operation, short-term rates return to base, immediately boosting consumption. The direct interest rate effect on consumption is reinforced by the gradual return to baseline of real disposable income.

Imports follow a path similar to GDP and are below base throughout the simulation period; they start to recover six years after the shock. The behaviour of exports is determined by the euro appreciation and the stronger effect is attained at the beginning of the simulation period. The effect on exports turns positive by the forth year of the simulation, two years after the exchange rate returns to base. The pass-through of domestic cost on export prices is generally low.

The budget balance deteriorates in the first two years of the simulation, returning slowly to base by the end of the ten-year period of simulation.

4.2 A Fiscal Policy Shock

The fiscal policy shock is a sustained increase in public consumption equivalent to 1 per cent of GDP (Figure 10.2). It is assumed that this increase corresponds only to an increase in procurement expenditure while wage expenditure remains constant.

The increase in public consumption raises output, employment and the components of domestic demand. The implied multiplier is around 0.8 for the first year and then rises throughout the simulation period. Prices respond sluggishly to the demand shock through the usual channels, but the effect on prices is rather low for the entire simulation period. The demand expansion raises the level of imports while the stabilizing impact of exports through erosion of the real exchange rate is limited. This is mainly due to a weak pass-through of domestic prices to export prices in the present model.

Without the operation of a fiscal rule, the path for the public debt is explosive. In our regular medium-run simulations, a fiscal rule allowing taxes to react to deviations of the debt ratio from its baseline value is normally in operation. The implementation of this rule stabilizes the model in the long run in the case of a fiscal shock. Moreover, in this simulation, the assumed exogeneity of interest rates and the absence of a monetary policy rule exclude the appearance of crowding out effects that normally should be present in a more realistic depiction of the working of the economy.

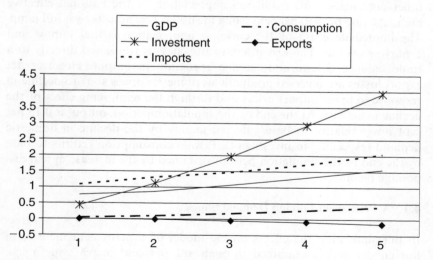

Figure 10.2a   Fiscal policy shock: permanent increase in government consumption of 1% of GDP

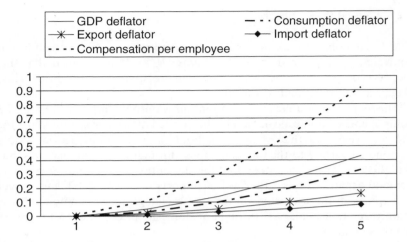

*Figure 10.2b   Fiscal policy shock: permanent increase in government
consumption of 1% of GDP*

4.3   An Exchange Rate Shock

In this simulation (results are depicted in Figure 10.3) we investigate the
effect of a 1 per cent appreciation of the euro for five years against all
other currencies. This entails an appreciation of the national effective
exchange rate by 0.30 per cent while the dollar rate adjusts by a full jump.
The immediate effect of the currency appreciation is that import and
export prices fall. The loss in competitiveness is translated directly to a
trade balance deterioration and a reduction in output. However net
export losses are reversed gradually as domestic prices start to decline in
response to lower import prices and through the reinforcing effect of the
decline in activity. At the end of the simulation period, output is 0.15 per
cent lower relative to base, affected mainly by the decline in domestic
demand (especially in investment). Private consumption returns to base
by the end of the simulation period, sustained by the increase in real disposable income.

4.4   A Permanent Foreign Demand Shock

In this simulation the effects on the model of a permanent increase in
foreign demand is examined through a 1 per cent increase in foreign
demand outside the euro area (Figure 10.4). In the Greek case, exports of
goods and services outside the euro area constitute more than 50 per cent

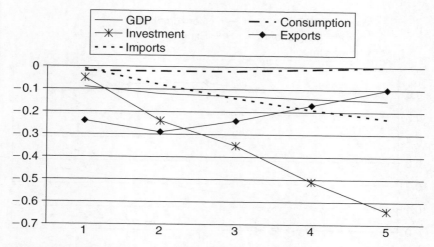

Figure 10.3a *Exchange rate shock: appreciation of the euro by 1% for five years*

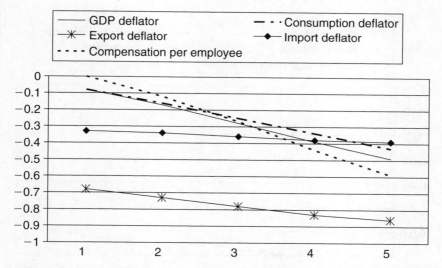

Figure 10.3b *Exchange rate shock: appreciation of the euro by 1% for five years*

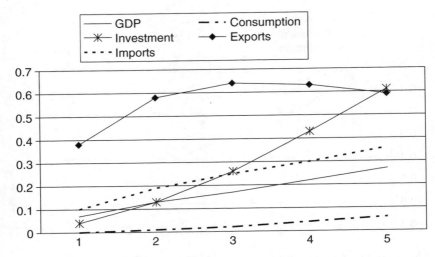

Figure 10.4a　Foreign demand shock: permanent increase in the extra-euro area world demand by 1%

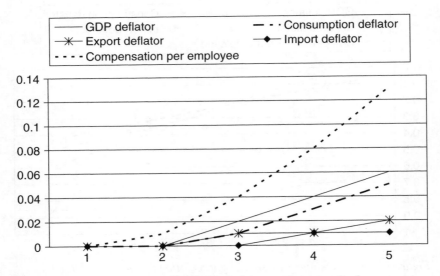

Figure 10.4b　Foreign demand shock: permanent increase in the extra-euro area world demand by 1%

of total exports. Hence the increase in our world market variable is 0.55. The increase in foreign demand leads to an increase in exports, which in the medium run reaches a level of around 0.6 above base consistent with the long-run unit elasticity of exports with respect to world demand. The increase in exports sets up an upward reaction of all the expenditure components. However the positive effect of rising demand and the consequent fall in unemployment has a sluggish and modest impact on wages and prices. Thus a rise in exports is maintained throughout the simulation period, as some minor competitiveness losses caused by the rise in domestic prices cannot erode the impact of the increase in foreign demand. The gradual increase in the components of aggregate demand boosts imports which, in turn, counterbalances the impact of exports on the contribution of the external sector to output growth. By the end of the simulation period, output is 0.27 per cent above base and the foreign sector contributes only 0.02 percentage points to this deviation.

4.5 A Permanent Oil Price Shock

This simulation shows the effect of a permanent 10 per cent increase in oil prices expressed in US dollars. The results presented graphically in Figure 10.5 are purely model-based but conditional on a constant real interest rates assumption in order to avoid a demand-boosting effect due to higher inflation.

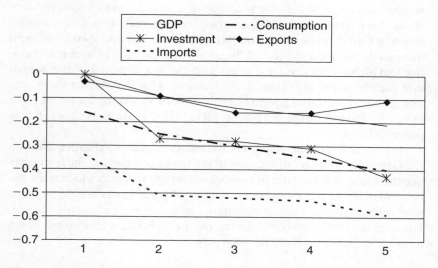

Figure 10.5a   Oil price shock (10% increase in oil prices, in US$)

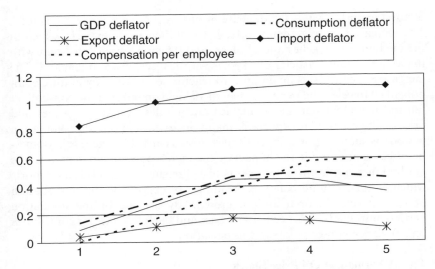

Figure 10.5b   Oil price shock (10% increase in oil prices, in US$)

The initial effect of the oil price rise is an increase in the level of import prices by 0.8 per cent, which builds up over time and levels off at around 1.1 per cent by the end of the simulation period. The impact of the oil price shock by the end of the simulation period on the GDP deflator and on the private consumption deflator is an increase of 0.36 and of 0.46 per cent above base, respectively. Higher prices reduce real disposable income, which in turn dampens consumer expenditure at first and then investment through the reinforcing effect of the accelerator. Nominal wages react positively to higher prices and real wages after the fourth period of the simulation slightly exceed the values of the base run. Moreover higher wages and unit labour costs shift aggregate supply upwards, reducing output at given prices. By the end of the simulation period GDP is around 0.2 percentage points below base.

This scenario does not represent the most realistic quantitative effect on the Greek economy of an increase in the world price of oil. Since in practice there is an institutional framework for setting fuel prices to market, the behaviour of the mark-ups and the terms-of-trade losses should be taken into account by additional exogenous adjustments and considerations. However the results are useful for tracing the main channels through which an oil price increase affects the economy.

5 CONCLUSIONS

Econometric models play an important role in the forecasting and the macroeconomic policy-making process of the Bank of Greece. In this chapter we have presented the structure and documented the use as well as the key properties of the current version of the Bank of Greece model. The model gives a rather accurate depiction of the dynamic behaviour of the main macroeconomic aggregates of the Greek economy. Moreover the model proved to be a useful tool in forecasting as well as in providing answers to questions related to the economic policy process. In this respect, the message that emerges from our experience using the model at the Bank of Greece is that the model can shed light on a wide spectrum of macroeconomic issues, especially in forecasting and in the support of the macroeconomic policy decisions of the members of the MPC.

The development of the model is a continuous activity at the Bank of Greece. Therefore the presented model should be considered more as a work in progress than as a finished product. In this conviction, possible extensions of the model could include a different and more sophisticated treatment of the expectations formation mechanism, which at present is modelled in a backward-looking manner, in order to be able to analyse and answer policy questions more accurately. In addition the desegregation of some equations, especially in the foreign and public sectors, is among our priorities in an aim to enhance the usability of the model in the policy process and to improve the information content of the forecast.

NOTES

1. Comments from Stephen G. Hall, Heather Gibson, George Tavlas and an anonymous referee are gratefully acknowledged. G. Pavlou provided excellent research assistance. The usual disclaimer applies.
2. Although financial deregulation began in the mid-1980s, the process was not completed until the mid-1990s.
3. In the sense that the BMPE involves close interaction between the Bank of Greece and ECB staff, while, in our internal forecasting rounds, the role of members of the MPC is prominent.
4. Dynamic homogeneity is accepted by the data and imposed in this equation.

REFERENCES

Brunner, K. and A.H. Meltzer (1972), 'A monetarist framework for aggregative analysis', Proceedings of the first Konstanz Seminar on Monetary Theory and Monetary Policy, *Kredit und Kapital*, Berlin: Duncker and Humblot, pp. 31–88.

Brunner, K. and A.H. Meltzer (1974), 'Money debt and economic activity', *Journal of Political Economy*, **80**, 951–77.

Fagan, G., J. Henry and R. Mestre (2001), 'An area-wide model (AWM) for the euro area', European Central Bank Working Paper, no. 42.

Garganas, N.C. (1992), *The Bank of Greece Econometric Model of the Greek Economy*, Athens: Bank of Greece.

11. Central Bank and Financial Services Authority of Ireland's model

Kieran McQuinn, Nuala O'Donnell and Mary Ryan

1 INTRODUCTION

The Irish component of the MCM (multi-country model) is estimated and maintained within the Economic Analysis, Research and Publications (EARP) department of the Central Bank and Financial Services Authority of Ireland (CBFSAI). The first edition of the model was initially estimated by a team of economists[1] between April 1998 and January 1999 over the period 1980–95 with quarterly ESA-79 data. An overview of the model is given in McGuire and Ryan (2000). The model is currently backward-looking, with expectations entering implicitly through lagged values of variables. To date, this version of the model has been used for the simulation exercises requested by the different working groups of the ECB and for domestic purposes. Between 2002 and 2003, the model was re-estimated over the extended period 1980–99 again with interpolated quarterly ESA-79 data. At the time of writing, the model is being reprogrammed in TROLL. The model currently has two main uses. It is used, firstly, as an input into forecasting exercises conducted by EARP and, secondly, for the analysis of different scenarios both for internal and external audiences.

The model forms an integral component of the Irish input into the ESCB broad macroeconomic projection exercise (BMPE) conducted by EARP. The model was first used as part of such an exercise in the spring of 2000. In this instance a non-model forecast was inputted as an update to the data and the model was solved for the resultant residuals. Where the residuals took on extreme values, the forecasts concerned were re-examined and, in certain cases, depending on the strength of non-model information, the forecasts were actually revised. Over time, however, the role played by the model in the projection exercise has diminished in view of the age of the model and, more recently, owing to the difficulties caused by the extreme values taken on by certain variables (such as the real interest rate) in an Irish context. It is expected that, once the new model is operational, its role will be expanded again. The lack of a long-run steady-state solution has also prevented the model from being used in a more extensive manner.

The scenario analyses conducted by EARP consider the impact on the Irish economy of changes in external circumstances, for example interest rate changes, exchange rate changes or an economic slowdown in Ireland's trading partners. Requests for such analyses arise from both inside and outside the CBFSAI. External requests arise from participation in ESCB projects while internal requests from within the CBFSAI can occur for a variety of reasons. For example, the Irish model has been used for stress-testing simulations conducted within the CBFSAI as a means of analysing the stability of the Irish banking system. To date, two sets of stress-testing exercises have been conducted using the macromodel. The first was in late 2000, while the second was conducted in summer 2003. The latter set of simulations included an exchange rate appreciation, a decline in equity prices (proxied by an increase in the user cost of capital) and a decline in world demand. Probabilities for the proposed shocks were then derived by interpolating density functions based on the historical data for the series in question.

An additional feature of the Irish modelling effort is the interpolation of quarterly data used in the model estimation. Official quarterly Irish national accounts are only available for some series from the mid-1990s onwards. As a result, a procedure based on Chow and Lin (1971) was used to interpolate components of the national accounts.[2] This procedure involved assembling an extensive range of annual data series, identifying and selecting indicator series for each data item and using these indicators to produce an inferred quarterly series using internally developed programmes. For example, quarterly data on the deflator for personal consumption are only available from 1990 onwards. The quarterly indicator used to interpolate the consumption series was the quarterly average of the retail sales index. Details of the procedure performed and the different indicators used in the Irish model-building exercise are available in McGuire, O'Donnell and Ryan (2002).

2   THE MODEL

The Irish model has a dual structure in that relationships between variables differ over different time horizons. An equilibrium structure is assumed for the economy which determines the long-run relationships. This structure is derived from economic theory but is tested rather than imposed on the data. The short-run relationships in the model are generated with less recourse to economic theory.[3] The long-run relationships are entered into the model as error correction terms in equations for the short-run development of variables. The model has not as yet reached the stage of having a long-run steady state. Notwithstanding the necessity for further work to ensure complete stability, the long-run properties of the model can still be usefully described in general terms.

The features of the model are essentially similar to the small-scale structural model described in Henry (1999). The level of real output is determined in the model as the interaction of aggregate supply and aggregate demand. Deviations of output from potential and unemployment from the natural rate cause wage and price adjustments to take place which return the model to a long-run neoclassical equilibrium. In this long run, aggregate supply is limited by the available labour supply and the production function of the economy so that the aggregate supply curve is vertical and the level of inflation is invariant to the equilibrium level of output.

The structure of the Irish model is now summarized in terms of the following main headings: (a) production function and factor demands, (b) components of aggregate demand, (c) prices and costs, (d) fiscal policy and the government sector, (e) trade and (f) monetary and financial sector.

2.1 Production Function and Factor Demands

In this section we discuss the long-run relationships for the supply side of the Irish model. The production function holds *in the long run* only. The economy can be off its production function at any point in time. This is because, in the short term, output is determined by demand and there is only a gradual adjustment of the demand for inputs. Thus the economy will only gradually move back onto the long-run production function. The model responds in this way because the factor demand relationships derived from the production function in the model are embedded as *long-run relationships* in the short-run factor demand equations. The sluggish adjustment of factor demands is both intuitively appealing and in line with the typical lagged response of employment to output across a range of economies.

The long-run behavioural relationships within the supply side of the Irish model are specified with a standard Cobb–Douglas (CD) production function specification with assumed constant returns to scale and Harrod-neutral technical progress. Other functional forms such as the constant elasticity of substitution (CES) have also been examined. In the long run, output, under the CD, is a function of capital and labour inputs and a constant rate of productivity growth due to labour-saving technical change:

$$\log(\text{full employment output}) = \log(\alpha) + \gamma^*(1-\beta)^*\text{Trend} + (1-\beta)^* \\ \log(\text{full employment level of labour}) \\ + \beta^*\log(\text{capital stock}), \qquad (11.1)$$

where the full employment level of labour is defined as the total labour force less the non-accelerating inflation rate of unemployment. This time-varying structural level of unemployment has been estimated using the Gordon (1997) approach as documented in Meyler (1999). The gap between the actual level of unemployment and this natural rate of unemployment helps to drive the economy back towards its long-run equilibrium through the wage and price equations of the model. The wage equation, for example, relates wage inflation to the gap between unemployment and the natural rate. If the natural rate is held constant then the Phillips curve, defined as the observed interaction between wage inflation and the actual unemployment rate, will be vertical. The failure actually to observe a vertical Phillips curve within the sample is attributed to movements in the natural rate, for example, the coexistence of falling unemployment and static wage inflation is explained by reductions in the natural rate.

A related concept of the unemployment gap variable is the output gap. This measures the difference between actual output and a measure of potential output. This measure of potential output is obtained by simulating the production function using current levels of capital stock and *potential* labour input, where potential labour input is the full employment level of labour defined above. This level of potential output is not equal to the long-run equilibrium level of output since the capital stock only adjusts slowly to its long-run level. Over time, as the capital stock adjustments take place, the two measures will converge. Consequently the output gap variable is related to the level of unused labour resources in the economy, which helps the model to adjust towards long-run equilibrium but does not represent this equilibrium at any point in time.

Using the parameter values from the estimation of (11.1), long-run equilibrium values are then derived for employment, capital stock and short-run marginal costs. Output prices are then scaled upwards by a parameter 'eta', which denotes the economy-wide assumption of imperfect competition, in order to arrive at an expression for long-run prices. These long-run values are then used as disequilibrium terms in short-run error correction models (ECM) for employment, investment and output prices.

There is no inherent mechanism to ensure that there is a stable equilibrium level of output in the long run. In order to achieve this there must be a stable equilibrium level of capital, which in turn implies that other variables settle down at stable levels, including both the real interest and the real exchange rate. The need for a stable real interest rate is intuitively sensible, but can be seen algebraically by noting that the marginal product condition from the production function results in the following: $\beta * GDP/capital\ stock = (r + \delta + v)$. This relates the marginal product of capital to the term in parentheses, which is the user cost of capital. This includes r, the real interest rate, along with the depreciation rate (δ) and a risk premium (v). The latter two elements are fixed so that, for GDP and capital stock to stabilize at their respective equilibrium levels, r must approach a stable value r^*. The requirement for a stable real effective exchange rate comes from the necessity for the components of aggregate demand to stabilize as a proportion of equilibrium output and to add up to equilibrium output in the long run: the net trade balance and consumption will not do so unless the real exchange rate stabilizes. The nominal level of interest rate and the exchange rate are exogenous variables in the model. The adjustment of these real variables, therefore, has to come about through developments in the domestic price level.

The only option as regards the nominal anchor for domestic prices would seem to be a link with external prices, given the small and open nature of the economy. The exchange rate is an exogenous variable and is used to translate foreign prices into domestic currency equivalents. These prices then work their way through a system of related price indices. In the final analysis, the level of external prices or inflation determines domestic price developments. If external inflation is set at a stable rate over a long-run simulation, the real interest rate and the real exchange rate will tend to settle down to equilibrium levels. The level of real output will then approach equilibrium through the mechanisms already described.[4]

2.2   Components of Aggregate Demand

Aggregate demand is made up of the usual output expenditure components. While government expenditure in real terms is treated as exogenous in the model, the other main elements are explicitly modelled.

Using neoclassical theory, personal consumption is modelled as having a long-run relationship with real private sector wealth. The resulting estimation conforms to this theory in that consumption is found to constitute a constant share of wealth.[5] Short-run deviations from the intertemporal household budget constraint are generated by changes in disposable income and credit availability, real interest rates and deviations from the long-run level of consumption.

Investment is determined by the gap between the actual and long-run equilibrium capital stock, with the latter being derived from the supply-side relationship between the marginal product of capital and the cost of capital. This term is used in the error correction term of the investment function, which also contains current and lagged changes in output. The latter adds an accelerator feature to the relationship. The actual level of the capital stock is obtained by the perpetual inventory method, whereby the current period's capital stock level is updated by taking the difference between last year's capital stock and depreciation levels and adding it to the contemporaneous level of gross investment. The annual depreciation rate is assumed to be 4 per cent.

The government and trade components of aggregate demand are described separately in Sections 2.4 and 2.5 of this chapter.

2.3 Prices and Costs

Given the small and open nature of the economy, the nominal anchor for domestic prices is a link with external prices. The exchange rate is an exogenous variable and is used to translate foreign prices into domestic currency equivalents. These prices then work their way through a system of related price indices. The nominal level of interest rates is also exogenous. In the final analysis, the level of external prices or inflation determines domestic price developments. If external inflation is set at a stable rate over a long-run simulation, the real interest rate and the real exchange rate should tend to settle down to equilibrium levels which, in turn, determine equilibrium output.

The three principal domestic wage and price equations in the model relate to wages per person employed, the GDP deflator and the consumption deflator. Other deflators relating to investment and government spending are derived from these and, where relevant, the import deflator within an ECM framework. Unlike other demand component deflators, the stock changes deflator is not separately determined, but rather is a residual item to ensure that the evolution of the individual deflators is consistent in aggregate with the GDP deflator so as to avoid 'adding-up' problems for nominal GDP and its components.

Wages and prices being the adjustment mechanism of the model in moving towards equilibrium, their long-run relationships and the degree of disequilibrium in the economy feature in their short-run behavioural equations. Long-run wages (total wages and salaries divided by total employment) are modelled using a wage mark-up model.[6] Long-run wages are set equal to output prices (GDP deflator) plus productivity (output per worker). The productivity term is adjusted to correct for possible distortions due to transfer pricing, and so is measured as real GNP per worker as opposed to GDP per worker. In the short run, wage dynamics are modelled as a function of the lag of wages, the deviation from the long run and the deviation from the time-varying NAIRU outlined in the supply side of the model. In general it was difficult to model the short-run dynamics of Irish wage inflation. For example, some variables were incorrectly signed and the coefficient on the error correction term, while correct, was very low. This may, in part, be due to the national rounds of wage bargaining in Ireland, which have been in place since 1988. These result in wage increases being agreed across most of the public and private sectors for a specified period of time (usually up to three years). An additional reason for the difficulties may be the close links between the Irish and UK labour markets.

The long-run level of the deflator is derived from an expression for short-run marginal costs which is multiplied by a competition parameter, as noted in the supply-side section of the model. As capital is assumed to adjust only sluggishly, it is regarded as fixed in the short run and so is treated as a constant in the production function when deriving short-run marginal costs. Wages per person employed, together with the level of output relative to the capital stock, are the principal factors in the short-run marginal costs function. The short-run movements in the GDP deflator depend principally on the ECM term, with lagged changes of the variables included.

The main concern of the long-run specification of consumer prices is to provide a means of capturing both internally generated price pressures and import price pass-through factors. The current long-run specification is based on a weighted average of domestic and foreign prices, although a purchasing power parity framework was also considered. Changes to foreign prices, arising from either trading partners' prices or the exchange rate, will feed into consumer prices via the import deflator and from there to the GDP deflator.[7] Short-run dynamics are represented in the usual ECM format.

Other deflators modelled within the Irish model include expressions for exports and imports, government consumption and capital formation and private capital formation. All of these are modelled as error correction models with relevant deviation from long-run equilibrium terms.

2.4 Fiscal Policy and the Government Sector

A basic fiscal block is included in the Irish model. The general government block is mainly made up of identities for variables such as public consumption, budget balance, public savings, net government lending and consolidated debt of the government. The interest payments on government debt are also exogenous in the model.

The only behavioural equation estimated in the government block is that for transfers to households. The change in transfers is specified as a function of lagged changes in transfers, the change in the unemployment level and the lagged change in nominal GDP. Indirect taxes in nominal terms are modelled as a product of an exogenous indirect tax rate and an indirect tax base. The tax base is composed of expenditure by households, by the government, firms' investment and exports. Direct taxes in nominal terms are modelled as the product of an exogenous direct tax rate and a direct tax base. The direct tax base depends on the total remuneration of employees, nominal transfers to households and other income. While direct and indirect tax rates are, at present, exogenous in the fiscal block, later versions of the model may include some sort of fiscal reaction function involving tax rates to help stabilize the model in long-run simulations.

2.5 Trade

The foreign trade block of the Irish model comprises long- and short-run equations for real imports and exports. Nominal imports and exports are identities obtained by multiplying the real variables by their respective deflators. Long-run relationships are established between trade volumes and measures of external demand and weighted domestic demand along with appropriate relative price measures. Short-run dynamics are represented by the standard ECM formulation, including the ECM term and lagged changes in the variables.

Long-run exports are modelled as a function of world demand and competitiveness. Data on world demand and competitors' prices are supplied by the ECB. The estimated results of this long-run relationship conform very closely with a priori expectations concerning a small open economy: Irish exports have a unitary elasticity with respect to world demand, while exports are highly price elastic *vis-à-vis* relative prices. In the associated short-run equation for exports, the long-run relationship is included as an error correction term.

The long-run imports equation is specified as a function of weighted demand and a relative prices variable. The weighted demand variable was constrained to have an elasticity equal to unity and relative prices yielded a relatively inelastic effect. The weighted demand variable is compiled with weights obtained from input–output tables and includes personal consumption, government consumption, investment and exports. The resulting short-run expression for imports includes the ECM term and changes in weighted demand.

In terms of the balance of payments, international transfers are an exogenous variable in the model. Given the value of nominal imports and exports, the remaining component of the current account is net factor income. In modelling net factor incomes, we have used a somewhat non-standard specification as, in the past, we found that net factor outflows are closely related to the levels of nominal exports. This is mainly due to the presence of the foreign-owned high-technology sector, where export earnings and factor income flows are very closely related. Remaining factor flows such as interest payments on the national debt are quite small in comparison with the outflow of profits from this sector. Thus net factor income is specified as a function of current and lagged nominal exports.

2.6 Monetary and Financial Sector

All interest rates used in the model are exogenously determined and are not currently linked to one another. Thus, for the purposes of any simulation conducted, all rates are changed. Short-term interest rates are adjusted for inflation using the consumption deflator.

3   SCENARIO SIMULATIONS

The aim of this section is to illustrate whole model properties by providing descriptions of different simulations, which have been performed on the model. The simulations consist of a monetary policy shock, a fiscal policy shock, a foreign demand shock, an exchange rate shock and an oil price increase. For the most part, the results presented are based solely on the model (with the exception of the oil simulation: see 3.5 below). In practice, if the results were being used as an input to policy formation, some might be augmented by judgmental input if judged appropriate.[8]

3.1 A Monetary Policy Shock

This simulation was part of an exercise carried out by the WGEM to assess the monetary transmission process. The short-term interest rate was increased by 100 basis points for two years. The long-term interest rate also increased following a simple interest parity condition and the exchange rate appreciated in line with an uncovered interest rate parity condition. The results for both real and nominal variables most affected by the scenario are presented in Figure 11.1.

Overall the effects on prices and output are small. Output remains below the baseline throughout the simulation period. The initial impact on GDP is a reduction of 0.2 per cent below the baseline in year 1, reaching its maximum effect in year 2. Considering the components of GDP,

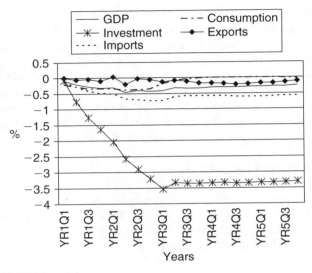

Source: Irish MCM model.

*Figure 11.1a   Simulation of a 100 bp increase in the short-term interest
rates for five years*

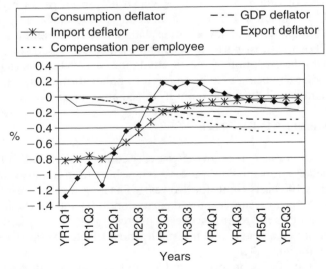

Source: Irish MCM model.

*Figure 11.1b   Simulation of a 100 bp increase in the short-term interest
rates for five years*

investment and imports are most strongly affected. Owing to the strong accelerator effect in the Irish model, the effect on investment remains strong by year 5 when it is 3.3 per cent below the baseline. Consumption falls below the baseline in the order of 0.30 per cent–0.36 per cent in the first two years, begins to recover above the baseline as the monetary policy shock ends, but then falls from year 5 onwards, as real income and real wealth are also falling.

Imports follow closely the pattern of GDP and begin to recover after year 2. Exports are undermined by the exchange rate appreciation before starting to recover towards the end of the five-year period.

Prices begin to respond immediately to the monetary shock. The trade deflators reflect the impact of the exchange rate appreciation; the export deflator falls by more or less the full amount of the appreciation, reflecting the high degree of price-taking behaviour. The private consumption deflator is close on 0.2 per cent below the baseline after five years. The GDP deflator falls steadily until year 5, reflecting the deflationary impacts of the shock.

Compensation per employee falls steadily under this scenario and, by year 5, it is almost 0.5 per cent below its baseline level.

3.2   A Fiscal Policy Shock

A simulation of a five-year increase in government consumption of magnitude 1 per cent of initial GDP is now described. The increase in government spending is assumed to take the form of an increase in goods and services purchased from the private sector and not an increase in government employment. Over a five-year period a 1 per cent of GDP increase amounts to an average increase in government spending of 5.2 per cent per annum. Figure 11.2 plots the evolution of the main variables affected by the increased government expenditure.

The increase in government spending boosts all elements of demand. The initial multiplier effect is just over 1. As the simulation horizon increases, lower unemployment eventually drives up wages. The consequent loss in competitiveness starts to erode exports, which are around 1.2 per cent below baseline after ten years. This slows the growth in output, which actually peaks in year 2 of the simulation.

3.3   A Foreign Demand Shock

In this simulation, the level of world demand is increased by 1 per cent for five years. In the Irish case, the increase is weighted by 0.6, the proportion of Irish exports which are sold outside the euro area. Figure 11.3 summarizes the temporal impact of the scenario.

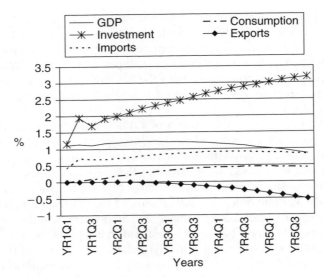

Figure 11.2a   *Simulation of a rise in real government consumption by*
1% of GDP for five years

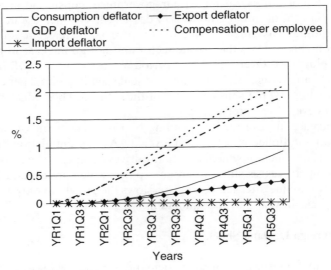

Figure 11.2b   *Simulation of a rise in real government consumption by*
1% of GDP for five years

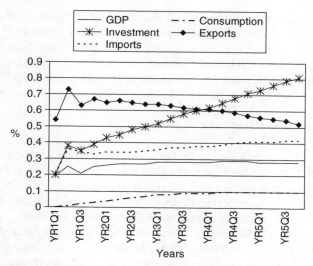

Source: Irish MCM model.

Figure 11.3a   Simulation of a 1% rise in export market volumes for five years

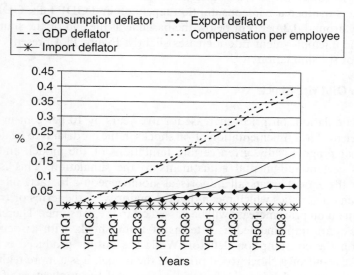

Source: Irish MCM model.

Figure 11.3b   Simulation of a 1% rise in export market volumes for five years

The increase in demand boosts all elements of the expenditure account through its impact on exports and investment. There is some small upward impact on the deflators. Unemployment falls slightly and wages increase but unit labour costs fall initially owing to an increase in productivity. After five years, investment is 0.8 per cent above the baseline, exports 0.5 per cent above, down slightly from their peak, and GDP 0.3 per cent above.

3.4 An Exchange Rate Shock

In this simulation, the euro strengthens for five years by 1 per cent against all currencies. In the Irish case, the shock is weighted by 0.715, which is the average of the non-euro area weights in Irish imports and exports. The appreciation has the expected downward impact on the trade deflators. The export deflator falls by almost the full amount of the shock, reflecting the high degree of price-taking behaviour. There is quite a small degree of pass-through from the imports deflator to the private consumption deflator, reflecting the low coefficient on the import deflator in the long-run private consumption deflator equation (0.205).

Exports and investment are reduced by the appreciation but consumption receives a slight boost from the increase in real wealth (due to the falling price level). Imports also increase slightly initially but fall below the baseline as the increase in consumption tapers off and GDP falls. GDP is down by around 0.2 per cent below the baseline at the end of the simulation. The unemployment rate increases slightly. Figure 11.4 presents the results for the simulation.

3.5 An Oil Price Shock

In this simulation, oil prices increase for five years by 10 per cent in US dollar terms. The implementation of oil shocks in the model has to be done somewhat pragmatically, given certain limitations of the model, and so involves certain judgmental adjustments to the simulation. This is so because the model treats all imports as homogeneous. In fact, oil has certain characteristics which mean that the majority of the terms of trade loss from an oil price increase will be passed on to the consumer. Therefore oil shocks are implemented as a terms of trade shock, with associated effects on the consumption deflator. While the output produced is not solely the result of a shock to oil prices in the model, it is a more realistic outcome to an oil shock and a better illustration of the application of the model in this regard.

The oil price increase causes the import deflator to rise by about 0.3 per cent over the baseline. The impact on the private consumption deflator is

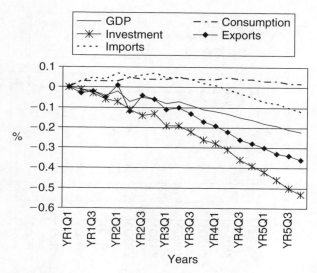

Source: Irish MCM model.

Figure 11.4a   *Simulation of a 1% rise in the euro effective exchange rate for five years*

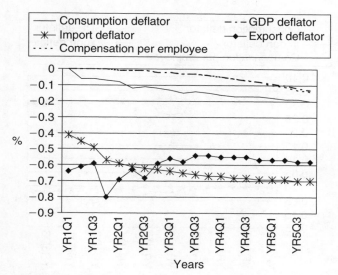

Source: Irish MCM model.

Figure 11.4b   *Simulation of a 1% rise in the euro effective exchange rate for five years*

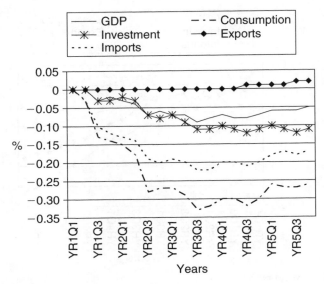

Source: Irish MCM model.

Figure 11.5a   Simulation of a 10% rise in the price of oil for five years

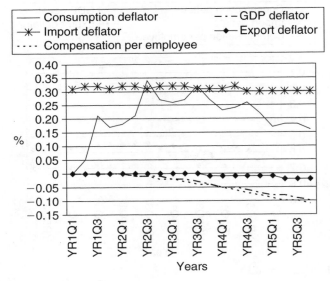

Source: Irish MCM model.

Figure 11.5b   Simulation of a 10% rise in the price of oil for five years

an increase of about 0.2 per cent, on average, over the five years. Both imports and private consumption fall steadily relative to their baseline levels, with imports down 0.2 per cent and consumption down 0.3 per cent by year 5. Investment is down by just over 0.1 per cent relative to its baseline level in year 5, reflecting the marginal decline in GDP over the same period. Figure 11.5 summarizes the impact of the oil price shock.

4   CONCLUSIONS

The rationale for undertaking economic modelling work is to assist policy makers through forecasts and simulations. The development work on a structural macroeconometric model has been undertaken in this context. It is very much 'work in progress' at present and it has not yet reached the stage where full use can be made of the model. Considerable advances have been made on a number of fronts, however, which provide a basis for further development and refinement. For example, procedures have been put in place to interpolate quarterly data from annual national accounts aggregates, so that this exercise can be repeated with relative ease. Diagnostic simulations designed to test the response of the model to various shocks and to determine its long-run steady-state properties have also been carried out. This process has helped to highlight the strengths and weaknesses of the model structure, determining the work programme for model improvement. The necessary software and econometric infrastructure have been put in place to allow for estimation and simulation, not only of internal models, but also of other models produced elsewhere, both inside and outside the Eurosystem.

As the model does not as yet converge to a long-run steady state, its main strength lies in the analysis of short-term dynamics. In that regard the model has been a source of valuable input both in the forecasting process and as a tool for scenario analysis within the EARP department of the CBFSAI. Model development has continued and a new model has been estimated over a longer time horizon (1980–99). At present, work is almost complete on the reprogramming of the re-estimated model, which incorporates some changes highlighted by the diagnostic simulations. In addition, the new model will include some extensions *vis-à-vis* its predecessor. For instance, the new model treats capital differently, in that a distinction is now made between non-residential and residential capital stock. This partly reflects the increased importance of the Irish property market since the mid-1990s and has entailed the addition of a housing model to the existing supply side of the Irish MCM template (see McQuinn, 2004). The addition of such a model will be of particular benefit, for instance, in the future performance of stress-testing exercises aimed at evaluating the sensitivity of the domestic property sector to changes in macroeconomic variables.

NOTES

1. The model team were Mairead Devine, John Frain, Daniel McCoy, Maurice McGuire, Aidan Meyler and Mary Ryan.
2. A RATS subroutine to implement the Chow and Lin interpolation procedure was developed in EARP and is available on the CBFSAI website (www.centralbank.ie). Please see 2/RT/04, 'A RATS subroutine to implement the Chow–Lin distribution/ interpolation procedure', J. Frain.
3. All relevant variables are initially included in the short-term dynamics with a wide range of lags but only those that are statistically significant are retained.
4. Initial estimation of the model may not yield a long-run steady-state solution. A number of refinements may have to be made to ensure this. These will typically include some policy reactions such as a fiscal policy rule designed to prevent an explosion in the debt to GDP ratio.
5. While real human wealth is calculated in the model, it does not feed back into the wealth variable in the consumption function. The wealth variable in the consumption function relates to financial wealth only. It should also be noted that more recently estimated long-run consumption equations include disposable income in addition to wealth.
6. An alternative formulation examined was a consumer-based model (using the personal consumption deflator and take-home wages). However it was felt that this latter approach did not yield significant improvements on the initial model.
7. There may be some role for domestic developments influencing the domestic price level, such as a change in the NAIRU. This does not cut across the idea that external prices form a nominal anchor in the sense that, in a very long-run simulation with the exogenous variables held constant, or growing at a realistic rate, the domestic rate of inflation will be determined by external developments.
8. The following assumptions underpin all the simulations: no monetary or fiscal rules are in operation, no changes to the exchange rate are made apart from those specified and wages are endogenously determined.

REFERENCES

Chow, G. and A. Lin (1971), 'Best linear unbiased interpolation, distribution and extrapolation of time series by related series', *Review of Economics and Statistics*, **53**, 372–5.

Frain, J. (2004), 'A RATS subroutine to implement the Chow–Lin distribution/ interpolation procedure', *Central Bank and Financial Services Authority of Ireland Technical Paper Series*, 2/RT/04.

Gordon R. (1997), 'The time-varying NAIRU and its implications for economic policy', *Journal of Economic Perspectives*, **11** (1), 11–32.

Henry, J. (1999), 'Euro area-wide and country modelling at the start of EMU', *Economic and Financial Modelling*, Autumn, 103–48.

McGuire, M. and M. Ryan (2000), 'Macroeconomic modelling developments in the central bank', *Central Bank of Ireland Quarterly Bulletin*, Spring, 77–90.

McGuire, M., N. O'Donnell and M. Ryan (2002), 'Interpolation of quarterly data for ECB/NCB multicountry modelling exercise – data update to 1999Q4', *Central Bank of Ireland Research Paper*, 1/R/02.

McQuinn, K. (2004), 'A model of the Irish housing sector', *Central Bank and Financial Services Authority of Ireland Technical Paper Series*, 1/RT/04.

Meyler, A. (1999), 'The non-accelerating inflation rate of unemployment (NAIRU) in a small open economy: the Irish context', *Central Bank of Ireland Technical Paper Series*, 5/RT/99.

12.   The Bank of Italy's quarterly model

Fabio Busetti, Alberto Locarno and Libero Monteforte

1   INTRODUCTION AND HISTORY

The Bank of Italy quarterly model (BIQM) is a new version of the model developed in the mid-1980s by a team of economists of the Research Department supervised by Albert Ando (Banca d'Italia, 1986). The architecture of this model had its foundations in previous modelling experience at the Bank, in particular M1BI (Banca d'Italia, 1970) and M2BI (Fazio and Sitzia, 1979) developed under the supervision of Franco Modigliani, but it also represented a major improvement in many respects. It integrated new time series results on cointegration and error correction specification; it reconstructed in detail the flow of funds of the economy; it benefited from the experience of the large-scale macroeconometric models of the 1980s, particularly the MPS of the US economy (Brayton and Mauskopf, 1985); it incorporated specific institutional mechanisms of the Italian economy. For example, the model's Phillips curve was adapted to the changes in the bargaining framework agreed upon by the social partners in July 1993, in particular the dismissal of automatic indexation and the substitute mechanism for recovering price increases in excess of the inflation target. Since the presentation of the first release, the BIQM has continuously evolved to take account of new data sources, changed institutional frameworks and a variety of expectations formation mechanisms and policy rules. More recently the model has been adapted to the ESA-95 standard of national accounts and to the introduction of the euro.

2   THE USES OF THE MODEL

The BIQM serves several purposes, the main one being to provide short- and medium-term projections. It is also used in policy evaluation exercises, for assessing the policy mix which is best suited for enhancing social welfare and in counterfactual analyses, in which actual developments in the economy or policy proposals are contrasted with fictitious alternatives so as to gain a better understanding of the costs and benefits inherent in economic actions. Finally the BIQM helps organize and coordinate economic analysis within the Research Department of the Bank of Italy.

The model contains some 800 equations, nearly 100 of which are stochastic. All equations are estimated by limited-information techniques, mostly ordinary least squares. A limited set of parameters, in particular some of those related to the user cost of capital, is calibrated. The software package used for estimation and simulation is Speakeasy/Modeleasy+.

3   AN OUTLINE OF THE THEORETICAL UNDERPINNINGS OF THE MODEL

The BIQM models separately the public and the private sector and, within the latter, distinguishes among energy, agriculture and the rest. As with most macroeconometric models, it is Keynesian in the short run, with the level of economic activity primarily determined by the behaviour of aggregate demand, and neoclassical in the long run, akin to the Solow model of exogenous growth. Along a steady-state growth path, the dynamics of the model stems solely from capital accumulation, productivity growth, foreign inflation and demographics; in the short run, a number of additional features matter, namely the stickiness of prices and wages, the putty-clay nature of the production process and inflation surprises.

In equilibrium, that is when no shocks affect the model, expectations are fulfilled and all adjustment processes are completed, the BIQM describes a full employment economy, in which output, employment and the capital stock are consistent with an aggregate production function, relative prices are constant and inflation equals the exogenous rate of growth of foreign prices. Money is neutral, though not super-neutral, and the model is stable.

The theoretical structure underlying the steady state is a traditional one. The supply sector can be thought of as being composed of producers who are price setters in output market and price takers in factor markets. Each producer, being endowed with the same Cobb–Douglas constant-returns-to-scale technology, knows the minimum average cost of his competitors and fixes the level of the mark-up so as to keep potential entrants out of business. Along a steady-state growth path, firms decide in each period the cost-minimizing factor mix and the level of domestic activity is then set to generate, given factor demands, a non-accelerating-inflation rate of unemployment. Life cycle consumers choose the desired addition to the real stock of total wealth, which is then allocated among foreign assets, physical capital and government debt,[1] and the real exchange rate adjusts so as to balance supply and demand and to clear capital markets. As consumers compute their lifetime resources without anticipating the need for the government to satisfy a long-run solvency condition, the stock of public debt is perceived to be part of total wealth and Ricardian equivalence does not hold.

A detailed description of the theoretical underpinnings of the BIQM is in Banca d'Italia (1986). Other useful descriptions of the main features of the model are Galli *et al.* (1989), Terlizzese (1994) and Siviero (1995).

3.1 Production Function and Factor Demands

The supply-side block of the BIQM hinges on a Cobb–Douglas production function and on the assumption that, since capital is non-malleable, the choice of productive factors is limited to the expansion of existing stocks. In each period, given demand expectations, firms set the desired addition to capacity. Cost minimization yields the optimal capital–output and labour–output ratios, k_t^* and l_t^* respectively, and the minimum average cost associated with one additional unit of production.

Desired (net) capital accumulation is therefore equal to $i_t^* = k_t^* \Delta v_{t+1}^e$, where v_t is the production output and the superscript e indicates expectation. Since it takes time to produce and deliver capital goods, actual and planned investment differ, with the former being a weighted average of the most recent values of the latter. Allowing for depreciation, expectations[2] and delivery lags, the previous expression becomes

$$i_t = \sum_{i=0}^{q} \beta_{1i} k_{t-i-1}^* v_{t-i} + \sum_{i=1}^{q+1} \beta_{2i} k_{t-i}^* v_{t-i}$$

where i_t denotes (gross) actual investment; in general, the first set of coefficients is positive while the remaining ones are negative. As is typical with models assuming that capital is putty-clay, investment reacts to changes in demand and changes in relative factor price differently: while in the first instance the shape of the response conforms to the accelerator principle, in the second it is smooth and monotone.

Associated with each vintage of capital is a fixed amount of labour which is needed to operate the new machinery and an efficient quantity of output which can be produced with it. The equations modelling employment and potential output are accordingly derived from the parameters of the investment function and from the sequence of vintages of new capital.

The demand for labour is determined in a stepwise procedure: first, as shown above, cost minimization determines the optimal labour-to-output ratio l_t^* for the planned addition to capacity Δv_{t+1}^e; then the labour requirement of the last vintage of *installed* rather than desired investment is derived; finally the demand for labour associated with the overall stock of capital is computed. Frictions and adjustment costs make total employment differ temporarily from the desired value. The labour demand function is then modelled as an error correction mechanism where the long-run employment is driven by the labour requirement associated with the existing capital stock.

The equilibrium relationship between desired investment and capacity, $i_t^* = k_t^* \Delta v_{t+1}^e$, represents the building block for modelling potential output as well. The optimal capital–output ratio may be viewed as a conversion factor mapping desired addition to production capacity into capital accumulation. By setting $k_t^* = 1$ in the investment equation, one can therefore obtain a measure of the desired *gross* addition to capacity which is consistent with capital accumulation: the level of potential output is obtained by cumulating the *net* addition to capacity corresponding to each vintage of capital; see Parigi and Siviero (2001).

3.2 Components of Aggregate Demand

The BIQM does not distinguish between households and firms; the explanatory variables in the equations modelling consumption accordingly refer to the private sector as a whole. Consumption of non-durables and durables is treated separately. The former is modelled consistently with the life cycle theory and is driven by permanent income, proxied by a weighted average of disposable income and wealth. Disposable income is computed by adjusting for the capital gains/losses on financial assets engendered by changes in the inflation rate. Since wealth is not measured at market value, the real interest rate is included among the explanatory variables. The demand for durables is driven by total consumption expenditure: its share depends on the relative price of durable goods and on the long-term interest rate.

The equation for housing investment relies on a variant of Tobin's *q* model: residential capital depends on the present value of the future streams of profits (proxied by the market price) of an additional unit of capital. Financing constraints are accounted for by using the expected real interest rate as an explanatory variable and a time trend is included to capture demographic effects on the total demand for houses; fiscal factors also play a role in the equation. The interaction between supply and demand for houses, the latter modelled as a portfolio allocation problem, determines the market price.

Equipment investment is modelled as described in Section 3.1. The equation for non-residential construction investment has an error correction specification with long-run homogeneity restrictions with respect to the output in the private sector; additional covariates are the real interest rate and a business confidence indicator.

3.3 Prices and Costs

The pricing strategies of firms are described by the equations modelling the private sector value-added deflators (at factor costs). Prices are set as a mark-up on marginal costs. In equilibrium, marginal and minimum average costs coincide and are proportional to unit labour costs. The mark-up is assumed to depend on the prices set by foreign competitors and on cyclical conditions, measured by the real exchange rate and the output gap, respectively. Deflators of aggregate demand components are modelled as a function of import and value-added deflators.[3]

A Phillips curve relation completes the price–wage block: wage inflation depends with unit elasticity on price changes, measured by a convex combination of expected and actual (past) inflation, and on the rate of unemployment. Specific features of the Italian wage setting are taken into account. The degree of utilized capacity is also included as a proxy for vacancies; a measure of union power is provided by the number of working hours lost due to strikes. Indirect taxes, social contributions and terms of trade have an impact on wages by affecting consumer prices. In equilibrium, the Phillips curve determines the NAIRU, while the price equation determines the factor shares in income distribution.

3.4 Fiscal Policy and the Government Sector

The model includes a detailed description of the items composing the government budget. No ad hoc policy rule is incorporated, but, whenever possible, the equations try and reflect the legal framework shaping the behaviour of the government sector. Those components of the budget balance which are more closely related to the implementation of fiscal policies, like consumption of goods and services and investment, are linked to GDP and to an exogenous variable capturing the discretionary impulses from the government. Automatic stabilizers turn out to be quite powerful and contribute to making the model border line stable.

Revenues are modelled both on a cash and on an accrual basis. The main items are direct taxes (disaggregated into taxes on wages, profits and capital income; and indirect taxes) distinguished according to whether they are levied on value added or on quantity sold; and social contributions, split into contributions paid by employers and contributions paid by employees. On the expenditure side, the main items are transfers (mostly pensions), wages and interest payments.

The financial behaviour of the public sector is described by the overall supply of government debt, distinguished according to maturity, and by the interest rate set on Treasury bonds. Borrowing requirements, net of changes in the stock of monetary base,[4] determine the total amount of new issues of Treasury securities, while yields-to-maturity determine the structure of government debt. The equation for the long-term interest rate reflects the desired composition of government debt and is consistent with the demand curve of the private sector. It sets the long-term rate as a function of the three-month Treasury bill rate and of a time-varying risk premium, which depends asymmetrically on interest rate volatility: when interest rates are rising, the risk premium which must be paid by the issuer increases; when interest rates are falling, the risk premium remains unchanged.

3.5 The Trade Equations

Several equations are devoted in the BIQM to modelling imports and exports. Services, agricultural goods and energy products are modelled separately from other goods. No distinction is made between trade with the euro area and trade with the rest of the world.

The modelling of the demand for imports and exports relies on the assumption of imperfect substitutability between foreign and domestic goods. In accordance with demand theory, imports may be viewed as the solution to the maximization problem of a representative consumer, who acts taking into account a budget constraint. Separability and homogeneity of the utility function ensure that the saving decision and consumption allocation – in particular the choice between domestic and foreign goods – can be treated separately. Absence of money illusion is imposed by considering relative prices and real income.[5] The scale variable driving imports is a weighted average of aggregate demand components, with exports and investments in machinery having the largest weights, in accordance with input–output tables; the degree of utilized capacity is included in the specification so as to capture the fact that sudden changes in domestic demand are initially more than proportionally met by foreign production.

Exports are modelled in a similar way: the scale variable is world imports and the degree of utilized capacity is used as a proxy for non-price competitiveness. Both imports and exports have unit elasticity as regards to their respective scale variables.

3.6 The Monetary and Financial Sector

The monetary and financial block of the BIQM fully tracks the flow of funds within the economy. It provides a detailed description of the portfolio decisions of economic agents: for given financial balances of the private and public sector, the former determined by consumption and investment choices and the latter by the objectives of the fiscal policy, the block generates gross flows of assets and liabilities and specifies how they are allocated among different instruments. Changes in the net foreign position are explicitly considered so that the model satisfies the private and public sector budget constraints with reference to total financial assets and total credit.

The theoretical framework underlying the monetary and financial block is to a large extent the one outlined in Ando and Modigliani (1975) and conforms to the methodology that is used to underlie the MPS econometric model. Agents make their financial choices hierarchically: they first choose the amount of money they want to hold in order to finance their transactions and then allocate their wealth among the remaining assets according to their risk–return preferences. Substitutability among assets is not perfect, since lenders and borrowers have their preferred point in maturity along the term structure, as suggested by the preferred habitat theory: returns vary from period to period depending on future expectations of the real interest rate and of the inflation rate, with volatility on financial markets and relative asset supply influencing the term premia. In order to ensure that agents satisfy their budget constraints, the demand function for a few assets (specifically those which seem to be more volatile) is derived as a residual, under the implicit assumption that they play the role of shock absorbers.

The monetary and financial section of the BIQM is composed of more than 200 equations, of which some 30 are stochastic. It describes the financial position of seven categories of economic agents (central bank, banks, government, households, firms, mutual funds and rest of the world)[6] and how their assets and liabilities are allocated among eight groups of instruments (currency, deposits, compulsory reserves, repos, short-term securities, long-term securities, loans, mutual funds shares). Each market is described by a demand function and an inverted supply equation, in which the endogenous variable is the relevant interest rate. The structure of the block is designed so as to provide a detailed account of the channels through which the central bank affects the economy via portfolio adjustment in the monetary and financial markets and therefore focuses on the market for shorter-term maturity instruments and on those 'intermediate' variables which are (or were) used as information variables for the conduct of monetary policy. The model therefore includes a detailed description of the working of the money market: the central bank controls liquidity conditions through open market operations and hence affects the inter-bank market and the market for Treasury securities. Term structure equations link the return on fixed-income long-term Treasury bonds to the three-month Treasury bill rate. For policy simulation purposes, the exchange rate responds to changes in the spread between domestic (euro area) interest rates and foreign rates and adjusts according to an uncovered interest parity relation.

3.7 A Summary of the Single Equation Properties of the BIQM

All equations in the BIQM are specified so as to ensure convergence to a steady-state growth path: demand components driven by domestic economic activity have unit elasticity with respect to output; exports increase one-to-one with world demand and are homogeneous with respect to domestic and foreign prices; prices and wages show no-money illusion, with the former linked to foreign inflation and the latter growing, in real terms, with trend productivity; capital and labour (in efficiency units) move in line with domestic value added.

The single-equation properties of the core equations of the BIQM are reported in Table 12.1. Given that the BIQM distinguishes between consumption of durables and of non-durables, between trade in goods and in services, between public and private sector, and disaggregates the latter into three subsectors, the figures listed Table 12.1 are to be interpreted as referring, not to single equations, but to blocks of equations. The table lists the responses (percentage deviations from baseline after 1, 2, 5 and 10 years) of the main variables to a permanent 10 per cent shock in their determinants. The employment equation and the Phillips curve refer to the non-farm non-energy private sector.

4 AN OUTLINE OF THE KEY CHARACTERISTICS

In order to evaluate the properties of the BIQM, a few exogenous variables have been subjected to shock and the response of the system analysed. The monetary policy experiment is conducted under the assumption that the policy tightening is not coordinated with other central banks and that exchange rates move according to a UIP condition.

4.1 A 100 Basis Point Shock to the Short-term Interest Rate sustained for Two Years

The monetary policy tightening induces a contraction in economic activity and a decrease in the price level. Output reaches a trough in the second year after the shock and gradually recovers thereafter, when the initial policy impulse vanishes. Investment is the component of aggregate

Table 12.1   *Response of main equations to 10% shock to key*
                 determinants‡

	Year 1	Year 2	Year 5	Year 10
Investment				
Output	8.2	19.9	16.2	10.2
Real user cost of capital	−1.1	−2.9	−5.5	−5.9
Employment‡				
Output	2.1	4.6	8.3	9.8
Real wages	0	−0.1	−0.6	−1.8
Output deflator				
Nominal wages	2.4	5.6	8.0	8.1
Import prices	1.3	1.8	1.9	1.8
Wages				
Consumption deflator	7.2	10.6	10.4	10.0
Unemployment rate*	−0.1	−0.1	−0.1	−0.1
Consumption deflator				
GDP deflator	6.7	9.8	9.3	9.2
Import prices	0.4	0.7	0.7	0.8
Export prices				
External prices	3.6	4.3	4.4	4.7
Domestic prices	5.8	5.6	5.6	5.2
Import prices				
External prices	9.1	9.1	9.1	9.1
Energy prices	0.9	0.9	0.9	0.9
Private consumption				
Disposable income	1.6	4.6	7.6	6.9
Wealth	0.2	1.1	2.7	3.0
Real interest rate	−0.2	−0.4	−0.6	−0.3
Export volume				
World demand	8.8	9.2	9.7	9.9
Competitiveness	4.9	9.8	17.5	21.6
Import volume				
Domestic demand	13.7	11.7	10.1	10.0
Competitiveness	−4.1	−8.0	−10.7	−10.8

Notes: (‡) Employment refers only to the private non-farm non-energy sector;
(*) temporary shock for one quarter.

demand which is most affected by the worsening of financing conditions, while consumption fluctuations are partly dampened by the positive effect on disposable income ensuing from the exchange rate appreciation and from the decrease in the price level. Net exports benefit from the contraction engendered by the initial shock and contribute to mitigating the slowdown in economic activity. The decrease in the import deflator is immediately reflected in the HICP, while it takes approximately two years for the slowdown in GDP growth to affect prices. The fall in output translates with some delay into job cuts: the increase in the unemployment rate becomes sizable only in the third year. This evidence is fully consistent with the price stickiness observed in oligopolistic markets and with capital being non-malleable: the first feature implies that changes in marginal costs are transmitted to prices slowly, with the mark-up buffering shocks to unit labour costs, while the second one justifies the smooth adjustment of labour demand and the limited response of both wages and productivity to shifts in factor prices.

4.2 A Five-year Increase by 1 per cent of GDP in Government Consumption

In the first year of the experiment, the fiscal stimulus results in a rise of GDP roughly in line with the size of the shock itself: while the surge in government consumption boosts, albeit modestly, consumption and investment, the deterioration in net trade compensates to a large extent the expansion in household and business spending. It takes a few years for the full effect of the initial shock to show up, since initially a sizable part of the increase in demand is met by foreign production. The Keynesian multiplier reaches its highest value of 1.39 in the third year and it takes even longer for domestic demand to reach its maximum.

Spurred by the surge in activity, inflation starts rising from the second year onwards and remains higher than in the baseline for most of the simulation horizon: under the assumption of fixed nominal short-term interest rates, which corresponds to a lax monetary policy stance, the rise in inflation engendered by the fiscal stimulus results in a decline in real interest rates and contributes to amplifying the impact on activity and prices of the initial shock. The reaction of capital accumulation follows the typical accelerator pattern; construction investment is the component whose response is more gradual and delayed. Investment is uniformly higher than in the baseline, fostered by the pick-up in real wages and the fall in real interest rates, both factors engendering a decrease in the relative cost of capital. Consumer spending increases as well, but less markedly, because the capital losses on (non-indexed) financial wealth, stemming from the acceleration of prices, attenuate the effects on disposable income of the policy-induced upturn. Net exports steadily decrease, reflecting first the expansion in imports driven by the delayed adjustment of production to the higher level of aggregate demand and then the deterioration in competitiveness ensuing from the increase in domestic prices. Labour dishoarding and the unfavourable change in relative factor prices delay the reaction of private sector employment to the fiscal stimulus. Excess demand in both labour and goods markets results in significant and persistent inflationary pressures: after five years the HICP is some 2 percentage points higher than in the baseline.

From the sixth year on, the vanishing of the fiscal impulse and the loss in competitiveness trim down the pace of expansion of economic activity. The increasing slackness in the labour market gradually engenders a reversal in the dynamics of unit labour cost; profit margins, which decreased initially, partially recover along with the slowdown in production costs. In the tenth year after the initial shock, inflation is lower than in the baseline; GDP, though still falling, seems to have more or less reached the trough and appears to benefit from the working of fiscal stabilizers and from the gradual recovery of competitiveness conditions.

4.3   A Five-year Increase by 1 per cent of Non-euro Area Imports

Exports rise in response to stronger foreign demand, but the response in GDP is sizably attenuated by the leakage due to the surge in imports. The market share of Italian goods shrinks slightly as world demand expands, because of the lag with which exports react to the shock and also as a result of the increase in domestic demand; the latter induces firms to shift their production to fulfil first domestic demand in the short term. As demand pressures build up, prices rise, with a one- or two-year lag, and competitiveness deteriorates, attenuating the initial boost provided by the rise in world demand. As the initial stimulus is reversed, output rapidly falls below baseline.

4.4   A Five-year 1 per cent Appreciation of the Euro Exchange Rate

The temporary euro appreciation engenders a contraction in exports, which persistently depresses GDP. Investment is, among the components of domestic demand, the one most sharply affected by the initial shock, also being hit by the increase in the real rental cost of capital associated with the reduction in inflation ensuing from the appreciation (nominal short-term interest rates are assumed to remain unchanged at their baseline levels); consumer spending, by contrast, does not react at all in the first half of the simulation horizon and then starts rising, benefiting from the increase in disposable income induced by the slowdown in price dynamics. Employment adjusts slowly to the lower level of economic activity, thanks also to the favourable change in the relative cost of labour. The current account initially improves, owing to the J-curve effect, but then deteriorates, reflecting the competitiveness loss following the appreciation of the domestic currency. Prices fall on impact as the exchange rate appreciates; the initial movement is subsequently amplified by the contraction in aggregate demand. As the initial shock vanishes, prices start reverting to the baseline values.

4.5 A Five-year Increase by 10 per cent in Oil Prices

The increase in oil prices is rapidly transmitted to the import deflator and hence to domestic prices. The surge in energy prices heavily affects real disposable income and consumption; the latter remains below baseline for almost the whole simulation period. The deterioration in competitiveness depresses exports (it should be emphasized, however, that this effect would be lower than estimated here if one took into account the impact of the oil price hike on the price of competitors). Output decelerates, and so does investment, because of the accelerator mechanism. The current account deteriorates, reflecting the worsening of the terms of trade. The slackness engendered by the economic slowdown gradually offsets the inflationary impulses associated with the increase in oil prices: four years after the initial shock, the GDP deflator is below the baseline value, which helps to restore competitiveness conditions and sustain disposable income. Prices rebound as soon as the initial rise in oil prices vanishes. Because of the persistent contraction in consumer spending and investment, it takes the whole simulation horizon for output to come back to its baseline values.

NOTES

1. Equities and private sector securities are not considered since they mostly cancel out in the consolidation of the balance sheet of households and firms.
2. The addition to capacity required to meet expected demand, Δv^e_{t+1}, is proxied by a distributed lag of value added.
3. The modelling strategy used to map supply and demand prices is derived from Klein (1983, pp. 24–8).
4. Other minor items relate to public sector borrowing requirements and new issues of Treasury securities, namely (changes in the stock of) post office deposits and public sector foreign debt.
5. Domestic and foreign prices enter the equation symmetrically, which is somewhat restrictive: factors like reputation, available servicing and retail outlets may induce people to react differently to identical changes in import and domestic prices. In addition, any individual good price is unlikely to have the same weight in the import and domestic price indices, so that some divergence between the two indices may simply result from individual good prices having different rates of inflation. Price homogeneity however is imposed in the equation, since it appears to be supported by statistical evidence.
6. In order to simplify the overall structure of the model, some short-cuts are used, the main one being the consolidation of the balance sheet of households and firms, which

sidesteps the need to model the equilibrium process in the stock market. This solution is consistent with the limited role that the equity market played until recently both as a source of financing for firms and as an investment opportunity for households.

REFERENCES

Ando, A. and F. Modigliani (1975), 'Some reflections on describing structures of financial sectors', in G. Fromm and L.R. Klein (eds), *The Brookings Model – Perspective and Recent Developments*, Amsterdam: North Holland.

Banca d'Italia (1970), *Un modello econometrico dell'economia italiana (M1BI)*, Rome: Banca d'Italia.

Banca d'Italia (1986), 'Modello trimestrale dell'economia italiana', Temi di discussione, no. 80.

Brayton, F. and E. Mauskopf (1985), 'The federal reserve board MPS quarterly econometric model of the US economy', *Economic Modelling*, 3, 170–292.

Fazio, A. and B. Sitzia (1979), *The Quarterly Econometric Model of the Bank of Italy. Structure and Policy Applications*, Rome: Banca d'Italia.

Galli, G, D. Terlizzese and I. Visco (1989), 'Un modello trimestrale per la previsione e la politica economica: le proprietà di breve e di lungo periodo del modello della Banca d'Italia', *Politica Economica*, 5, 3–52.

Klein, R.L. (1983), *Lectures in Econometrics*, Amsterdam: North-Holland.

Parigi, G. and S. Siviero (2001), 'An investment-function-based measure of capacity utilization. Potential output and utilised capacity in the Bank of Italy's quarterly model', *Economic Modelling*, 18, 525–50.

Siviero, S. (1995), 'Deterministic and stochastic algorithms for stabilisation policies with large-size econometric models', PhD dissertation.

Terlizzese, D. (1994), 'Il modello econometrico della banca d'Italia: una versione in scala 1:15', ricerche quantitative per la politica economica 1993.

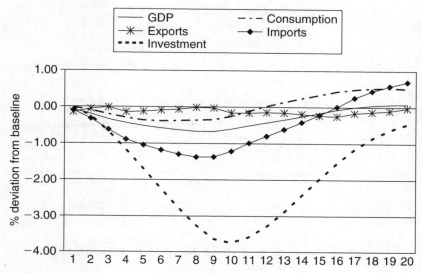

Figure 12.1a   Monetary policy shock (real effects)

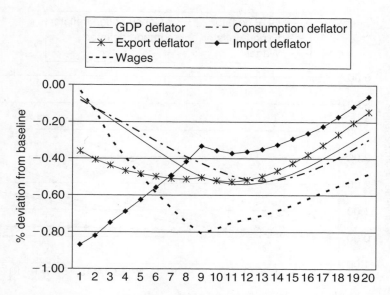

Figure 12.1b   Monetary policy shock (nominal effects)

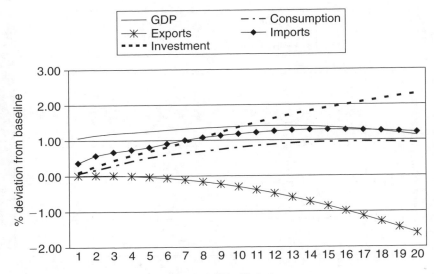

Figure 12.2a   Fiscal policy shock (real effects)

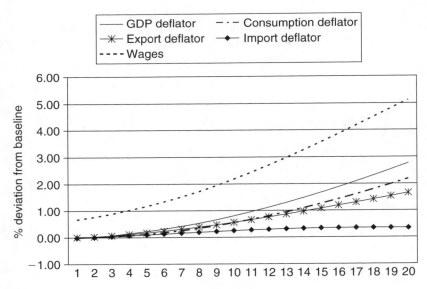

Figure 12.2b   Fiscal policy shock (nominal effects)

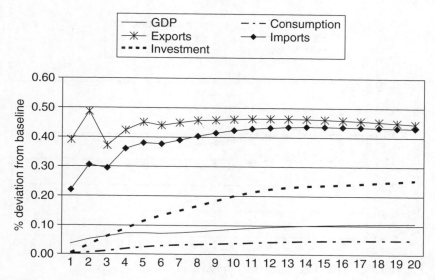

Figure 12.3a   World demand shock (real effects)

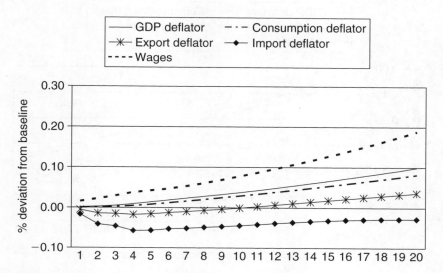

Figure 12.3b   World demand shock (nominal effects)

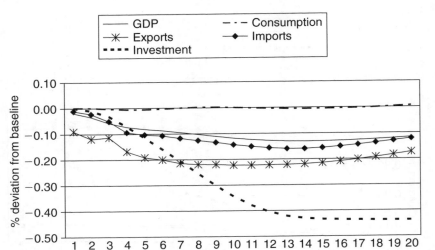

Figure 12.4a   Euro exchange rate appreciation (real effects)

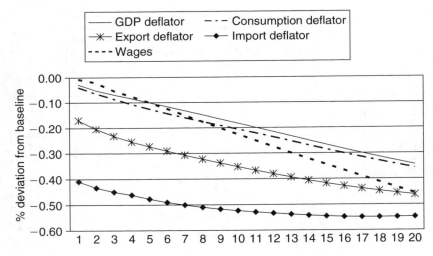

Figure 12.4b   Euro exchange rate appreciation (nominal effects)

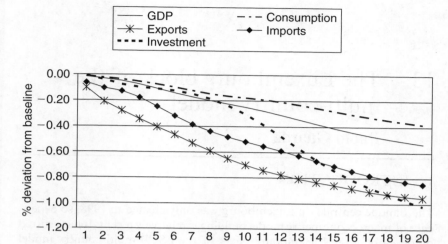

Figure 12.5a   Oil price shock (real effects)

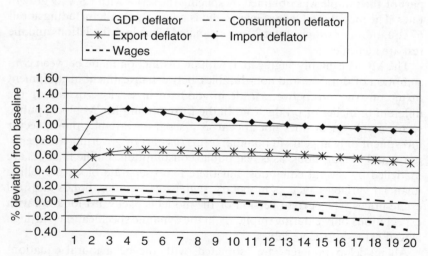

Figure 12.5b   Oil price shock (nominal effects)

13. The Luxembourg block of the multi-country model

Paolo Guarda

1 INTRODUCTION

The Banque centrale du Luxembourg was only created in 1998, so experience of macroeconometric model building is relatively recent. It has centred on developing the Luxembourg block of the ESCB multi-country model (MCM). The current version of this block is annual, as Luxembourg has not yet published quarterly national accounts. Most equations are estimated over the period 1970–2000; however, since ESA-95 national accounts for Luxembourg are only available for 1985 onwards, the earlier part of the sample was obtained by splicing the series with ESA-79 growth rates. The model is coded in Eviews and is relatively small, including about 67 equations, of which about 20 are estimated behavioural relations and the rest are identities.

The MCM is highly aggregated, with no distinction made between consumption of durables and non-durables, between investment in equipment or in construction, between trade in goods or in services, or among the different branches of production. In the Luxembourg MCM block, public sector employment does not appear as a separate variable; public sector investment only appears in nominal terms (as part of government expenditure) and is exogenous, as is real public consumption. Public finances are modelled by several equations, but there is no separate block modelling financial variables such as monetary aggregates, equities, bonds and real estate prices. The current version of the model is backward-looking, with expectations only entering implicitly in the dynamic specifications through lagged values of the variables.

All model parameters are estimated, with the behavioural equations usually specified as error correction mechanisms. The Engle–Granger two-step procedure was usually followed in estimation. In the first step, a static cointegrating regression serves to identify the long-run equilibrium consistent with economic theory. In the second step, a lagged error correction term incorporating deviations from this equilibrium is introduced in a dynamic specification, which also includes terms modelling the short-term dynamics that are justified on empirical rather than theoretical grounds. In both steps restrictions were imposed where necessary to ensure that estimated coefficients are consistent with economic theory or that dynamic homogeneity is preserved.

2   USES OF THE MODEL

The model is used both in the forecasting process and for policy analysis. In the macroeconomic projection exercise, the model not only provides a consistency check but also makes it possible to update projections rapidly using newer assumptions. In the forecasting process, the model also plays a central role in assessing the impact of various sources of uncertainty by simulating alternative scenarios. In terms of policy analysis, the model has been used internally to assess the consequences of tax reforms and of exchange rate fluctuations. The model has also contributed to a study of monetary policy transmission published as van Els *et al.* (2001) as well as work on inflation persistence in the euro area.

3   AN OUTLINE OF THE THEORETICAL UNDERPINNINGS OF THE MODEL

The theoretical underpinnings of the model closely resemble those of the AWM documented in Fagan *et al.* (2001). Thus the MCM embodies the neoclassical synthesis by combining Keynesian properties in the short run with neoclassical properties in the long run. Given nominal rigidities and costs of adjustment, output is demand-determined in the short run, but the long-run supply curve is vertical. The level of output in the long run is determined by an economy-wide Cobb–Douglas production function with two factors of production (capital and labour) and exogenous technological progress (a deterministic time trend). By assumption, this long-run production function features constant returns to scale.

Given that Luxembourg is part of the European Monetary Union, interest rates and exchange rates are exogenous in the Luxembourg MCM block, as are all foreign variables. Since the national economy is both very small and very open, activity fluctuates strongly with the level of foreign demand (measured by an index of real imports among Luxembourg's trading partners). Since the exchange rate is fixed, domestic prices and wages in the long run are determined by foreign prices (meaning both the price of Luxembourg's imports and the prices set by foreign competitors on Luxembourg's export markets).

3.1   Production Function and Factor Demands

The constant-returns-to-scale Cobb–Douglas production function can be written:

$$Y = Ae^{(1-\beta)\gamma T}K^{\beta}N^{1-\beta}$$

where Y is real output, K is the real capital stock (calculated by the permanent inventory method), N is total employment (including the self-employed) and T is the deterministic time trend associated with labour-augmenting technical progress. The production function parameters A, β and γ were recovered by imposing cross-equation restrictions in estimating a system of simultaneous equations representing the supply side. This included two factor demand equations (for investment and employment) derived from the first-order conditions of the representative firm's profit maximization problem (assuming factor markets are perfectly competitive). A third equation determined the output price as a mark-up on marginal cost (consistent with imperfect competition on the market for output). Following Willman and Estrada (2002), the supply side can be written as follows:

$$\ln(N) = \frac{\ln(A)}{1-\beta} + \frac{1}{1-\beta}\ln(Y) - \frac{\beta}{1-\beta}\ln(K) - \gamma T$$

$$\ln(K) = (1-\beta)\ln\left(\frac{\beta}{1-\beta}\right) - \ln(A) + \ln(Y) + \frac{1}{1-\beta}\ln\left(\frac{W}{P_K}\right) - \frac{1}{1-\beta}\gamma T$$

$$\ln(P) = \ln(\eta) - \ln(1-\beta) - \frac{1}{1-\beta}\ln(A) + \frac{\beta}{1-\beta}\ln\left(\frac{Y}{K}\right) + \ln(W) - \gamma T$$

where P is the price of output (measured by the GDP deflator), η is the mark-up on marginal cost, W is the nominal wage rate and P_K is the nominal user cost of capital (see below).

The marginal productivity conditions for capital and for labour appear as error correction terms in the dynamic equations for investment and employment, ensuring consistency with the underlying theoretical framework of the supply side. Similarly the equilibrium condition for prices appears as an error correction term in a dynamic equation for the GDP deflator. Note that these equilibrium relations only hold in the long run, with the short-run dynamics of investment, employment and prices determined in part by other factors, including fluctuations in aggregate demand.

For example, the short-run dynamics in the *investment* equation include a standard accelerator effect from aggregate output. However the long-run component of investment adjusts the capital stock towards its desired level in long-run equilibrium, matching the capital–output ratio with the real user cost of capital. The latter is measured as a weighted average of short- and long-term interest rates adjusted by a constant rate of depreciation (chosen to be consistent with the method used in calculating the capital stock) and then multiplied by the ratio of the total investment deflator to the GDP deflator.

The short-run dynamics of the *employment* equation also feature an accelerator effect, as well as an auto-regressive component and a term reflecting short-run wage developments. The long-run component, instead, adjusts employment to the level consistent with the inverted production function at the long-run equilibrium.

3.2 Components of Aggregate Demand

Real GDP is broken down into the standard six expenditure components. *Private consumption* is a function of real disposable income, real financial wealth and the real long-term interest rate. Disposable income is measured as the sum of compensation of employees and public sector transfers to households minus direct taxes paid by households (including social security contributions). Real financial wealth is measured as cumulated savings, under the assumption that households own all assets in the economy (public debt, net foreign assets and private capital stock). This may be an unrealistic assumption in an economy as open as that of Luxembourg, but there is no alternative measure available, as financial accounts have not yet been published. In any case, empirical results suggest the wealth measure based on this assumption has a statistically significant effect on consumption with the sign anticipated by economic theory. *Public consumption* is exogenous in real terms, but its deflator is endogenous, depending on the GDP deflator, so that nominal public consumption is also partly endogenous.

Gross fixed capital formation is determined by the investment equation described in the previous section, which incorporates the gap between actual and desired capital stock. *Changes in inventories* are determined by a separate estimated equation, which tends to restore a constant ratio of cumulated inventories to real GDP in the long run.

Exports of goods and services are a function of the level of real world demand addressed to Luxembourg as well as of a measure of the competitiveness of Luxembourg's exports. World demand is measured by a weighted average of real imports of Luxembourg's 17 main trading partners (both euro and non-euro countries) using appropriate trade weights. The long-run elasticity of exports to this world demand indicator is constrained to unity. Competitiveness is measured by the ratio of the export deflator to foreign competitors' export prices (a weighted average of the export deflators of the same 17 trading partners).

Imports of goods and services depend on an indicator of demand for real imports and on relative prices. The import demand indicator is calculated as a weighted sum of real domestic final demand components with weights set to their average import content (1998–9). The long-run elasticity of imports to this demand indicator is constrained to unity. Real imports also depend on the ratio of import prices to domestic prices (as measured by the GDP deflator). Finally movements in Luxembourg's nominal effective exchange rate have short-run effects on the volume of imports.

3.3   Prices and Costs

The model adopts a monopolistic competition setting, allowing the representative firm to retain some market power so that it sets prices as a mark-up over marginal cost. In this context, the key price index is the deflator of GDP at factor cost (excluding indirect taxes and subsidies). As described in the supply side, in the long-run equilibrium the GDP deflator depends on marginal cost, which is a function of parameters estimated simultaneously with the equations for labour demand and investment. The short-run price dynamics reflect not only movements in the wage rate but also changes in import prices, allowing the mark-up to vary with changes in competitiveness.

Other domestic prices, meaning the deflators of private consumption, public consumption and total investment, are modelled as weighted averages of the GDP deflator and import prices. Static homogeneity conditions are imposed on all these estimated price equations, ensuring that only relative prices are relevant in the long-run (a form of the law of one price holds). The deflator for changes in inventories is derived as a residual so that nominal GDP is to equal the sum of its nominal components.

The wage equation reflects the first-order condition for profit maximization in long-run equilibrium, incorporating labour productivity and the output price in the error correction term. However the short-run dynamics include several other factors affecting wages, including cyclical movements in the mark-up, labour productivity and unemployment. These are consistent with a bargaining framework in which unions and firms negotiate wages and firms then set the level of employment. The data are consistent with full dynamic homogeneity, ensuring that the steady state is independent of inflation and productivity growth, as is required for the Phillips curve to be vertical in the long run.

Finally, in terms of external prices, the import deflator is modelled in the long run as a weighted average of oil prices, foreign competitors' prices and the GDP deflator (the latter captures pricing-to-market behaviour). Fluctuations in Luxembourg's nominal effective exchange rate have a short-run impact on the import deflator. The export deflator is determined in the long run as a weighted average of competitors' export prices and the GDP deflator.

3.4 Fiscal Policy and the Government Sector

The fiscal block includes only one estimated equation on the expenditure side. This determines government transfers to households as a share of nominal GDP. While this may seem to give government expenditure a pro-cyclical bias, it does correspond to current practice in planning overall public expenditure. Of the other three expenditure categories, public consumption is exogenous in real terms, and public investment and interest paid on public debt are exogenous in nominal terms (for projection purposes these are drawn from the government's published stability programmes). On the revenue side, the model determines five separate categories of tax receipts by multiplying their respective tax base by an (exogenous) effective tax rate. Thus direct taxes paid by households are linked to gross income (the sum of compensation of employees and transfers to households). Direct taxes paid by firms are based on firms' gross operating surplus. Social security contributions (paid by households and by firms) are based on compensation of employees. Indirect taxes are based on nominal GDP. Other government net revenue is left exogenous.

3.5 Trade

The current account is the sum of the trade balance (determined by export and import equations described previously), net factor income and transfers from the rest of the world. Net factor income is modelled by a separate estimated equation linking it to lagged values of the stock of net foreign assets. Net transfers from the rest of the world are exogenous. The stock of net foreign assets is calculated by cumulating the current account.

3.6 Monetary and Financial Sector

As indicated above, interest rates and exchange rates are exogenous in the current version of the model. It would be difficult to incorporate a money demand equation in the model, as Luxembourg's financial sector (and its money creation) mainly serves non-residents. Equations determining financial asset prices (that is, equities, bonds and real estate) may be added in the future.

4   AN OUTLINE OF THE KEY CHARACTERISTICS

This section describes the structure of the model in terms of its behaviour in five key simulations. These include a monetary policy shock, a fiscal policy shock, a foreign demand shock, an exchange rate shock and an oil price shock. Unless otherwise indicated, results presented graphically are expressed as percentage deviations from the baseline simulation.

Simulation 1: Monetary Policy Shock

This simulation involves a two-year increase in nominal short-term interest rates by 100 basis points. Long-term interest rates respond according to the expectations hypothesis and the euro exchange rate appreciates in line with an uncovered interest parity condition. Interest rates and the exchange rate return to baseline at the beginning of the third year of the simulation. Foreign demand and prices deviate from baseline until year 5 to reflect spillover effects within the euro area as described in van Els *et al.* (2001).

As illustrated in Figure 13.1a, the impact on GDP is fairly small, with a maximum divergence from baseline of −0.24 per cent in the third year of the simulation. In this year, interest rates and the exchange rate return to their baseline values, and output follows by year 6 of the simulation. Private consumption drops −0.36 per cent below baseline in year 2 and is much slower to return to baseline because real disposable income falls until year 4 of the simulation and does not return to baseline until year 9. Note that interest payments on public debt are exogenous (they are negligible in Luxembourg), so they are unaffected by the interest rate shock and cannot contribute to supporting disposable income. The most dramatic effect is on real investment, which declines by nearly 2 per cent in year 3 of the simulation before recovering smoothly once interest rates return to baseline. There is a slight downward dip in investment in year 7, which is due to the rise in the user cost of capital once foreign prices return to baseline in year 6, favouring the recovery of the import and investment deflators. The fall in exports is greatest in the third year (when the exchange rate returns to baseline) reaching −0.45 per cent. By year 7 exports are slightly above baseline, reflecting the improvement in competitiveness due to lower prices. The fall in imports, reaching −0.73 per cent in year 3, exceeds that in

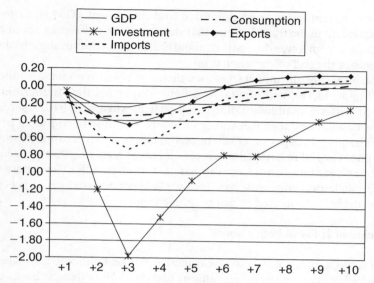

Figure 13.1a   Effects of a two-year 100 bp increase in short-term interest rates (real categories)

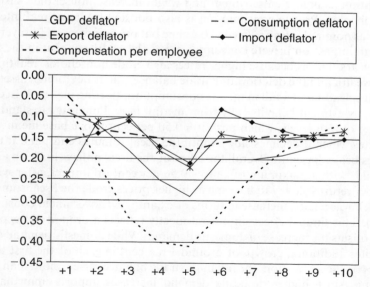

Figure 13.1b   Effects of a two-year 100 bp increase in short-term interest rates (nominal categories)

exports, reflecting lower consumption and investment. This leads to an improvement in the trade balance that stabilizes GDP, offsetting about half the impact from lower domestic demand and pushing output slightly above baseline at the end of the simulation.

The impact of the monetary policy shock on prices is even more moderate (Figure 13.1b), with the GDP deflator displaying the familiar hump-shaped pattern, gradually falling until year 5, when it is −0.29 per cent below baseline and then recovering smoothly. The drop in consumer prices reaches only −0.18 per cent (also in year 5) before slowly returning towards baseline. The fall in compensation per employee reaches −0.41 per cent in the same year and then returns to baseline more rapidly. The export and import deflators drop below baseline by −0.22 per cent and −0.21 per cent, respectively (both in year 5) before recovering.

Simulation 2: Fiscal Policy Shock

This simulation involves a five-year increase of real public sector expenditure by 1 per cent of the initial value of real GDP. Note that the backward-looking nature of the model limits its appropriateness for analysing fiscal shocks, so results should be interpreted with caution. Figure 13.2a shows that the increase in government spending initially boosts private consumption as higher employment and wages increase households' disposable income. Private consumption is also boosted by lower real interest rates as nominal rates are fixed at baseline but prices increase. However the overall impact on private consumption is only +0.01 per cent in the first two years. This is because higher prices also erode households' real financial wealth and the deteriorating trade balance causes net foreign assets to decline, leading to a fall in private consumption, starting in year 3. In contrast, investment benefits fully from the fall in real interest rates and the higher output levels, which push it +0.50 per cent above baseline in year 1, after which it declines slowly until the fiscal stimulus ends, and it then drops below baseline. Overall the effect of the fiscal policy shock on GDP is mild, with a maximum of only +0.56 per cent on impact, after which output returns slowly to baseline as higher prices erode the fiscal stimulus (which was a fixed increase in terms of ex ante *real* government consumption). This limited effect on output mostly reflects a drop in net exports that offsets the increase in domestic demand. While domestic demand contributes additional growth of around 1 per cent in each of the first three years of the simulation, the fall in the trade balance offsets more than half of this, since higher domestic demand increases imports immediately, while exports initially remain close to baseline. As illustrated in Figure 13.2b, the increase in prices drives wages +0.62 per cent above baseline by

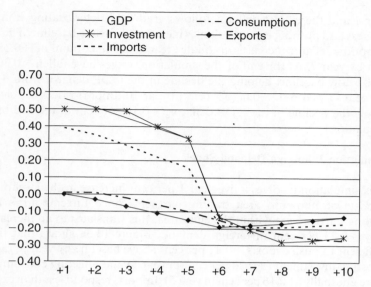

Figure 13.2a   Effects of a 1% increase in government consumption (real categories)

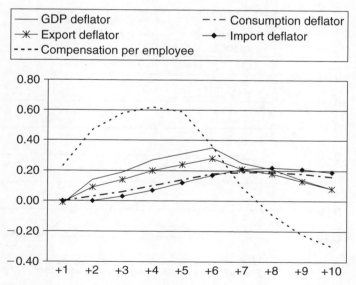

Figure 13.2b   Effects of a 1% increase in government consumption (nominal categories)

year 4 and the export deflator follows gradually, deteriorating competitiveness and pushing export volumes increasingly below baseline. The consumption deflator increases gradually, reaching a maximum of +0.19 per cent by year 7. At the end of the simulation, wages have fallen −0.30 per cent below baseline, helping the decline in the GDP deflator from +0.35 per cent in year 6 to +0.08 per cent in year 10. Import prices are slow to follow the decline in the GDP deflator (+0.19 per cent at the end of the simulation).

Simulation 3: Foreign Demand Shock

This simulation involves a five-year 1 per cent increase in the level of real imports of non-euro area trading partners. Since Luxembourg's main trading partners are within the euro area, this translates to an increase of only +0.23 per cent in foreign demand. Figure 13.3a shows that this is sufficient to push exports +0.42 per cent above baseline by year 3, rapidly boosting investment (+0.20 per cent in year 3) and affecting consumption more gradually (+0.16 per cent in year 5). Imports respond less than exports but with a similar profile, peaking +0.42 per cent above baseline in year 4. Overall, GDP rises +0.16 per cent above baseline on impact and reaches +0.19 per cent in years 3 to 5. This impact is probably underestimated, as

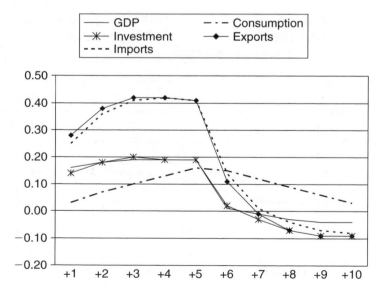

Figure 13.3a   Effects of a permanent 1% increase in the level of non-euro area world demand (real categories)

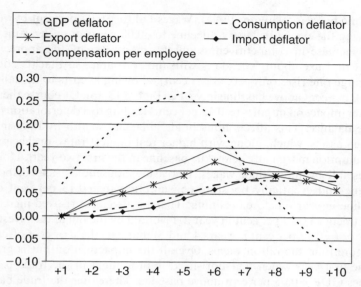

Figure 13.3b   *Effects of a permanent increase in the level of non-euro area world demand (nominal categories)*

spillovers in intra-euro trade and prices are ignored in this simulation and are likely to be significant for Luxembourg.

Wages rise above baseline (Figure 13.3b), peaking at +0.26 per cent in year 5 before declining. The consumption and import deflators rise continuously, reaching +0.08 per cent and +0.09 per cent at the end of the simulation. This reflects the GDP deflator's slow return to baseline after peaking at +0.15 per cent in year 6. Once foreign demand returns to baseline, the deterioration in competitiveness pushes exports below baseline in year 7 and they are at −0.09 per cent at the end of the simulation. Imports and investment follow a similar adjustment, but consumption is still +0.03 per cent above baseline in year 10, reflecting lower real interest rates and higher real wealth (boosted by the accumulation of capital stock and net foreign assets). At the end of the simulation, wages have just declined below baseline and the export deflator is following gradually (+0.05 per cent).

Simulation 4: Exchange Rate Shock

This simulation involves a five-year appreciation of the euro by 1 per cent. This is directly transmitted to the oil price in euros, depressing import prices and the consumption deflator, which are both −0.16 per cent below baseline by year 5 (Figure 13.4a). Wages fall to −0.07 per cent by year 6, allowing the export deflator to decline to –0.08 per cent in the same year. This increase in competitiveness offsets the impact of the appreciation (most of Luxembourg's trade is with the euro area, so that its effective exchange rate rises only +0.48 per cent), allowing exports to actually rise +0.10 per cent above baseline in year 2 (Figure 13.4b). Of course there is a greater impact on imports (+0.12 per cent) leading to a deterioration of the trade balance. This affects households' financial wealth by lowering net foreign assets, which, along with higher real interest rates, pushes private consumption marginally below the baseline in the first two years. However prices fall by more than wages, increasing households' real disposable income and eventually boosting consumption to +0.13 per cent above baseline in year 6 before declining. There is also a short-lived increase in investment (+0.19 per cent in year 2) favoured by the fall in the investment deflator (−0.13 per cent in years 4 and 5) that cuts the user cost of capital by more than the fall in wages. Overall the impact on output is greatest in the first year, when the short-lived improvement in the trade balance pushes GDP +0.05 per cent above baseline. Thereafter the trade balance deteriorates but domestic demand expands, stabilizing output until the exchange rate returns to baseline. This temporarily boosts the export deflator (+0.14 per cent above baseline in year 6), cutting net exports further. By the end of the simulation, exports and imports are still marginally above baseline, with the trade balance below baseline.

Simulation 5: Oil Price Shock

This simulation involves a five-year 10 per cent increase in oil prices expressed in US dollars. Note that, given the theoretical structure of the MCM, a rise in oil prices is more a competitiveness shock than a supply-side shock, as it cannot affect factor substitution except in so far as it has different effects on nominal wages and the investment deflator. Oil prices enter the model directly in the equation determining the import deflator, thereby affecting the GDP deflator and all the other key deflators. As illustrated by Figure 13.5a by year 6, the GDP deflator is +0.60 per cent above baseline and the consumption deflator is at +0.76 per cent. The increase in labour costs (+0.55 per cent in years 7 and 8) drives up the export deflator (+0.47 per cent in year 6), leading to a continuous fall in exports (−0.34 per cent) and a drop in real GDP (−0.08 per cent) (see Figure 13.5b). Private consumption is stable in the first year as the fall in real interest rates offsets lower real disposable income. Consumption then declines continuously to −0.67 per cent in years 7 and 8 before recovering slowly. Investment declines immediately, reaching a trough (−0.76 per cent) in

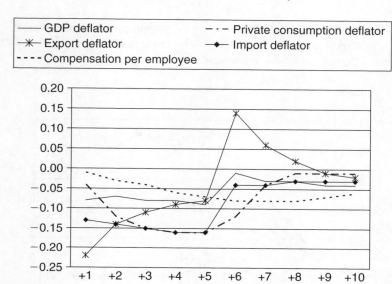

Figure 13.4a   Effects of a five-year 1% appreciation of the euro vis-à-vis all other currencies (nominal categories)

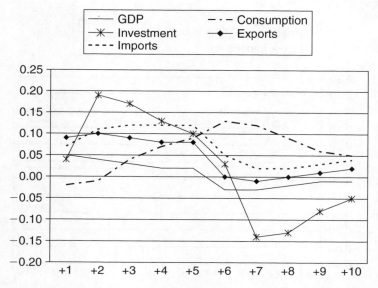

Figure 13.4b   Effects of a five-year 1% appreciation of the euro vis-à-vis all other currencies (real categories)

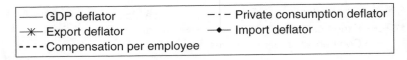

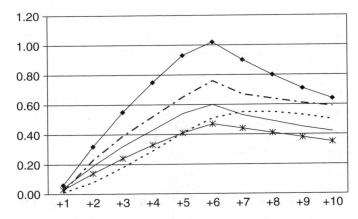

*Figure 13.5a   Effects of a permanent 10% increase in oil prices
(nominal categories)*

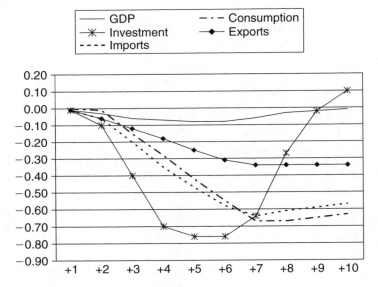

*Figure 13.5b   Effects of a permanent 10% increase in oil prices
(real categories)*

year 5 and then recovering rapidly as oil prices return to baseline. Following year 7, exports and imports are both slow to climb back to baseline. GDP declines furthest (−0.08 per cent) in years 5 and 6, when domestic demand is weakest. At the end of the simulation, private consumption is still −0.63 per cent below baseline, but lower imports allow the trade balance to largely offset this shortfall in domestic demand. Note that the drop in GDP is probably overstated, as the simulation is run in isolated mode. In reality an oil price shock is likely to increase foreign competitors' import and export prices, reducing the effect on Luxembourg's competitiveness.

REFERENCES

Fagan, G., J. Henry and R. Mestre (2001), 'An area-wide model (AWM) for the euro area'. ECB Working Paper No. 42.
van Els, P., A. Locarno, J. Morgan and J.-P. Villetelle (2001), 'Monetary policy transmission in the euro area: what do aggregate and national structural models tell us?'. ECB Working Paper No. 94.
Willman, A. and A. Estrada (2002), 'The Spanish block of the ESCB multi-country model', ECB Working Paper No. 149.

14.   MORKMON: a macroeconomic model of the Netherlands' economy

Peter van Els

The MORKMON model was developed at De Nederlandsche Bank (DNB) in the early 1980s and has undergone various changes and extensions over the years.[1] The current version of the model is described in van Els and Vlaar (1996). Since the publication of this report, equations have been updated in the light of recent economic history when necessary, but the structure of the model has remained broadly unaltered. Further changes are currently under consideration because of ESA-95 and changes in the availability of monetary data.

1   THE USES OF THE MODEL

MORKMON is used in short-term forecasting, in conducting policy and scenario analyses, and in counterfactual simulation exercises.[2] These activities serve DNB's internal process of policy preparation. Forecast horizons cover a short period of up to two years ahead in most cases, although just occasionally they cover slightly longer horizons. An example is the ex ante assessment of a new cabinet's economic policy package at the beginning of its four-year term. Projections are a combination of model-generated and judgmental information. Judgmental sources include available off-model information taken from new releases of cyclical and price indicators, or from predictions based on other in-house or external models. Scenario analyses usually address topics such as the transmission of monetary policy; the implications of fiscal and budgetary policies for output and inflation; labour market policy, social security regulation and wage formation; the macro implications of asset price developments; and explaining the development of bank credit and monetary aggregates. MORKMON projections represent DNB's contribution to the ESCB's broad macroeconomic projection exercises. Furthermore DNB publishes MORKMON projections and scenario analyses in the June and December issues of its *Quarterly Bulletin*. These projections help the Bank inform the public about the most likely short-term outlook of the Dutch economy and the main risks that surround it.[3]

2   A BIRD'S EYE VIEW OF MORKMON

The model is estimated using quarterly data over a sample period starting from 1970q1. MORKMON is not derived from one single and fully coherent theoretical framework to which the model converges in the long run. Its structure is of a somewhat more eclectic nature, aiming to balance the various demands related to theoretical rigour, data congruency and institutional detail. When using the model, the emphasis is on the short term. However, through the use of error correction mechanisms, plausible long-run relationships between the model variables have been imposed. MORKMON consists of some 400 equations of which 70 are estimated behavioural equations. Most equations have been estimated using ordinary least squares, although the multivariate portfolio models for households, firms and pension funds have been estimated using Iterated SUR (see van Els and Vlaar, 1996).

An important feature of MORKMON is the degree of detail of its monetary submodel. This is built around the financial balance sheets of seven distinct sectors (households, non-financial firms, pension funds and life insurance companies, banks, the public sector, the central bank and the foreign sector). Financial behaviour of households, non-financial firms, and pension funds and life insurance companies is captured by estimated multivariate dynamic portfolio models of the Brainard–Tobin type, which describe the allocation of financial wealth over the various assets, including liquid assets, shares, bonds and foreign assets. Loans demanded by households and firms are mainly provided by banks and pension funds and life insurance companies. The share of loans provided by banks depends, among other things, on the cyclical stance of the economy. The yields of the various assets and liabilities (liquid assets, savings deposits, short-term bank credit) reflect the interest rate-setting behaviour of banks and, hence, depend on market rates and banks' financial position. Financial asset prices and house prices are endogenous, so that household wealth may be measured at market value. The equations explaining the behaviour of domestic stock prices are based on the dividend growth model according to which the current stock price reflects the discounted sum of future dividend income flows, taking into account that new issues of shares also influence their price. Hence stock prices respond to changes in interest rates, profitability and a cyclical indicator. House prices react to changes in real disposable household income, long-term interest rates, the price of rents and the deflator of residential investment. The monetary submodel also comprises a system of equations explaining the investment income flows (dividend and interest payments) received and paid by each of the sectors. These flows are fully in line with the sectoral holdings of assets and liabilities, thereby contributing to a consistent modelling of the income channel of monetary transmission.

Like many other macromodels, MORKMON is Keynesian in the short run, with output and employment mainly demand-determined owing to the presence of price and wage rigidities. On the supply side, potential output and employment are determined by a CES production technology. Here we make a distinction between the market sector, where employment responds more strongly to changes in real wages, and the semi-public sector, which is relatively insensitive to the real wage. Labour supply is endogenous and responds to changes in demographics, the replacement rate (the remuneration of working-age people who do not have a job relative to the wage received by workers) and the unemployment rate (discouraged worker effect). The rates of unemployment and capacity utilization directly influence prices, wages and components of aggregate demand (investment, exports and imports), thereby fostering a convergence of actual and potential output on the one hand, and actual employment and labour supply on the other. The set-up of the model does not, however, imply a return to a well-defined long-run neoclassical equilibrium or steady-state growth path but ensures that imbalances between potential and actual output and employment are of a temporary nature. The equilibrium unemployment rate is implicitly endogenous, depending, amongst other things, on the level of the replacement rate, the terms of trade and the rate of income tax payments and social security contributions.

Private consumption depends on real disposable household income and real financial and non-financial wealth measured at market value, taking into account differences in propensities to consume out of wage income, transfer income and investment income. The direct substitution effect is captured by the inclusion of the long-term interest rate in the equation. In the short run, private consumption is affected strongly by changes in the unemployment rate. Moreover consumers raise their spending somewhat when government financial balances improve. The government financial balance and the change in the unemployment rate partly capture (endogenous) confidence effects on private consumption.

Non-residential investment depends on the user cost of capital (a combination of short- and long-term interest rates), firms' profitability and output. The dynamics of investment are also affected by short-run changes in total sales and by fluctuations in the rate of capacity utilization, which proxy the accelerator effect. Residential investment is determined by real disposable household income, long-term interest rates and house and rent prices. Another factor of importance relates to the (exogenous) impact of building programmes initiated by the government. Inventory formation, acting as a buffer for demand shocks in the short run, is modelled via the so-called 'Fair approach' (Fair, 1984). According to this approach the optimal inventory stocks-to-sales ratio depends on the real interest rate. In MORKMON, an average of short- and long-term interest rates represents the cost-of-capital effect on inventory formation. Exports depend on world demand and relative export prices. Cyclical factors (when the domestic economy is weak producers seek to raise exports) and profitability also affect exports. Imports mainly depend on sales, relative import prices and the rate of capacity utilization.

Prices of expenditure categories depend on the cost of production, competitors' prices and the rates of capacity utilization and unemployment. Competitors' prices and cyclical indicators reflect the mark-up of prices over the costs of production. The latter consist of unit labour costs, capital costs and the costs of importing energy and non-energy commodities and intermediate services. In the long run, expenditure prices are homogeneous in the costs of production and competitors' prices. Wage formation reflects a wage-bargaining framework where, in equilibrium, the wage rate depends on consumer and producer prices, productivity, the unemployment rate, the replacement rate and the rates of income tax and social security premiums paid by employees and employers.[4]

The public sector is modelled in some detail. A distinction is made between the government sector on the one hand and social security funds on the other; for each of these the model describes the various categories of revenues and outlays. Non-transfer government outlays are more or less fixed in real terms, broadly in line with the current practice of budgetary policy making. The model is, however, easy to adjust to reflect different fiscal regimes or forms of fiscal discipline. Social security transfers are split into unemployment benefits, disability programmes, pay-as-you-go pensions, early retirement programmes and health care. On the government revenue side, income taxes, corporate taxes and indirect taxes are modelled separately. Regarding social security funds, the model distinguishes between social security contributions paid by employers and by employees. This allows their differing effects on wage formation and wage costs to be taken into account in a proper way. The simulations presented below abstract from specific fiscal solvency rules and should be interpreted as outcomes conditional upon unchanged fiscal policy parameters. Note that outlays and revenues are endogenous in the model with the exception of government investment and material consumption, in line with standard practices. An exogenous category defined as 'other' captures elements not accounted for in the rest of government outlays.

Expectations are backward-looking. Expectation formation mechanisms are sometimes modelled through 'third or signalling' variables. For instance, a worsening of current government financial balances and unemployment is taken to signal gloomy expectations of households with respect to their future spending power, and hence decreases private consumption. In simulations, forward-looking behaviour is often introduced by design, by imposing forward-looking response patterns generated by outside models for external variables such as exchange rates, foreign prices and long-term interest rates. Explicit forward-looking behaviour in, for instance, wage formation, private consumption and investment has been found to be of relatively limited importance in the Netherlands.[5]

The transmission of monetary policy operates through various channels. In the short run, prices are mainly affected by the response of the exchange rate. Cost-of-capital effects on residential and non-residential investment and on inventory formation dominate the impact of monetary policy on output in the short and medium term. The strength of other channels, such as the intertemporal substitution effect on private consumption and wealth effects on consumption due to asset price responses, crucially depends on the magnitude of the change in long-term interest rates. The income channel, which relates to the investment income flows triggered by the changes in interest rates and the accompanying portfolio reallocation, is relatively small and operates with a fairly long lag.

Table 14.1 provides an overview of the main short-, medium- and long-run elasticities and semi-elasticities in most of the behavioural equations of MORKMON that have been discussed in this section.

3   FULL MODEL SIMULATION PROPERTIES

MORKMON's system properties are analysed by conducting five simulation experiments:

1. a two-year 100 basis points increase in the short-term interest rate,
2. a five-year increase in real government consumption by 1 per cent of initial GDP,
3. a five-year 1 per cent increase in non-euro area world demand,
4. a five-year 1 per cent appreciation of the euro *vis-à-vis* all other currencies,
5. a permanent 10 per cent increase in oil prices.

Table 14.1 Single equation simulation results: effects in percentages of a
1 per cent or 1 percentage point increase in explanatory factor

	Impact in quarter				
	1	4	8	16	40
Labour demand market sector					
Output private sector	0.04	0.25	0.57	0.99	1.00
Real product wage	0.00	−0.08	−0.29	−0.64	−0.70
Labour demand semi-public sector					
Output semi-public sector	0.22	0.48	0.79	1.00	1.00
Real product wage	0.00	−0.03	−0.09	−0.14	−0.15
Labour supply (% point of population 15–64)					
Replacement rate	0.00	−0.02	−0.05	−0.06	−0.07
Unemployment (% point of population 15–64)	0.00	−0.04	−0.11	−0.18	−0.20
Non-residential investment					
Output	0.00	0.00	0.46	0.91	1.00
Capacity utilization (% points)	0.00	1.83	2.72	3.01	2.96
Long-term interest rate (% points)	0.00	−1.57	−2.14	−2.15	−2.07
Short-term interest rate (% points)	0.00	0.00	−0.28	−0.63	−0.69
Residential investment					
Real disposable household income	0.00	0.63	0.78	0.80	0.80
Long-term interest rate (% points)	0.00	−1.69	−3.44	−3.70	−3.70
Relative price of rents	0.00	0.75	0.93	0.96	0.96
Relative price of houses	0.00	0.32	0.40	0.41	0.41
Private consumption					
Real disposable household income	0.00	0.57	0.92	0.95	0.95
Household wealth at market value	0.00	0.03	0.05	0.05	0.05
Long-term interest rate (% points)	0.00	−0.28	−0.31	−0.31	−0.31
General government financial balance (% GDP)	0.00	0.20	0.32	0.33	0.33
Unemployment rate (% points)	0.00	−0.43	−0.03	−0.00	−0.00

Table 14.1   (continued)

	Impact in quarter				
	1	4	8	16	40
Gross output enterprises (inventory formation)					
Total sales	0.82	1.08	1.08	1.08	1.08
Cumulated inventory stock	0.00	−0.08	−0.08	−0.08	−0.08
Long-term interest rate (% points)	0.00	−0.07	−0.07	−0.07	−0.07
Short-term interest rate (% points)	0.00	−0.07	−0.07	−0.07	−0.07
Exports goods excluding energy					
Relevant world demand	0.81	0.81	0.91	0.98	1.00
Relative export price	−0.69	−0.69	−0.92	−1.08	−1.12
Imports goods excluding energy					
Total sales	1.10	1.10	1.07	1.04	1.01
Relative import price	0.00	−0.25	−0.39	−0.57	−0.74

The results of these experiments are summarized in Figures 14.1 to 14.5 at the end of this chapter. The reporting horizon covers a five-year period. The design of the simulation exercises is based on a set of common assumptions regarding the feedback on policy instruments and the responses of long-term interest rates and exchange rates. In Simulations 2 to 5, policy-controlled and market interest rates are exogenous over the reporting horizon and remain unchanged at baseline values. Except for Simulations 1 and 4, exchange rates remain unchanged at baseline values over the reporting horizon. In Simulation 1, no monetary policy rule is implemented and the responses of long-term interest rates and exchange rates follow from using the (forward-looking) expectations hypothesis and uncovered interest parity condition, respectively. We apply no fiscal policy rules in any of the simulations and models are operated in isolated mode without taking into account international spillovers. We briefly explain the main results next.

The two-year 100 basis points *increase in short-term interest rates* shows moderate effects on output and prices in the Netherlands. In the first and second years, the exchange rate channel almost completely dominates the impact on prices reflecting the fact that the Netherlands is a small open economy. The GDP response in the first year is also mainly related to the worsening of the competitive position due to the appreciation of the euro exchange rate. However the cost-of-capital channel, which operates through residential and non-residential investment as well as through inventory formation, also significantly affects GDP and becomes the dominant channel for real activity from the second year onwards. Other channels of transmission such as the direct substitution channel and the asset price channel (house, stock and bond prices) via private consumption are not very important because of the moderate response of the long-term interest rate. This response reflects the assumption of term structure effects consistent with the expectations hypothesis.

The *increase in real government consumption* by 1 per cent of initial GDP is followed by a substantial drop in unemployment, as about 40 per cent of the impulse directly relates to an increase in government employment. In the design of the simulation we abstract from direct crowding out of private sector employment. Lower unemployment temporarily boosts private consumption. Investment increases because of positive accelerator effects. Real GDP initially increases by slightly more than 1 per cent thanks to positive spillovers on private spending. Lower unemployment leads to higher wage demands and hence to higher price levels. It also encourages non-active agents to participate in the labour market. However higher real product wages eventually begin to erode the positive employment effects. The increase of labour supply and the endogenous crowding out of private sector employment eventually force unemployment gradually back towards its baseline level. Furthermore private savings increase in the long run as the worsening of the government financial position has a direct negative impact on private consumption.

The effects of a 1 per cent *increase in non-euro area world demand* are very straightforward. This shock boils down to a 0.45 per cent increase in total relevant world demand for the Netherlands. Exports move broadly in line with world demand. Owing to lower unemployment (real) wages and prices are somewhat higher. Domestic demand is a bit higher, but also triggers additional imports. On balance, GDP is about 0.2 per cent higher over the simulation period.

The 1 per cent *appreciation of the euro* lowers real GDP by almost 0.1 per cent. Initially the reduction in economic activity is triggered by lower exports in particular. In the medium term domestic demand and net trade both contribute to the reduction in real GDP. Lower foreign prices gradually, feed into domestic prices and wages. After five years the HICP is down by 0.3 per cent.

Finally a permanent 10 per cent *rise in oil prices* leads to higher consumer prices and hence triggers a negative response of consumer spending, with spillovers on investment. Eventually GDP is about 0.2 per cent lower than base and consumer prices are 0.5 per cent higher. Despite the negative impact on economic activity, government finances slightly improve thanks to higher government revenues from domestic consumption and exports of natural gas.

4   THE FUTURE OF MORKMON

As the model is used extensively for both forecasting and policy analysis, a substantial amount of resources is dedicated to updating and maintaining it. The most important improvement that we would like to implement in the near future is to strengthen the model's theoretical consistency, based on current best practices, and thus further improve the long-run simulation properties of the model. This is required because, as forward-looking elements become more and more pivotal in terms of explaining economic behaviour, the long-term features of the model need to be well defined and understood by the modeller.

Other changes involve allowing explicitly for confidence indicators in the model, in order to contribute directly to policy discussions which often revolve around changes in consumer confidence. Similarly, as issues of financial stability acquire a more prominent role in the Bank's functions, our models need to adjust accordingly. An obvious example of this is the explicit modelling of the financial accelerator which in the current version of the model is only proxied. Finally, as best modelling practices are currently viewed to move in the direction of dynamic general equilibrium models, we will, in the future, be required to consider the parallel use of such models alongside MORKMON.

NOTES

1. See for instance Fase *et al.* (1992).
2. A more detailed record of the interaction between model use, model building and policy making at DNB is provided in van Els (2000).
3. Assuming unchanged interest and exchange rates and unchanged fiscal policy settings.
4. On this framework, see Graafland and Huizinga (1999), and Broer *et al.* (2000).
5. See Bikker *et al.* (1993).

REFERENCES

Bikker, J.A., P.J.A. van Els and M.E. Hemerijck (1993), 'Rational expectation variables in macroeconomic models: empirical evidence for the Netherlands and other countries', *Economic Modelling*, **10**, 301–14.
Broer, D.P., D.A.G. Draper and F.H. Huizinga (2000), 'The equilibrium rate of unemployment in the Netherlands', *De Economist*, **148**, 345–71.

van Els, P.J.A. (2000), 'Policy making and model development: the case of the Nederlandsche Bank's model MORKMON', in Frank A.G. den Butter and Mary S. Morgan (eds), *Empirical Models and Policy-Making: Interactions and Institutions*, London: Routledge, pp. 76–92.

van Els, P.J.A. and P.J.G. Vlaar (1996), 'MORKMON III: een geactualiseerde versie van het macro-economisch beleidsmodel van de Nederlandsche Bank', WO&E Onderzoeksrapport no. 471.

Fair, Ray C. (1984), *Specification, Estimation and Analysis of Macroeconometric Models*, Cambridge MA/London: Harvard University Press.

Fase, M.M.G., P. Kramer and W.C. Boeschoten (1992), 'MORKMON II, the Nederlandsche Bank's quarterly model of the Netherlands' economy', *Economic Modelling*, **9**, 146–204.

Graafland, J.J. and F.H. Huizinga (1999), 'Taxes and benefits in a non-linear wage equation', *De Economist*, **147**, 39–54.

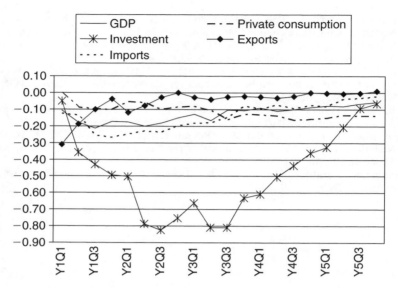

Figure 14.1a   Effects of a two-year 100 bp increase in short-term interest rates (real categories)

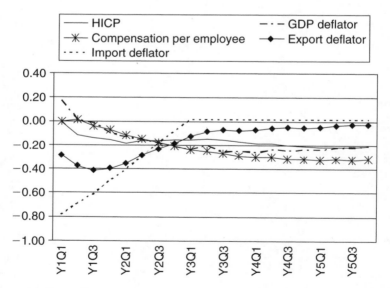

Figure 14.1b   Effects of a two-year 100 bp increase in short-term interest rates (nominal categories)

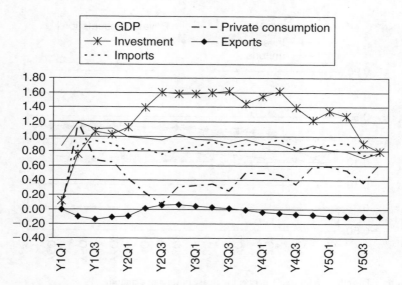

Figure 14.2a   Effects of a five-year increase in real government consumption by 1% of initial GDP (real categories)

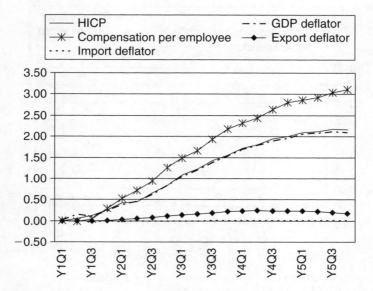

Figure 14.2b   Effects of a five-year increase in real government consumption by 1% of initial GDP (nominal categories)

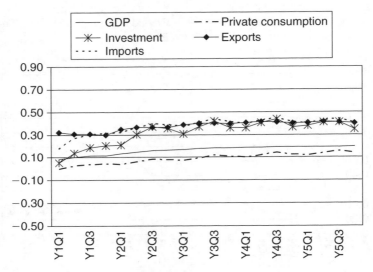

Note: The effects refer to a 1 per cent increase in foreign demand.

Figure 14.3a   Effects of a five-year increase in foreign demand outside the euro area (real categories)

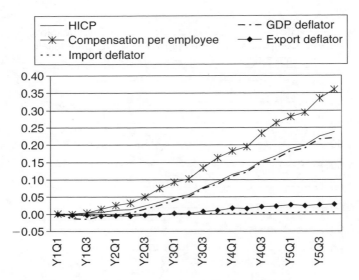

Note: The effects refer to a 1 per cent increase in foreign demand.

Figure 14.3b   Effects of a five-year increase in foreign demand outside the euro area (nominal categories)

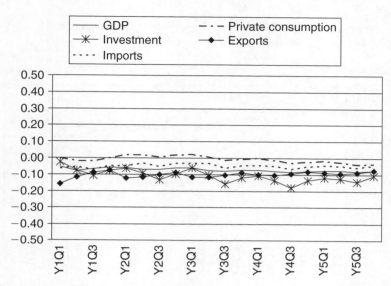

Figure 14.4a   Effects of a 1% appreciation of the euro vis-à-vis *all other currencies, sustained for five years (real categories)*

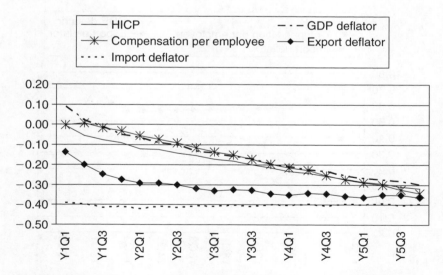

Figure 14.4b   Effects of a 1% appreciation of the euro vis-à-vis *all other currencies, sustained for five years (nominal categories)*

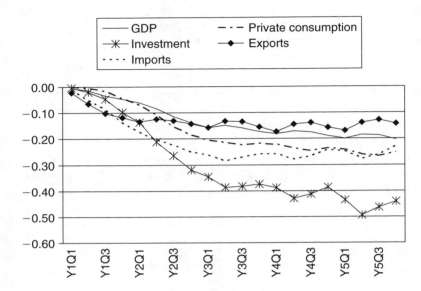

*Figure 14.5a   Effects of a permanent 10% increase in oil prices
            (real categories)*

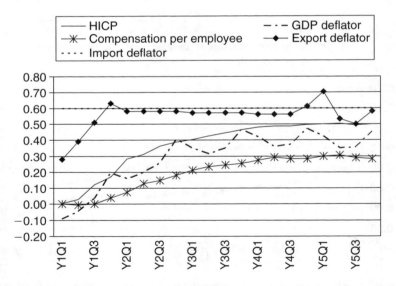

*Figure 14.5b   Effects of a permanent 10% increase in oil prices (nominal
            categories)*

15. The Austrian quarterly model

Gerhard Fenz and Martin Spitzer

1 INTRODUCTION

Until it joined the European System of Central Banks (ESCB), the Oesterreichische Nationalbank had no strong incentive to undertake the considerable task of building a macroeconomic model for forecasting purposes, as this task was performed by two domestic research institutes. From the late 1970s onwards, the Oesterreichische Nationalbank relied mainly on individual models for different sectors and problems. In the late 1990s, an annual macromodel was expressly built to contribute a forecast of the Austrian economy within the ESCB projection exercise. As a next step, the development of the Austrian Quarterly Model (AQM) proceeded in close cooperation with the ECB over a period of two years, from 2002 to 2003. Of course the specification of the AQM is not fixed but constantly under review, so that it is extended and re-estimated in light of new data and new developments in modelling technology.

2 USES OF THE MODEL

The purpose of the AQM is twofold. Firstly, it produces forecasts of the Austrian economy up to three years ahead for the ESCB projection exercise. The model-based estimates of future economic developments may undergo revisions to incorporate experts' judgmental assessments. This is typically the case when faced with structural breaks or discretionary policy measures which cannot be captured econometrically. Forecasts are published twice a year, in June and December.

Secondly, the AQM provides simulations of different scenarios including policy measures or external shocks. These simulation exercises are carried out for international institutions such as the ECB, the OECD or the IMF as well as for internal economic analysis at the Oesterreichische Nationalbank.

3   AN OUTLINE OF THE THEORETICAL UNDERPINNINGS OF THE MODEL

The structure of the AQM reflects the general features of the modelling strategy of the multi-country model (MCM) developed at the ESCB.[1] One element of this strategy involves the decision to build a relatively small-scale model to keep the structure simple enough for projection and simulation purposes while incorporating a sufficiently detailed structure to capture the main characteristics of the Austrian economy. Another element of the modelling strategy is to embody the 'neoclassical synthesis', a combination of Keynesian short-run analysis and neoclassical long-run analysis popularized by Samuelson (1967). More precisely, the short-run dynamics are estimated to conform to empirical evidence, while the long-run relationships are derived from theoretical optimization. An aggregate neoclassical production function is the central feature of the long-run behaviour with a vertical supply curve. The neoclassical relationships ensure that the long-run real equilibrium is determined by available factors of production and technological progress. Therefore real output growth in the long run is independent both of the price level and of inflation. Imperfections in the markets for goods and labour prevent the economy from returning instantaneously to the long-run equilibrium. Thus the economy converges slowly towards its equilibrium in response to economic shocks. Simulation exercises with the AQM typically show that the adjustment process is rather long, reflecting past experience in the Austrian economy and the fact that expectations formation is strictly backward-looking in the current version of the model. Extensions to include forward-looking elements in the price and wage block are straightforward.

The main behavioural equations are estimated using the two-step Engle–Granger technique. Long-run relationships are estimated in levels (non-differenced time series) and then enter the dynamic equations as error correction terms. There is no calibration, as all parameters are econometrically estimated. The simulation and projection features of the AQM are driven by 38 behavioural equations. An additional 107 equations contain linking relationships, identities and transformations to ensure consistency and a sufficiently detailed analysis. Overall 217 variables enter the model.

3.1   The Production Function and Factor Demand

Consistent with the neoclassical framework, the long-run aggregate supply curve is assumed to be vertical and the long-run equilibrium is solely supply-driven. The economy is assumed to produce a single good (Y). The technology is described by a standard constant-returns-to-scale Cobb–Douglas production function with two input factors, capital (K) and labour (L). Technological progress is exogenously given at a constant rate (γ) and enters in the usual labour-augmenting or Harrod-neutral manner. The long-run properties of the model can be derived by standard static optimization techniques. A representative firm maximizes profits (Π) given the technology constraints:

$$\max \Pi(Y, L, K) = P \cdot Y - W \cdot L - CC \cdot K$$

$$s.t. \quad Y = \alpha K^{\beta} \cdot L^{1-\beta} \cdot e^{(1-\beta)\gamma T}$$

where P denotes the price level, W the wage rate, CC the nominal user cost of capital, α a scale parameter, β a technology parameter and T a time index. For estimation purposes we use seasonally-adjusted quarterly ESA-95 data for employment, GDP, the GDP deflator and compensation to employees (as a measure of labour income). Quarterly ESA-95 data are only available from 1988Q1. In order to extend the data to 1980Q1, we used growth rates from ESA-79 data. This procedure causes a break in some time series around 1988, making it necessary to introduce shift dummies in certain equations. Data for the gross capital stock were provided by Statistics Austria. Employment data include both employees and the self-employed, whereas our measure of labour income includes only employees. Therefore we used compensation per employee as a proxy for the 'wages' of the self-employed to calculate total labour income. For estimation purposes, the employment figures were adjusted for full-time equivalents. The nominal user cost of capital, CC, is defined as the sum of the real interest rate, the depreciation rate and a risk premium:

$$CC/ITD = LTI/400 - \pi + \delta_{KSR} + RP$$

where ITD denotes the investment deflator, LTI long-term interest rates, π the inflation rate, δ_{KSR} the depreciation rate of the capital stock and RP the risk premium. The inflation rate π is defined as a moving average of annual changes in the investment deflator over the current and the past four quarters. The risk premium is approximated by the trend component of the difference between the marginal product of capital and the sum of the real interest rate and the average depreciation. The average risk premium is slightly above 0.5 per cent per quarter and shows an increasing trend during the 1990s.

Solving the maximization problem above leads to a nonlinear three-equation system of first order conditions which determines the long-run values of prices, employment and the capital stock.[2] Table 15.1 reports the estimated parameters of the supply block.

Table 15.1   Estimated coefficients of the supply block

Coefficient	Symbol	Estimate
Output elasticity of capital	β	0.366987
Scale parameter	α	1.704339
Technical progress	γ	0.004192

In modelling investment, we used the ratio of investment to the optimal capital stock (which should equal the sum of the depreciation rate and the equilibrium growth rate of the economy in the long run) as an ECM term. Since the real interest rate has a strong influence on the optimal capital stock via the real user cost of capital, the investment equation represents the main transmission channel of monetary policy in the model. Short-run dynamics are dominated by accelerator effects represented by an autoregressive term and a coefficient on real output growth that is larger than one.

The equilibrium level of employment depends solely on the supply side and is obtained by inverting the production function. In the short run, employment moves procyclically with contemporaneous GDP growth. Furthermore it is assumed that firms, on the basis of bargained wages, can choose their desired level of employment. Thus increases in real wages lead to a lower employment level.

In the long run, the labour force follows demographic developments and is given exogenously. In the short run, cyclical fluctuations in output lead to variations in employment but also trigger responses in labour supply. The effect of output variations on the unemployment rate is cushioned by a procyclical reaction of the labour force, a pattern which was especially clear in past Austrian data. The second important short-run determinant in the labour supply equation is real wage growth. As real wages in Austria are known to be very flexible, they tend to reinforce the procyclical behaviour of labour supply.

3.2   Demand Components

Consistent with the permanent income hypothesis, private consumption is a function of real disposable household income and real wealth in the long run. Disposable income comprises the following components: compensation to employees, other personal income (gross mixed income and property income), transfers received and paid by households and direct taxes paid by households. The bulk of financial wealth is illiquid assets, which amount to about one-quarter of total assets. Taking this fact into account yields a reasonable asset-to-income ratio of about 2, in line with other international studies (see Muellbauer and Lattimore, 1995). Nominal short-term interest rates also determine the equilibrium level of consumer expenditures, capturing substitution effects and credit constraints. Consumption is not further disaggregated into durables and non-durables owing to data constraints. The period 1991 to 1997 is characterized by a pronounced decline in the household savings ratio, from 12 per cent to just above 7 per cent. The decline can only be partly explained by the rise in the wealth-to-income ratio and probably reflects changes in household habits and preferences. In order to capture this shift in preferences, a negative trend was introduced in the long-run consumption equation.

The ratio of inventories to output shows on average a declining trend over the 1990s. Alongside this trend, the evolution of inventories is determined by the costs of adjusting production, costs of holding inventories and running out of stock or backlog costs (see Holt *et al.*, 1960). Estimation results show that inventories behave procyclically in Austria. More inventories imply higher holding costs but reduce the probability of running out of stock or backlog costs. The level of inventories that equalizes this counteracting cost increases with economic activity, causing a simple accelerator effect.

3.3 Price Equations

The long-run properties of the price block are jointly determined by two key variables, the deflator of GDP at factor costs and the nominal wage rate. In addition, external price developments are mainly captured by the import price deflator. Other domestic price deflators like the private consumption deflator and the investment deflator feature long-run unit elasticity with respect to these key variables. This assumption of static homogeneity implies that the corresponding error correction terms are modelled in terms of relative prices.

The long-run behaviour of the GDP deflator at factor costs is given by the supply block. The corresponding coefficient of the error correction term implies an adjustment to the equilibrium of 14 per cent per period. Prices in a small open economy like Austria should also depend strongly on foreign price pressures. Foreign competitors' prices were not included in the static steady-state solution of the supply block but enter through import price inflation. The estimated coefficient is rather low, but import prices tend to be more volatile than domestic prices, reflecting the high volatility of exchange rates and commodity prices.

In the AQM, the nominal wage rate is approximated by average compensation per employee as recorded in National Accounts data. These quarterly data are adjusted to full-time equivalents using interpolated annual data. A typical feature of the Austrian labour market is the declining income share of labour. During the sample period, the share dropped from almost 68 per cent in 1980 to slightly less than 60 per cent in 2000. This conflicts with the assumption of a Cobb–Douglas production function with constant returns to scale which implies constant factor income shares in equilibrium equal to the output elasticities β and $(1-\beta)$. A trend in the long-run wage equation starting in 1988Q1 accounts for this fact. The central feature of the short-run dynamics is a Phillips curve linking wage growth to the deviation of the unemployment rate from a constant NAWRU which is exogenous to the model.[3] However the long-run Phillips curve is vertical. The contemporaneous inflation rate measured by the GDP deflator at factor costs is highly correlated with nominal wage growth leading to a rigid behaviour of real wages in simulation exercises. We therefore decided to use only lagged inflation as this better reflects the high real wage flexibility characteristic of the centralized wage setting process in Austria.

The private consumption deflator is a central price variable with strong feedbacks, especially via real wages and real wealth. In the long run, the private consumption deflator depends on the GDP deflator at factor costs, with static homogeneity imposed. In the case of the private investment deflator, long-run unit elasticity with respect to the GDP deflator at factor costs and the import deflator was imposed. This reflects the higher import content of this GDP component compared to private consumption.

3.4 The Government Sector

The role of the public sector is captured by various variables. Among the most prominent are government consumption, government investment, transfers paid and received by households, direct taxes paid by households and firms and indirect taxes. In the long run, the ratio of government consumption to GDP and of public to private investment is assumed to be constant, in short-run analysis both variables are exogenous.

For long-run simulations, the model incorporates a fiscal policy rule with respect to direct tax rates along the lines of the Maastricht public debt criterion of 60 per cent. However in most simulation exercises fiscal policy is assumed to be exogenous and the fiscal closure rule is not activated and only standard automatic fiscal stabilizers are at work.

The ratio of transfers received by households to GDP is a function of the unemployment rate, which is assumed to mirror the cyclical position of the economy. Transfers received by households act as the main automatic stabilizer in the model. An increase in the unemployment rate according to the EUROSTAT definition by 1 per cent causes additional transfers to households of about 0.5 per cent of nominal GDP. The ratio of transfers paid by households to GDP is typically assumed to be constant in simulation exercises.

3.5 The Monetary Sector

A typical macroeconomic model for an economy with an independent monetary policy incorporates a monetary policy rule. By choosing a target level for a nominal anchor this rule ensures a nominal equilibrium by defining an appropriate feedback rule for nominal interest rates. Typical examples for nominal target variables are price levels or, more recently, inflation rates. As long as monetary aggregates are not addressed by interest rate rules there is no specific role for money in this kind of model. Thus monetary aggregates typically influence neither output nor prices. Assuming that the velocity of money is constant, money supply in the AQM can be thought of as moving in line with nominal GDP. Since Austria is part of the euro area and monetary policy decisions are based on an assessment of euro area-wide conditions, a national interest rate rule is not appropriate. Thus interest rates are typically kept exogenous in projection and simulation exercises. Credit demand follows real developments. Feedbacks from the credit market to the real economy are not taken into account.

3.6 The Foreign Trade Block

In modelling real exports, long-run static homogeneity with respect to foreign demand was imposed, in the case of real imports with respect to a modified domestic demand variable. This boils down to modelling export and import market shares in the long run.

The foreign demand variable is defined as the demand on Austrian export markets weighted by trade shares. Changes in the market share of Austrian exporters are explained by a price-competitiveness variable and a time trend. Competitiveness is measured by the ratio of Austrian export prices to competitors' prices. The time trend reflects rapidly increasing trade links in the past.

The modified domestic demand variable is calculated by aggregating real GDP components (with the exception of real imports) weighted by their respective import content, as appears in the current input–output table. In the long run, import market shares depend negatively on a competitiveness variable defined as the ratio of import prices to the GDP deflator at factor costs. Again a time trend had to be introduced, capturing the surge in trade volumes in the recent past. Moreover the special role of oil prices had to be considered. Real imports are very inelastic with respect to oil prices. To control for this fact, the effect of the price-competitiveness variable on real imports was corrected for oil prices.

The equilibrium levels of the Austrian export and import deflators are determined by competitors' export and import prices which are assumed to be exogenous and domestic prices. Competitors' import prices are defined as a weighted sum of our trade partners' export prices weighted by their import shares; competitors' export prices are a double weighted sum of the export prices of countries also exporting to Austrian export markets. The first weight is the export share of a competing country on a specific export market. The second weight is the share of that market in total Austrian exports. In modelling the steady-state import deflator, static homogeneity was imposed with respect to competitors' import prices, the GDP deflator at factor costs and oil prices. The steady-state export deflator depends on competitors' export prices and the GDP deflator at factor costs.

4   AN OUTLINE OF THE KEY CHARACTERISTICS

For a better understanding of the key characteristics of the AQM, five representative simulation exercises are performed to analyse fiscal, monetary and external shocks. All simulations are run without imposing the fiscal closure rule that limits growth in public debt or a monetary closure rule that stabilizes prices. Thus interest rates and nominal exchange rates are assumed to remain constant at their baseline levels over the whole simulation horizon as well as direct taxes and transfers paid by households as a percentage of GDP. Automatic stabilizers work only through transfers received by households and are assumed to depend positively on the unemployment rate. Exogenous (that is, constant) nominal interest rates imply that real interest rates are endogenous via changes in inflation. The backward-looking behaviour of inflation expectations can thus lead to highly variable real interest rates and user cost of capital in simulations. This can generate a relatively strong reaction of real investment to a shock. The 'no change in monetary policy' assumption also explains counterintuitive responses of real investment in some simulation exercises.[4]

The monetary policy shock was carried out according to the harmonized design of the WGEM monetary policy transmission exercise. The special feature of this simulation is that international spillover effects are explicitly considered. The design of the remaining four shocks (fiscal policy shock, foreign demand shock, exchange rate shock and oil price shock) are described in detail in van Els *et al.* (2003). They were run in isolated mode, that is to say, international spillovers and exchange rate effects were disregarded. These effects are of course crucial transmission channels in a small open economy like Austria. Thus the corresponding simulation results have to be interpreted as partial solutions. All simulations are limited to five years.

4.1 Monetary Policy Shock

The uniform simulation design agreed on in the course of the WGEM monetary policy transmission exercise was based on an increase in the short-term interest rate by 100 basis points for two years and a subsequent return to baseline for the remaining three years. Changes in short-term interest rates triggered changes in long-term interest rates in line with a simple interest parity condition. Furthermore it was agreed that nominal exchange rates of the euro follow a simple uncovered interest rate parity condition. International spillovers from other euro-area countries were explicitly taken into account.

As can be seen in Figures 15.1a and 15.1b, the cumulated effects of the monetary policy shock on economic activity are strongest in the second and third year (-0.3 per cent). Initially the dampening effects of net exports are strongest, but from the second year onwards, the fall in domestic demand dominates. Consumer prices are 0.2 per cent below baseline after two years.

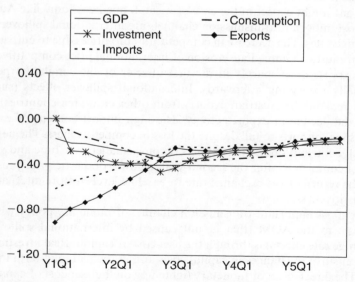

Figure 15.1a   Real effects of a monetary policy shock

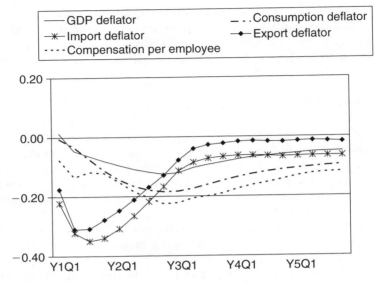

Figure 15.1b   Nominal effects of a monetary policy shock

After the end of the shock, GDP and prices return slowly towards their baseline levels.

As one might expect in the case of a small open economy like Austria, the most important transmission channels are international spillovers and exchange rates. The decrease in competitors' euro prices due to euro appreciation causes an immediate erosion of international price competitiveness. Real exports drop sharply in the first quarter of the simulation period, gradually recovering afterwards. International spillover effects (such as lower demand for Austrian exports from other euro-area countries) reinforce the decline in export activity. The high import content of exports causes real imports to fall despite the loss in competitiveness. The negative growth contributions of net exports become smaller over time and vanish almost completely after the second year as lower domestic price pressures and the return of the exchange rate to baseline levels restore international competitiveness.

The most important transmission channel of monetary policy which is intrinsic to the AQM (that is, not caused by international spillover or exchange rate effects) is through the user cost of capital. Real investment is very sensitive to changes in capital costs and in the real long-term interest rate. The direct effect of monetary tightening on the user cost of capital via nominal interest rates is amplified by the indirect effect via lower inflation.

Other direct transmission channels are mainly present in the household sector. The substitution effect which reflects the increase in relative costs of present versus future consumption dominates the wealth effect which captures the fall of the market value of household's financial wealth. Since households are net lenders, income out of wealth increases as financial yields rise. But the overall effect of the income channel is small. The fall in households' real disposable income is mainly due to weaker employment and lower gross mixed income.

4.2   Fiscal Policy Shock

Figure 15.2 shows the effects of an increase of government consumptions by 1 per cent of baseline real GDP for five years. A surge in government consumption automatically causes an increase in output. Employment is affected with a certain lag, triggering a consistently increasing deviation of the unemployment rate from the exogenous NAWRU. Short-run dynamics according to the Phillips curve lead to an increase in wage inflation. Higher wages and the rise in domestic demand cause a general pick-up in prices. Real investment activity is boosted for two reasons. First, output expansion operates directly by the common accelerator effect and, second, higher inflation rates imply lower real interest rates and therefore a lower user cost of capital. Households' real disposable income rises as employment

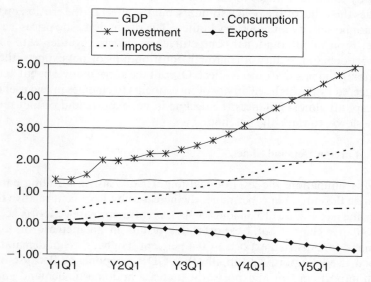

Figure 15.2a   Real effects of a fiscal policy shock

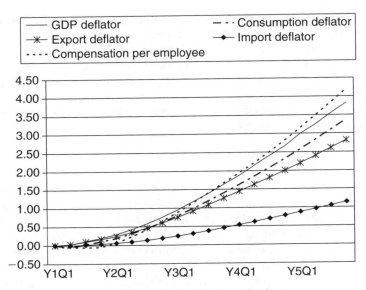

Figure 15.2b   Nominal effects of a fiscal policy shock

expands and other personal income increases. This is only partly offset by
slightly lower real wages in the first few years. Higher inflation gradually
erodes the value of the policy stimulus, but the effect of the erosion on total
economic activity remains very limited. The rise in domestic prices leads to
an erosion of international competitiveness which, together with higher
import demand, reduces the growth contributions of net exports, thereby
damping the positive output effect. Overall the surge in investment activity
(triggered by the high sensitivity of investments to changes in real user costs
of capital) almost balances the decline in net exports and output returns
only slowly towards the baseline.

4.3   Foreign Demand Shock

In this simulation, the level of real imports of Austria's trading partners
outside the euro area is permanently increased by 1 per cent relative to the
baseline (see Figures 15.3a and 15.3b). As extra-euro area exports account
for 40 per cent of total exports, this results in an increase of foreign
demand for Austrian exports of 0.4 per cent. Higher foreign demand triggers a rise in exports and in all other GDP components. Because of the
high import content in exports, the increase in domestic demand and the
loss in international price competitiveness (domestic prices are rising faster

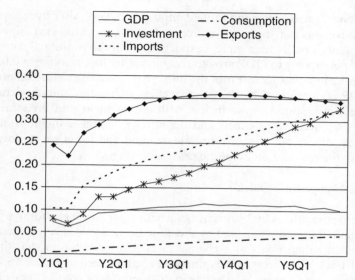

Figure 15.3a   Real effects of a foreign demand shock

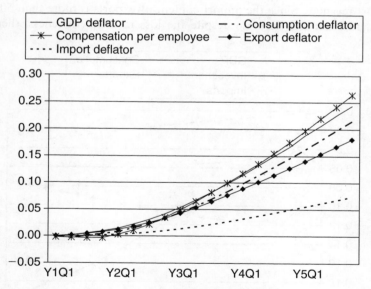

Figure 15.3b   Nominal effects of a foreign demand shock

than import prices), demand for real imports picks up. After five years, the cumulative effect of the positive foreign demand shock on real imports is only slightly smaller than on real exports. Overall the additional contribution of net exports to GDP growth remains rather low, peaking at 0.05 per cent in the first two years. From the third year onwards, additional growth of GDP is dominated by the positive effect of rising domestic demand. Private consumption grows in line with employment and investment is boosted by accelerator effects and the impact of higher inflation on the user cost of capital. Higher domestic demand and lower unemployment increase the pressure on domestic prices and wages.

4.4   Exchange Rate Shock

The euro strengthens by 1 per cent against all other currencies for five years. The simulation is implemented by shocking the nominal effective exchange rate and nominal bilateral exchange rates that enter the model (that is, USD/EUR). The effects of this simulation can be seen in Figure 15.4. An immediate consequence is a decline in extra-euro area competitors' export and import prices in euros. The effect of the appreciation is a deterioration of international competitiveness, reducing market shares and decreasing export revenues. Since the import content of exports is more than 50 per cent, real imports decrease despite the loss in competitiveness, thereby

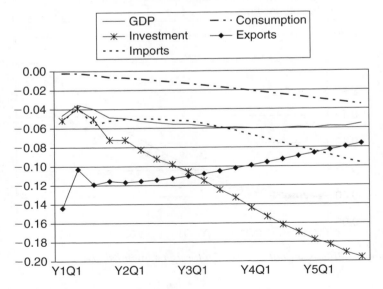

Figure 15.4a   Real effects of an exchange rate shock

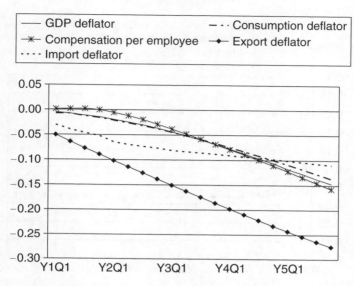

Figure 15.4b   Nominal effects of an exchange rate shock

reducing the negative growth effects of net exports. Lower demand and declining import prices cause a general reduction of price pressures over the simulation period, leading to a gradual recovery of international competitiveness. After five years, negative contributions of net exports to GDP growth have vanished. The drop in prices increases the real user cost of capital and causes investment activity to fall. The almost monotonic deterioration of investment activity causes imports – contrary to exports – to decline further until the end of the simulation period.

4.5   Oil Price Shock

The rise in oil prices by 10 per cent in US dollar terms initially increases import prices by 0.5 per cent and the domestic price level by slightly more than 0.1 per cent. The strong negative reaction of imports in the first two quarters causes GDP to rise thanks to a larger contribution of net exports. Within the first three quarters, foreign prices begin to drive the domestic price level above baseline. The loss in international competitiveness causes exports to drop below baseline. A second important, although counterintuitive, effect is through the lower user cost of capital. Since nominal interest rates are kept constant, higher domestic inflation reduces real interest rates, thereby creating a favourable situation for investment.

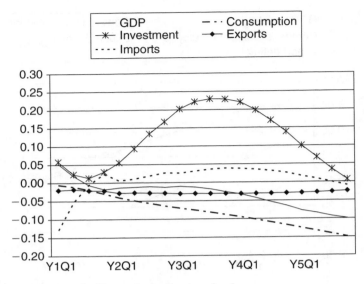

Figure 15.5a   Real effects of an oil price shock

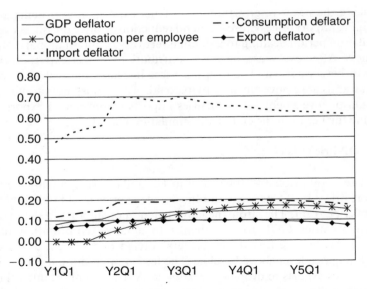

Figure 15.5b   Nominal effects of an oil price shock

Higher investment stimulates imports, further reducing the contribution to growth from net exports. Real private consumption declines throughout, reflecting the erosion of real compensation per employee and a fall in employment. After five years, the GDP deflator is 0.13 per cent above the baseline and real GDP is about 0.1 per cent below.

5 CONCLUSIONS

The AQM in its current versions has already proved to be a very versatile tool within the range of models used at the Oesterreichische Nationalbank. Possible directions for further developments are obvious. One involves developing a more detailed representation of the public finance block to disaggregate the financial determinants of the model. Another project currently under way analyses the long-run properties of the model. Finally an extension to forward-looking behaviour is planned for a later stage.

ACKNOWLEDGMENT

We would like to thank Jerome Henry, Peter McAdam, Martin Schneider, Johann Scharler, Thomas Warmedinger and an anonymous referee for helpful advice and the ECB for their hospitality during the work on this chapter. The views and findings of this chapter are entirely those of the authors and do not necessarily represent those of Oesterreichische Nationalbank.

NOTES

1. See Fagan *et al*. (2001) and Willman and Estrada (2002).
2. A permanent dummy starting in the first quarter of 1996 was introduced in the price equation. This date marks the start of a period of wage moderation. A second dummy covering 1980 to 1988 controls for the fact that ESA-79 data had to be used for this period.
3. The trend unemployment rate is calculated using the method advocated in Elmeskov (1993).
4. Moreover, since the inflation rate in the user cost of capital term is defined as a moving average of annual inflation rates over the current and the past four quarters, and prices behave rather stickily in simulations, responses of investments in simulations exercises with the AQM over a period of five years often appear to be rather monotonic and long-lasting.

REFERENCES

Elmeskov, J. (1993), 'High and persistent unemployment: assessment of the problem and its causes', OECD Economics Department working paper 132.

Fagan, G., J. Henry and R. Mestre (2001), 'An area-wide model (AWM) for the euro area', ECB Working Paper Series (42).

Holt, C.C., F. Modigliani, J.F. Muth and H.A. Simon (1960), *Planning Production, Inventories and Work Force*, 1st edn, Englewood Cliffs, NJ: Prentice-Hall.

Muellbauer, J. and R. Lattimore (1995), 'The consumption function: a theoretical and empirical overview', in M. Hashem Pesaran and Mike Wickens (eds), *Handbook of Applied Econometrics-Macroeconomics*, Cambridge, MA: Blackwell Publishers, pp. 221–311.

Samuelson, P. (1967), *Economics, An Introductory Analysis*, 7th edn, New York: McGraw-Hill Book Company.

van Els, P., A. Locarno, J. Morgan and J.-P. Villetelle (2003), 'The effects of monetary policy in the euro area: evidence from structural macroeconomic models', in I. Angeloni, A. Kashyap and B. Mojon (eds), *Monetary Policy Transmission in the Euro Area*, Cambridge: Cambridge University Press, pp. 91–106.

Willman, A. and A. Estrada (2002), 'The Spanish block of the ESCB-multi-county model', ECB Working Paper Series (149).

16. The annual macroeconometric model of the Banco de Portugal

Gabriela Lopes de Castro

1 INTRODUCTION

This chapter briefly describes the main features and uses of the Annual Macroeconometric Model (AMM). Since spring 2001, this model has been the main macroeconomic forecasting tool used by the Banco de Portugal. The projections for the Portuguese economy are generated using additional models, namely a small-scale quarterly inflation-forecasting model[1] and some bridge models, which are intended to provide non-causal forecasts for the short-term quarterly developments. In addition, a small-scale model incorporating forward-looking elements is being developed, mainly oriented to provide simulations of fiscal policy changes.

The reason why an annual rather than a quarterly model was chosen, is mainly the lack of consistent and reliable quarterly time series for the Portuguese economy with the sufficiently long period of time that is required for econometric estimation.[2] Moreover we have to estimate causality links with a degree of detail that is not possible with a quarterly frequency, in particular in the case of general government variables. Indeed one of the special features of the model is its very comprehensive and fully integrated block of public finances.

Since 2001, some progress has been made in the AMM. Besides some improvements in the model equations, other important developments are still being carried out, namely, improvements in the financial block of the model. Additionally some work has also been devoted to the possible introduction of forward-looking elements that might improve the results for some simulation and for the convergence towards the long-run path. Therefore, this document and the results presented here may be revised as a result of further work.

2 USES OF THE MODEL

The AMM is currently used as the main tool to produce short- and medium-term projections and to assess the impact of shocks on key economic variables. In particular, the AMM is used in the preparation of economic projections up to three years ahead and in the simulation of alternative scenarios in the context of the biannual Eurosystem projection exercise. These projections are published twice a year in the bank's quarterly bulletin. The AMM is also used in the analysis of various policy measures and in risk analysis.

3 AN OUTLINE OF THE THEORETICAL UNDERPINNINGS OF THE MODEL

The theoretical structure underlying the AMM is relatively standard, ensuring that nominal shocks are neutral to the economic activity in the long run, but have real impact in the short run. The model is divided into three sectors: public sector, farm and non-farm private sectors.

Potential output is defined on the basis of a Cobb–Douglas production function for the non-farm private sector with constant returns to scale on three productive factors (labour, capital and oil imports, as an intermediate factor) and labour-augmenting technological progress.[3] Using this equation, potential output is achieved when employment is equal to its long-run level, which depends on the NAIRU and on the exogenous assumptions for the population and for the activity rate.[4]

In the short run, owing to some rigidity in wages and prices, GDP and employment are determined by aggregate demand. However deviations of demand from the long-run level of output trigger a process of wage and price adjustment that drives the model to the long-run equilibrium; that is, product and employment tend to converge to their long-run levels. As both interest rates and exchange rates are exogenously determined, the response to a change in domestic/external relative prices also plays a role in ensuring the return to the long-run equilibrium.

The behavioural equations were estimated on the basis of historical data, typically from 1980 onwards. However some dynamic specifications were also calibrated to improve the forecasting performance of the model.[5] The long-run relations enter the dynamic equations in the form of an error correction term to ensure that the dependent variables converge to the long-run equilibrium path. These long-run conditions were estimated imposing a set of structural economic constraints to hold in the long run. AMM is a backward-looking model as most of its behaviour equations include lagged values of the dependent variables, imposing some inertia in the model.

The model incorporates over 100 behavioural equations and accounting identities, structured in five blocks: expenditure, production and labour market, disposable income, financial and general government blocks. The database used to estimate the model was built from three different sources: (a) estimates produced by Banco de Portugal for the period 2002–3; (b) the new series of national accounts produced by the Portuguese statistical office, Instituto Nacional de Estatística, for the period 1995–2001, based on the ESA-95; (c) from 1977 to 1994, the national accounts were extrapolated using the annual historical series produced by the Banco de Portugal.

3.1 Production Function and Factor Demands

Starting from a Cobb–Douglas production function for gross output in the non-farm private sector (Q_{pri}) with labour (L_{pri}), capital (K_{pri}) and oil as an intermediate input (M_{oil}),

$$Q_{pri} = BK_{pri}^{\theta_1}(L_{pri}e^{\gamma t})^{\theta_2}M_{oil}^{\theta_3}, \quad \theta_1 + \theta_2 + \theta_3 = 1$$

the derived (Cobb–Douglas) function specifies value added (Y_{pri}) depending on labour, capital and the relative price of the intermediate good.

$$Y_{pri} = AK_{pri}^{1-\alpha}(L_{pri}e^{\gamma t})^{\alpha}\left(\frac{Poil}{PYcf_{pri}}\right)^{-\mu}$$

where

$$A = (1 - \theta_3)(B\theta_3^{\theta_3})^{\frac{1}{1-\theta_3}}, \quad \alpha = \frac{\theta_1}{\theta_1 + \theta_2}, \quad \mu = \frac{\theta_3}{\theta_1 + \theta_2}$$

This production function implies a potential output depending on oil price and thus changes in this price are considered as a supply shock.[6] The coefficient for the labour share was calibrated on the basis of the observed average wage income share in the period 1983–2000.

The long-run specification for the non-farm private investment equation is consistent with the Cobb–Douglas approach, that is, in the long run, capital stock is proportional to output, with its ratio depending only on the expected cost of capital in real terms (the expected real interest rate and a depreciation rate).[7] The dynamic equation for investment includes two error correction terms, ensuring that, in the long run, investment and the capital stock grow at the same rate as GDP.

In the long run, the level of employment is given, depending on the assumptions for the NAIRU and for the participation rate. The cyclical component of employment depends on real wages adjusted for trend productivity and on the output gap. Private sector real wages are consistent with the constant labour share implied by the Cobb–Douglas function and their growth equals average productivity growth in the long run.

3.2   Components of Aggregate Demand

Regarding aggregate demand, expenditure on real GDP is split into five components. *Private consumption* is divided into consumption of non-durables, consumption of durables and housing rents. The consumption of non-durables, which incorporates the existence of consumers with and without liquidity constraints in the economy,[8] is computed as a weighted average of real disposable income and potential GDP (obtained from the supply side plus the observed farm private GDP and public GDP) as a proxy for the permanent income. This equation also includes the short-term interest rate in real terms and inflation.[9] The household's disposable income excludes housing rents and is adjusted by the amount of capital redemptions paid by households. This adjustment is intended to take into account the impact on private consumption of the increase in household indebtedness observed in the recent past. The specification of private consumption of durables, which is similar to the one for non-residential investment, is a function of the stock of durables, the short-term interest rate plus the depreciation rate and the real disposable income (excluding rent and adjusted for capital redemptions). In the short run, the consumption of durables is also a function of the unemployment rate as a proxy for consumers' confidence. Housing rents are in line with the evolution of the stock of housing.

Public consumption is broken down into civil servants' wages, intermediate consumption and consumption of fixed capital.

Gross fixed capital formation (GFCF) is split into general government GFCF, private residential and private non-residential GFCF. The long-run private non-residential investment is consistent with the production function, as mentioned above. In the short run, it is also a function of changes in private GDP and changes in interest rates. The private residential investment is a function of nominal lending rate to households and of the adjusted real disposable income, with a unit coefficient. Finally public investment is exogenous.

Total exports are split into goods and services. This breakdown is justified by the different behaviour of these categories of exports. In addition, given the significant weight of exports of tourism services in the Portuguese economy, an additional breakdown is considered: tourism services and other services. Exports of goods, in the long run, are determined by the external demand (with a unit elasticity) and a measure of competitiveness that is proxied by the ratio between external and internal unit labour costs, which is an adjustment channel for the equilibrium in the economy. Reflecting a strong empirical regularity in the Portuguese economy, exports in the short run are negatively influenced by the evolution of private consumption, reflecting some substitution between sales in domestic and in external markets.

Imports of goods and services are modelled as a function of global demand components weighted by their relative import content and an indicator of price competitiveness defined as the ratio between import and internal demand prices.

3.3 Prices and Costs

In the long run, real wages in the private sector increase in line with the average productivity growth, which is consistent with the constant labour share implied by the Cobb–Douglas function. This relation enters the dynamic equation as an error correction term, as does the gap between the unemployment rate and its structural level (NAIRU) and a target value for inflation rate.[10]

In the long run, the private consumption deflator excluding energy is defined as a weighted average of unit labour costs and import prices.[11] The short-run dynamics also include spillover effects from changes in energy prices. Energy prices depend on the hypothesis assumed for fuel prices and exchange rates.

The purchasing power parity condition is considered in the ECM of exports and import prices equations, thus exchange rate variations tend to be fully transmitted to domestic prices in the long run. As regards the imports deflator, it is worth mentioning that oil prices are considered separately from the remaining import prices. Finally the GDP deflator is obtained as the weighted average of demand component deflators.

3.4 Fiscal Policy and the Government Sector

The AMM includes a very detailed description of the items composing the general government budget (for example, taxes on households, firms, goods and services and social contributions, in the case of revenue; public consumption, interest paid by general government, different types of transfers to households and firms, in the case of expenditure). Expenditure and revenue equations were designed to reflect institutional arrangements and fiscal rules. The public finance block is linked to the other blocks of the model, therefore allowing for the automatic computation of second round effects of changes in fiscal policy instruments. Moreover it has been designed to fully ensure consistency between the macroprojections and the detailed public finance forecasts, as presented by the Banco de Portugal in the context of the Eurosystem projection exercise.

The degree of detail of the general government accounts makes it possible to simulate the overall impact in the Portuguese economy of different fiscal policy measures, for instance changes in income tax rates, VAT, social transfers and public consumption. Most of the equations and rules used in this block were drawn from previous studies made at the Banco de Portugal on the impact of cyclical fluctuations on the budget balance and on the estimation of fiscal elasticities.[12]

Most of the variables on the revenue side react contemporaneously to real and nominal changes in the economy. Some capital revenues, however, are fixed in nominal terms in the first year. On the expenditure side, most of the variables are set exogenously, as they reflect policy options (for example, number of civil servants, real intermediate consumption, real public investment) or structural developments of the economy (number of pensioners, for instance).

3.5 Trade

Trade flows are estimated in a standard fashion, depending on a competitiveness indicator involving trade prices and, in addition, on domestic demand components weighted by their import content, in the case of imports of goods and services, and on the external demand relevant for the Portuguese economy, in the case of exports of goods.

The current account plus capital account in AMM is structured as follows: the trade balance in goods and services is obtained from the export and import equations (volumes and prices). Net private external transfers, mainly composed of emigrants' remittances, are a function of the international environment of the Portuguese economy, measured by the weighted average of GDP of the main countries. The net income balance depends on the level of net international investment position of the Portuguese economy, as well as on the evolution of interest rates. Finally net public transfers are exogenously determined, as they mainly correspond to predetermined transfers from the EU.

3.6 Monetary and Financial Sector

In its standard version,[13] the financial block includes estimated equations for banking credits and deposits of households. Banking credit to households is divided into housing credit and remaining credit. The first depends on nominal housing investment and on the nominal interest rate. The remaining credit is a function of nominal private consumption of durables. Redemptions of households' debt are explicitly derived in the financial block, as they are used to adjust disposable income.

Finally, in order to check the overall financial consistency of the projection exercises carried out with the AMM, a table with flows of funds among firms, households, general government and the external sector is also produced as an additional diagnostic tool.

4   AN OUTLINE OF THE KEY CHARACTERISTICS

The aim of this section is to present the results of simulations of shocks.

4.1   Monetary Policy Shock

The monetary policy shock presented in Figures 16.1a and 16.1b corresponds to an increase of 100 basis points in the nominal short-term interest rate for two years. The long-term interest rate is adjusted to a term structure scheme and the exchange rate appreciates in line with an uncovered interest rate parity condition.[14]

The increase in nominal interest rates reduces demand through lower private consumption and lower investment, respectively, to a minimum

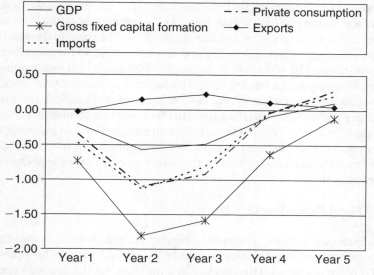

Figure 16.1a   Real effects of a monetary policy shock

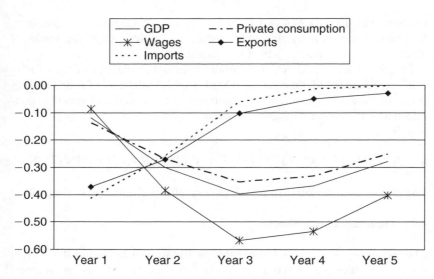

Figure 16.1b   Monetary policy shock (impact on deflators and wages)

of −1.1 per cent and −1.8 per cent in the first two years.[15] The effect on demand is slightly compensated by a small increase in exports, which reflects some substitution effect between sales in domestic and external markets.[16] In comparison with the baseline, GDP decreases in the first two years to a minimum of −0.6 per cent. As a consequence of the decrease in GDP, employment declines to a minimum of −0.3 per cent in the first three years, inducing a reduction in disposable income, which also affects private consumption. The reduction in demand is translated into lower domestic prices through wages, reinforced by the decrease in the first year in import prices, as a consequence of the euro appreciation. Therefore the private consumption deflator deviates from the baseline to a minimum of −0.35 per cent three years later. The return of the interest rate to its initial level after two years leads to an increase in consumption and investment to its baseline levels, which also induces the adjustment of domestic prices to the baseline path.

4.2   Fiscal Policy Shock

The fiscal policy shock presented in Figures 16.2a and 16.2b, is specified as an increase in real public expenditure on goods and services by 1 per cent of GDP for five years. This shock shows the short-term Keynesian properties of the model, since the increase in public expenditures stimulates real

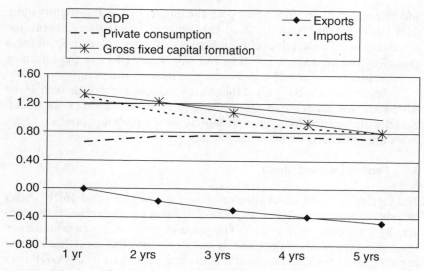

Figure 16.2a   Real effects of a fiscal policy shock

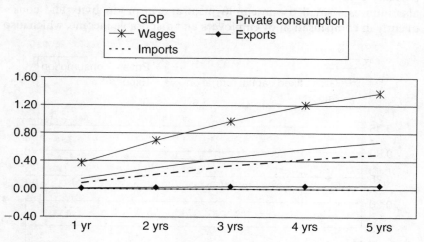

Figure 16.2b   Fiscal policy shock (impact on deflators and wages)

demand, both directly and indirectly through second-round effects in private consumption and in investment. On the other hand, the strong impact in demand is slightly compensated by the decrease in exports, which reflects the aforementioned substitution effect between sales in domestic and external markets. In the first year, the impact on GDP is slightly more than 1 per cent and from the third year onwards it starts to adjust to the baseline path. This GDP evolution is due to the loss of competitiveness caused by the increase in inflation and wages as well as to the return of investment, after its initial overshooting, to its long-run path.

However it should be stressed that backward-looking models such as the AMM are not adequate to assess the impact of such a shock. In fact, a model with forward-looking expectations would probably produce faster crowding-out effects on private expenditure.[17]

4.3   Foreign Demand Shock

The foreign demand shock, presented in Figures 16.3a and 16.3b, corresponds to an increase in real imports of trading partners outside the euro area by 1 per cent for five years. The share of non- euro area countries in Portuguese exports is approximately one-third, thus this shock has a direct impact of 0.25 per cent on exports in the first year. As a result, GDP rises by 0.05 per cent *vis-à-vis* the baseline in the first year. There are also some positive indirect effects in GDP through consumption and investment, partially compensated by the increase in imports. The increase in GDP also induces a small rise in employment and in productivity and consequently in compensation of employees and disposable income, which also

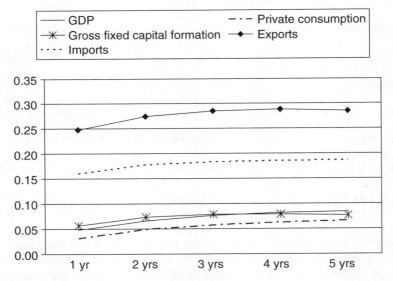

Figure 16.3a   Real effects of a foreign demand shock

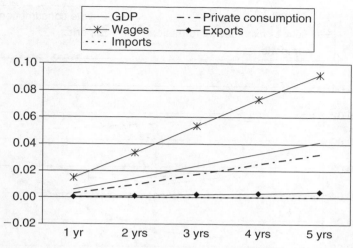

Figure 16.3b   Foreign demand shock (impact on deflators and wages)

contributes to the slight increase in private consumption. GDP exhibits a fast convergence, reaching its long-term path in the third year (0.08 per cent above the baseline). This shock also has a small but permanent effect on domestic deflators and a larger effect on wages, which is 0.1 per cent above baseline after five years.

4.4   Exchange Rate Shock

The exchange rate shock presented in Figures 16.4a and 16.4b, is undertaken as an appreciation of the euro effective exchange rate by 1 per cent for five years. The appreciation of the euro is quickly passed through the import and export deflators. The loss of competitiveness translates into a slight reduction of exports and, consequently, GDP, investment and imports. On the other hand, the decrease in consumer prices, reflecting the import deflator evolution, is transmitted to the other nominal variables, which induces a temporary increase in real disposable income and consequently causes some increase in consumption. Additionally the consumption pattern also reflects a slight increase of permanent income, due to the reduction of oil prices in euros. Thereafter the decrease in inflation tends to balance the exchange rate effects, explaining the return of GDP to its baseline path.

The much larger effects on prices than on real variables are consistent with previous studies of the Portuguese economy.[18] Firstly, the fluctuations of the nominal exchange rate in a small economy like the Portuguese one tend to be quickly transmitted to prices and thus the real exchange rate is

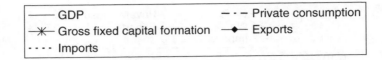

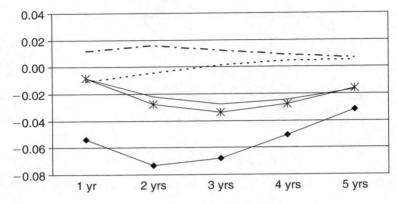

Figure 16.4a   Real effects of an exchange rate shock

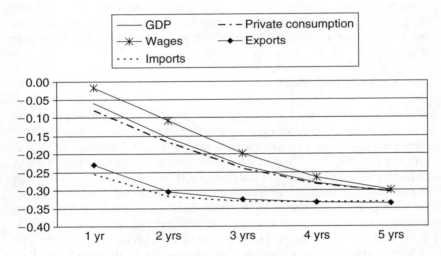

Figure 16.4b   Exchange rate shock (impact on deflators and wages)

just temporarily affected. Secondly, an appreciation of the euro against the US dollar, besides representing a competitiveness issue, also corresponds to a positive shock to terms of trade, given the important share of imports expressed in this currency (oil prices and other commodities).

4.5   Oil Price Shock

A temporary (five-year) increase of 10 per cent in oil prices, presented in
Figures 16.5a and 16.5b, is transmitted immediately to the import deflator

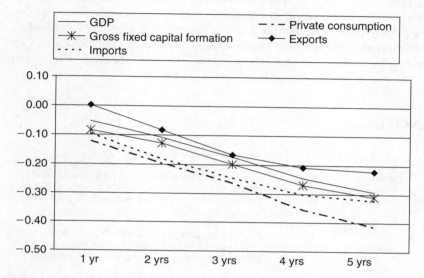

Figure 16.5a   Real effects of an oil price shock

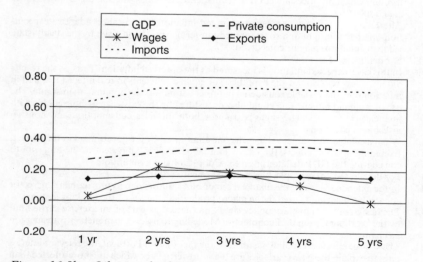

Figure 16.5b   Oil price shock (impact on deflators and wages)

(by approximately 0.75 per cent vis-à-vis the baseline) and, hence, to domestic prices. As this shock decreases the potential output of the economy, reflecting the functional form of the production function, it will produce long-term effects in the real variables. The capital stock has to adjust to the new long-term level of GDP, which implies a reduction in investment. The increase in prices affects real disposable income and consequently private consumption decreases. Exports also show a reduction, which is mainly due to the loss of competitiveness as a consequence of the increase in domestic unit labour costs. The trade balance deteriorates, reflecting the worsening of the terms of trade.

NOTES

1. This model plays a key role in the narrow inflation projection exercise.
2. It is worth mentioning that a quarterly macroeconometric model, with a structure similar to the AMM, is being developed. Currently, the work is being devoted to the estimation and simulation of the model, as the development of a consistent quarterly database has already been completed. In the near future, this new model is likely to play a prominent role in the forecasting process.
3. See Bruno and Sachs (1985).
4. The NAIRU is assumed to be constant, in line with previous findings for the Portuguese economy (Luz and Pinheiro, 1993; Gaspar and Luz, 1997; Marques and Botas, 1997).
5. For example, the quarterly inflation model, mentioned above, was used to calibrate some parameters of the AMM.
6. This approach allows the solving of the problem of traditional models where the oil price is just considered as a competitiveness feature, not accounting for the mechanisms through which oil prices affect GDP permanently. On this issue see, for instance, Jones *et al.* (2004).
7. Alternative approaches to measure expected inflation (for instance, adaptive expectations, perfect foresight or a constant medium-term expectation given by the steady-state value of inflation) may be considered.
8. For details, see Luz (1992).
9. In this case, expected inflation is measured as the observed inflation. Thus, as the results did not allow rejection of the hypothesis of equal coefficients in real interest rate and in inflation rate, the variable considered in this equation was the nominal interest rate. The use of nominal interest rate could also be justified by the existence of households with financial constraints. The same is true for both durables consumption and housing investment equations.
10. When available, this target value is the one announced by the government in the budget.
11. Excluding taxation effects, the use of unit labour cost is equivalent in the long run to considering the GDP deflator given the Cobb–Douglas assumption.
12. For details, see, for example, Neves and Sarmento (2001).
13. In the extended version, the financial sector block allows one to project banking sector consolidated accounts used in the macro prudential analysis of the banking system.
14. The design of the monetary policy shock was agreed as part of an exercise carried out by the Working Group on Econometric Modelling to assess the monetary transmission mechanism.
15. These large effects are mainly justified by the fact that, in Portugal, the relevant interest rates to explain these two variables are the short-term ones, which are more affected than the long-term interest rates in this monetary policy shock.

16. It is worth mentioning that these shocks are without spillover effects.
17. For more details, see Félix (2004).
18. For more details, see Esteves (2003).

REFERENCES

Bruno, M. and J. Sachs (1985), *Economics of Worldwide Stagflation*, Cambridge, MA: Harvard University Press, chs 2–3.

Esteves, P. (2003), 'Monetary conditions index for Portugal', Banco de Portugal, *Economic Bulletin*, June.

Félix, R. (2004), 'A small-scale model with forward-looking elements for the Portuguese economy', mimeo.

Gaspar, V. and S. Luz (1997), 'Unemployment and wages in Portugal', Banco de Portugal, *Quarterly Bulletin*, December.

Jones, D., P. Neiby and I. Paik (2004), 'Oil price shocks and the macroeconomy: what has been learned since 1996', *Energy Journal*, **25** (2), 1–32.

Luz, S. (1992), 'The effects of liquidity constraints on consumption behaviour: the Portuguese experience', Banco de Portugal, working paper no. 3–92.

Luz, S. and M. Pinheiro (1993), 'Unemployment, job vacancies and wage growth', Banco de Portugal, *Quarterly Bulletin*, June, **15** (2).

Marques, C. and S. Botas (1997), 'Estimation of the NAIRU for the Portuguese Economy', Banco de Portugal, working paper no. 6/97.

Neves, P. and L. Sarmento (2001), 'The use of cyclically adjusted balances at Banco de Portugal', Banco de Portugal, *Economic Bulletin*, September.

17. The Bank of Finland's macroeconomic model BOF5

Hanna-Leena Männistö

1 INTRODUCTION

One of the two main research areas of the Bank of Finland is modelling of monetary policy, where the focus is on the treatment of uncertainty and expectations in quantitative calculations and models used in monetary policy analysis. This research strategy already started to be evident in the mid-1990s, when the present version of the Bank's structural domestic model was built, and explicit modelling of expectation formation was introduced.

This chapter briefly documents the present fifth version of the Bank of Finland macroeconomic model, BOF5, and its parallel aggregative version, BOFMINI. In constructing the model, consistent treatment of expectations is emphasized. Intertemporal optimization with rational expectations is taken as the starting point, and Euler equations are applied in the estimation of the key behavioural equations. Consistent treatment of technology on the supply side has been another important aim. A detailed analysis of the model, including some simulations that illustrate the properties of the model and an outline of the derivation of the key equations, is presented in Willman *et al.* (2000), which also briefly describes the evolution of the BOF model since the early 1970s. A full list of equations is presented in Willman *et al.* (1998).

2 USES OF THE MODEL

The Bank of Finland's BOF model is designed to simulate the Finnish economy in an aggregative way and to produce quantitative information on responses of the economy to various types of impulses originating, for example, in the world economy or in economic policy measures. The BOF model has been used regularly by the Bank's Economics Department for forecasting and policy analysis: BOF4 (documented in BOF4, 1990) since the late 1980s and thereafter BOF5 since 1996 (Willman and Männistö, 1997). Model development is a joint effort of the Economics Department and the Research Department. On a rotating basis, on average two econo-mists of the modelling and forecasting team visit the Research Department each year to work in model development together with the Research Department staff.

In recent years, an aggregate version of the BOF5 model, called BOFMINI, has been applied. It is a medium-sized quarterly macroeco-nomic model. The economics of the BOFMINI model is the same as that of the BOF5 model, but, in BOFMINI, the private sector is not disaggre-gated into manufacturing and the rest of the private sector, and the gov-ernment sector is not disaggregated into the central government, local government and social security funds. This markedly reduces the number of variables and identities in the model (the number of equations in the BOF5 is about 400, in the BOFMINI about 240), without affecting key simulation properties.[1]

The BOFMINI model has been used in the Bank's forecasting process, in both the internal and the Eurosystem BMP exercise, amounting to four forecasting rounds per year. The internal forecast report, including the full set of model tables, is made publicly available. Sensitivity analysis and alternative scenarios are regularly produced with the model to shed light on risk analysis. In producing the baseline, the model is used as an integrating device, so that off-model input and judgment are also discussed in the theoretical framework provided by the model. Input from short-term models and indicators as well as judgmental information are taken on board, especially for the short-term forecast. A detailed public finance satellite spreadsheet is linked to the model in the forecasting process with feedback. The forecasting team discusses the forecast issues and numbers in a scheduled set of meetings, and decides on the need for further itera-tion. The baseline is used in the policy assessment process as input, often accompanied by policy analysis or alternative scenarios. In addition, the baseline is used in the monitoring process as a point of reference for new information.

The GMM method is used in the estimation of the Euler equations that are applied in the key behavioural equations. Model data are based on the quarterly National Accounts and other publicly available sources, but for some variables data have been constructed specifically for the BOF model. The model databank is part of the Bank's economic time series databank, accessible to the Bank's staff involved in forecasting, monitoring or model-ling. The model is coded in LBS (CEF) software.

3   AN OUTLINE OF THE THEORETICAL UNDERPINNINGS OF THE MODEL

The theoretical starting point adopted in constructing the BOF5 is that it represents the neoclassical synthesis. By this, we mean that, in the short run, owing to the relative rigidity of wages and prices, production, income and employment are determined by aggregate demand. Thus the short-run properties of the model are Keynesian. In the course of time, however, wages and prices respond to possible discrepancies between demand and supply, and consequently the product and labour markets tend to converge to full employment and purchasing power parity between domestic and foreign currency prices.

The applied Euler approach means that the key behavioural equations (11 in BOFMINI, 15 in BOF5) are derived on the basis of intertemporal optimization by households and firms. The Euler equation for consumption is derived from the behaviour of a utility-maximizing consumer, and that for investment from the behaviour of a profit-maximizing firm. Via an intertemporal optimizing agent problem, and assuming adjustment costs both in changes of levels and in deviations from the desired level, we derive forward-looking equations for, for example, prices, demand for labour and demand for money. Also the equations for inventory investment, housing investment and the real price of housing are forward-looking. In addition the long-term interest rate is determined as the weighted average of expected short-term interest rates. Moreover model-consistent inflation expectations make wage formation forward-looking. The labour unions are assumed to maximize expected real after-tax wages over the contract period. Thus inflation expectations enter the negotiated wage rate equation with the coefficient one. Wage drift over the negotiated wage is a function of the real wage gap and the unemployment rate.

Backward-looking counterparts, included in the model as alternative equations, are derived as transformations of the estimated equations, under the assumption of static expectation formation.[2] In most cases, an analytic transformation is applied, but, in a few cases, an error correction has been estimated. In simulating the model, either alternative for expectation formation can be chosen. In preparing the medium-term macro forecast, we use the backward-looking transformations, but inflation expectations are treated as forward-looking in the sense that exogenous leads of inflation are updated several times during the forecast round. In policy analysis and alternative scenarios, we impose model-consistent expectations.

3.1 Components of Aggregate Demand

The behaviour of the household sector is based on intertemporal maximization of utility under a flow budget constraint, with wealth composed of housing wealth, money balances and debt. In addition the possibility that the ability of households to foresee future flows of income as imperfect has been taken into account. These assumptions imply that private consumption depends on current-period real disposable income, real wealth and the present value of the expected stream of future real income. The demand for actual real money balances depends on the weighted averages of past and future consumption streams and on nominal interest rates.

The interaction of the demand and supply of housing services plays an important role in the wealth channel mechanism and hence in the transmission of monetary policy to the household sector. The equilibrium condition for the demand for and the supply of housing services determines the rental price of housing and it depends positively on permanent income and negatively on the existing housing stock. The market price of housing is the discounted present value of the determinants of the rental price of housing and is therefore forward-looking. However, as it is assumed that the demand for housing services reacts slowly to changes in permanent income, this relationship also includes a strong backward-looking element. In this equation, monetary policy affects the market price of housing directly through the interest rate used in discounting. The market price of housing affects the household sector wealth via the value of the housing stock and the accumulation of the housing stock.

The construction of new dwellings is a function of the market price of housing relative to production costs (Tobin's q). In addition, changes in the interest rate also have a direct effect on housing investment. This direct link is associated with the cost of financing during the construction period. The household sector flow budget constraint defines the net borrowing requirement; that is, the accumulated changes in the outstanding debt of the household sector.

For the household sector, the interest rate applied in the model is the rate of new bank loans. It is a function of both the short-term and the long-term market rate, with more weight on the former, reflecting the fact that the majority of household sector bank loans are linked to short-term Euribor rates. As is evident from the narrow definition of household sector wealth, there is no explicit equities market in the BOF model. Instead, in stock price simulations, we shock the wealth variable directly.

3.2 Production Function and Factor Demand

The behaviour of firms is based on profit maximization. In the first stage, firms maximize the value of their expected future profit streams subject to their respective production functions,[3] product demand functions, adjustment costs associated with investment and the credit ceiling. The credit ceiling reduces the size of the discount factor. Intertemporal profit maximization results in forward-looking fixed investment functions so that investment depends on both future and past differences between the marginal product and the rental price of capital. The main determinant of the rental price of capital is the real interest rate. Marginal products of capital are calculated from estimated production functions and depend positively on the output–capital ratio. Hence, for example, as a result of a demand shock, the accumulation of the capital stock gradually decreases the marginal product of capital and the incentive for additional investment.

The desired demand for labour input can be solved by the inverted production function. The second stage of the minimization of adjustment cost functions produces equations for actual labour demand. Labour input is modelled in hours worked, and a simple transformation, with some lags, is estimated for numbers employed. The labour force reacts to changes in labour demand via the encouraged worker hypothesis.

3.3 Prices and Costs

The first-stage maximization also defines the desired price levels for exportables and for commodities sold in domestic markets as a mark-up over short-run marginal costs of production. Marginal costs include raw material costs and the ratio of nominal labour costs to the marginal product of labour, measured in terms of the capital–labour ratio. Hence a positive demand shock causes an upward price pressure via the decreasing marginal product of labour.[4] The second stage of the minimization of adjustment cost functions produces equations for actual export prices and producer prices, as well as labour demand, with both forward- and backward-looking elements. A similar type of equation is also derived for inventory investment by assuming increasing costs associated with deviations of inventories and production from desired levels.

The input–output identity for production with the assumption of fixed input shares is used in solving for value-added deflators. Likewise prices for demand components are obtained as weighted averages of sectoral producer prices and import prices, adding impacts of changes in effective indirect tax rates. The national consumer price index is modelled to include the imputed housing cost term and, finally, the harmonized index of consumer prices, with a narrower basket, is defined.

3.4 Trade

The private sector meets two demand functions: the foreign demand for exportables, that is, the exports of goods equation and domestic demand for import-competing products. In line with the small open economy hypothesis, the price elasticity of exportables is high.[5] Domestic demand for domestically produced goods and services is obtained indirectly as the difference between total domestic demand and imports. Imports, in turn, are a function of an input–output estimate of import demand (that is, demand components multiplied by a constant import share) and relative prices. As the price elasticity of imports is low, there is low substitutability between domestically produced and imported goods.

Although the main determinant of export prices is the short-run marginal cost of production, the high price elasticity of exports does not allow wide deviations from purchasing power parity in the long run. For instance, if relative export prices are too high, the volume of exports, and hence production, decreases. In the case of infinite long-run price elasticity of exports, this process continues until costs are restored to a level consistent with competing world market prices, mainly through wage responses to lower demand for labour. This mechanism also explains why the exchange rate impact on domestic prices is strong, as shown in Simulation 4 below.

3.5 Fiscal Policy and the Government Sector

In the goods and production factor markets, the model contains three domestic behavioural sectors: the household sector, the corporate sector and the government sector. Fiscal policy is either exogenous or endogenized through simple policy rules. General government income, outlay, net lending and debt accumulation are modelled, but, as explained above, the forecast paths are produced by iterating with the public finances satellite. In simulations other than the forecast baseline, effective tax rates as well as government expenditure, other than interest outlays and unemployment benefits, are exogenous.

3.6 Monetary and Financial Sector

In developing the financial block of the BOF model, the preceding BOF4 model was built to reflect the fact that Finnish financial markets were deregulated in the mid-1980s and the focus shifted from excess demand for bank loans to the supply and demand of broad money, the determination of money market interest rates and the term structure of interest rates. As in the BOF4, the agents in the BOF5 model are households, firms, banks, other financial institutions, the government sector, the central bank and foreign investors, and the financial block reflects a straightforward application of the monetary tradition of financial modelling. A fixed exchange rate regime is now incorporated, but, prior to the EMU, the option to vary the central bank decision variable was used in the BOF4 simulations, and the model was also solved assuming a floating exchange rate regime. Perfect capital mobility, implying uncovered interest parity, was the benchmark case.

4   AN OUTLINE OF THE KEY CHARACTERISTICS

In the simulations below, no policy reaction is assumed, and exchange rates are fixed throughout. In particular, fiscal policy does not respond. In practice, we keep tax rates at the baseline level and government expenditures fixed in real rather than nominal terms (full indexation of nominal exogenous variables). In the interest rate and exchange rate simulations below, negotiated wages are fixed during the first year of the simulation period, reflecting a typical situation with wage contracts fixed over a one-year period. Wage drift is already endogenous from the start of the simulation.

The shocks are temporary, lasting only two years in the first simulation and five years in all the other simulations, whereas the actual simulation period is much longer. In the simulations below, to avoid permanent nominal interest rate shocks, we let the short-term rate follow a fixed real interest rate rule starting in the eighth year of the simulation.[6] This results in bringing the real short-term rate in line with the baseline in the very long run, and bringing the expected long-term rate in line with average future short rates in the long run. The shocks are unanticipated at the start of the simulations, but the reversal of the shock is anticipated. As the model is rather linear, the asymmetries that might arise if the shocks were of the opposite sign are minor, given the nature and small size of the shocks and given the rather balanced baseline.

4.1   Monetary Transmission Simulation

Figures 17.1a and 17.1b present results for a monetary policy simulation. The imposed shock is a 100 basis point increase in the short-term interest rate for two years, accompanied by a temporary appreciation of the exchange rate as implied by the uncovered interest parity condition.

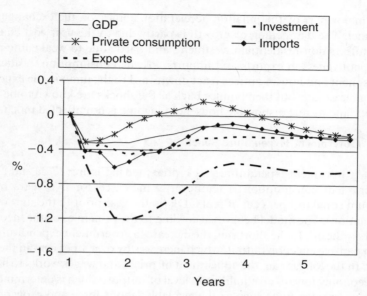

Figure 17.1a   Temporary (two-year) 1 percentage point increase in interest rates, difference from baseline

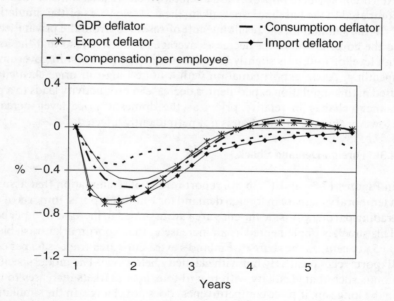

Figure 17.1b   Temporary (two-year) 1 percentage point increase in interest rates, difference from baseline

The major part of the inflation deceleration comes via the exchange rate channel. The dampening of growth is partly due to the user cost channel that affects non-residential investment, and partly due to weakening price competitiveness in exports and imports. Private consumption, residential investment and housing prices react downward to the jump in the expected real interest rate, but then bounce back as the shocks are known to be temporary and as real disposable household income is not affected much.

4.2   Government Expenditure Shock

In the government expenditure shock, presented in Figures 17.2a and 17.2b, government consumption is temporarily increased for five years by an amount equal to 1 per cent of real GDP (in the year prior to the start of the simulation). The model behaves according to the principles of the 'neoclassical synthesis'. In the short run, the increase in government expenditure has an expansive effect on output, which increases by over 1 per cent in the first year. In the longer run, the adjustment of prices and wages works to adjust the economy toward an equilibrium level of output, which is determined by supply considerations such as the available labour force and exogenously determined technical progress. Government balance weakens somewhat, even if employment improves and unemployment-related transfers decrease compared to the baseline, especially in the first two years of the simulation.

In the simulation, the resultant shift of resources from the private sector to the government sector decreases average productivity, so that the long-run level of output is slightly lower than without the burst in government spending. As an export equation with a finite long-run price elasticity is used in this simulation experiment, a decrease in productivity leads to a permanent change in relative prices as the domestic price level increases. However the rate of inflation is not permanently affected.

4.3   Foreign Demand Shock

In Figures 17.3a and 17.3b, we report results of a simulation that assumes a temporary increase in foreign demand for Finnish exports. Imports of our trading partners outside the euro area are assumed to increase by 1 per cent. This shock is implemented as an increase in the export market variable by 0.65 per cent, as the share of Finland's extra-euro area trade is 65 per cent. Exports react positively but with elasticity below one. The model specification is such that elasticity with regard to export markets increases to 0.85 in the long run, if price competitiveness does not change. In the simulation, the positive demand shock leads to higher wages and deterioration in competitiveness. As the elasticity of the export volume with regard to

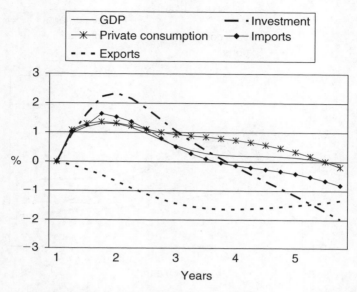

Figure 17.2a   *Temporary (five-year) increase of 1% of real GDP in public consumption, difference from baseline*

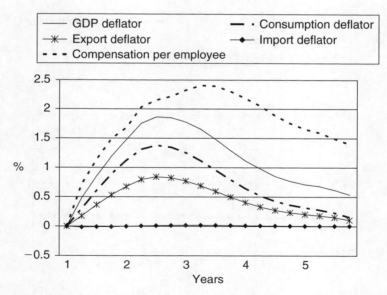

Figure 17.2b   *Temporary (five-year) increase of 1% of real GDP in public consumption, difference from baseline*

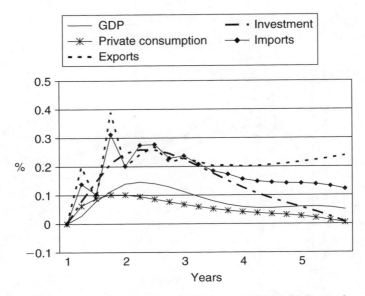

Figure 17.3a Temporary (five-year) 1% increase in world demand,
difference from baseline

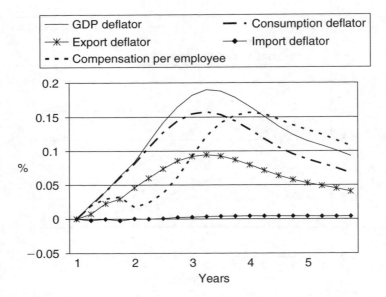

Figure 17.3b Temporary (five-year) 1% increase in world demand,
difference from baseline

relative prices is high, the export volume increases only sluggishly. Qualitatively the results are straightforward: an increase in demand causes an increase in prices.

4.4 Appreciation of the Exchange Rate

In this simulation (see Figures 17.4a and 17.4b) the euro is assumed to appreciate by 1 per cent against all other currencies, implying an appreciation of 0.6 per cent in the trade-weighted competitiveness indicator for Finland. A rather fast and full pass-through is assumed here, according to the original model design. Our current practice is to assume a much more gradual pass-through to import prices (50 per cent in four years instead of 100 per cent in four years as in the reported simulations) as a result of changes brought about by the EMU.

The appreciation is quickly passed through to import and export prices. As wages also respond to restore price competitiveness, domestic prices adjust to an approximately 0.5 per cent lower level in three years' time. (In a backward-looking case, by comparison, the full 0.6 per cent adjustment would take place in four years' time.) The rate of inflation will ease by 0.2 percentage points in the first two years. There will be a slowing in growth

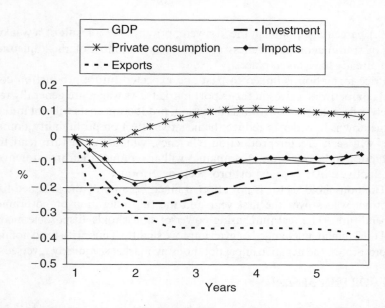

Figure 17.4a   Temporary (five-year) 1% appreciation of euro effective exchange rate, difference from baseline

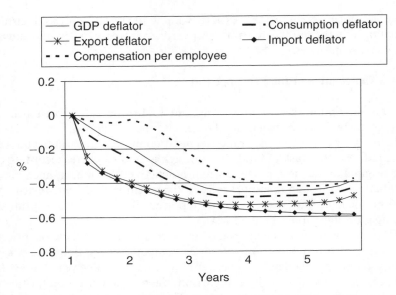

Figure 17.4b   Temporary (five-year) 1% appreciation of euro effective exchange rate, difference from baseline

of 0.1 percentage points in the first year, primarily as a result of a weakening of trading competitiveness. By the third year, most of the adjustment will already have taken place.

Price formation is linked to past and expected future production costs and competitors' prices in the export markets. As wages are generally relatively inflexible in a downwards direction, production costs will not initially come down. In order to reduce the negative effect on profitability, companies will seek greater production efficiency, which will in turn lead to a reduction in labour input. Companies will also reduce their investments in productive capacity as export prospects deteriorate.

The household sector is not affected much because of the assumed fixed contract wages over the first year and the full indexation of government expenditures. The real purchasing power of households' disposable income will thus remain unchanged or even improve slightly. Thus, with fixed nominal interest rates, the negative impact on housing markets is quickly reversed.

4.5   Oil Price Shock

In Figures 17.5a and 17.5b, we report the results of a temporary 10 per cent increase in the price of oil. As the weight of energy in our import price

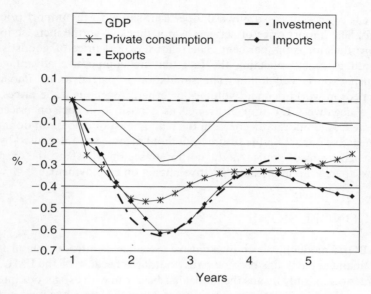

Figure 17.5a   Temporary (five-year) 10% increase in the price of oil, difference from baseline

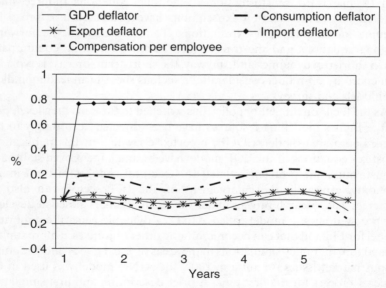

Figure 17.5b   Temporary (five-year) 10% increase in the price of oil, difference from baseline

index is 9 per cent, we apply a 0.9 per cent shock to the import price of goods. The import price of services is not shocked, so the increase in the import deflator is 0.8 per cent. The relative export price of goods is not allowed to react, reflecting the fact that no competitive advantage to Finnish exports will follow. The simulation is partial as no impact is assumed on world demand volumes or other exogenous trade prices. We find a negative GDP impact as well as a positive impact on prices, as expected. A temporary decrease in the real interest rate does not dominate the negative impact on the future household income stream, caused by the worsened terms of trade. As the corporate sector adjusts to the oil price shock, there is an immediate negative impact on employment.

5 CONCLUSIONS

The BOF5 model has been in extensive use since its introduction in 1996. The financial block has become partly outdated because of the EMU, but in practice this only means the model has been run with exogenous interest rates and exchange rates in recent years. Over the years, we have consistently used the rational expectations algorithm in policy simulations and scenarios, whereas the stepwise iterative forecast simulations have been run with the backward transformations of the Euler equations. In forecasting, iterated exogenous inflation expectations have been used as a proxy for genuine model-consistent expectations. The difference in the forward-looking equations and the transformed backward-looking counterparts lies in short-run dynamics and, anyway, the short-term forecast is typically influenced by off-model considerations such as short-term leading indicator models and surveys.

As the focus on monetary policy has switched to the euro-area level, part of the Bank's modelling resources have been directed accordingly to the Bank's euro-area model, EDGE, reported elsewhere in this publication. Most key equations of the BOF model have by and large proved stable and robust, but some problems related to structural changes in the Finnish economy, especially the enlargement of the ICT sector, can also be detected. The research project under way at the Bank is aimed at developing a new domestic model called AINO, a dynamic general equilibrium model for Finland that can become, among other objectives, a more sophisticated tool for policy simulations in the areas of fiscal policy and structural labour market issues. In autumn 2004, the AINO model was used in the forecast process for the first time. A brief description and first simulation results of the AINO model can be found in Kilponen *et al.* (2004).

NOTES

1. However, Euler equations for the private sector demand for capital and labour in BOFMINI have slightly different elasticities than the disaggregative counterparts in the BOF5.
2. See Willman *et al.* (2000, pp. 299–302) and Willman *et al.* (1998, pp. 149–53) for details.
3. In BOF5, the functional form of the value-added production function for manufacturing is Cobb–Douglas and, for the rest of the private sector, CES. In BOFMINI, the functional form for the private sector is CES. The input share of raw materials is assumed constant in volume terms.
4. MPL (marginal productivity of labour) and SMC (marginal costs of production) are analytically solved via the CES production function. In the short run, with a positive demand shock, hours worked increase relatively more than the capital stock, causing the MPL to decrease and the SMC to increase.
5. The model can be simulated alternatively under the assumption of infinite or finite long-run price elasticity of exports.
6. The nominal rate reacts to changes in inflation so that the real interest rate remains as in the baseline. The results are rather robust with regard to when, after the reporting period, the rule is switched on. Without the rule, the simulations might run into convergence problems.

REFERENCES

Kilponen, Juha, Antti Ripatti and Jouko Vilmunen (2004), 'Aino: the Bank of Finland's new dynamic general equilibrium model of the Finnish economy', *Bank of Finland Bulletin*, **78**(3), 71–9.

The BOF4 Quarterly Model of the Finnish Economy (1990), Bank of Finland, D:73.

Willman, Alpo and Hanna-Leena Männistö (1997), 'The BOF5 macroeconomic model of the Finnish economy', *Bank of Finland Bulletin*, **71**(5), 7–12.

Willman, Alpo, Mika Kortelainen, Hanna-Leena Männistö and Mika Tujula (1998), 'The BOF5 macroeconomic model of Finland, structure and equations', Bank of Finland discussion papers, 10/98.

Willman, Alpo, Mika Kortelainen, Hanna-Leena Männistö and Mika Tujula (2000), 'The BOF5 macroeconomic model of Finland, structure and dynamic microfoundations', *Economic Modelling*, **17**, 275–303.

Index